PRAISE FOR THE LAWS OF CREATIVITY

"Drawing on decades of experience, Joey Cofone has distilled the elements of creativity into an excellent, easy-to-use guide. *The Laws of Creativity* provides a roadmap for unleashing the creative force inside you."

—**JAMES CLEAR,** author of the worldwide bestseller, *Atomic Habits*

"Creativity is not magic: it's a skill that you can develop with practice. *The Laws of Creativity* is a comprehensive exploration of the curiosity, discipline, playfulness, and persistence necessary to usher new ideas into the world, and Joey Cofone is a brilliant guide."

—**JOSH KAUFMAN,** bestselling author of *The Personal MBA, The First 20 Hours,* and *How to Fight a Hydra*

"After 35+ years of designing, I confirm these laws hold true. *The Laws of Creativity* contains a valuable set of tools for creatives and non-creatives alike."

—**CHIP KIDD,** award-winning designer and author of *GO: A Kidd's Guide to Graphic Design*

"A comprehensive, witty—and accurate—deconstruction of creativity and how to grow something from nothing. *The Laws of Creativity* will change the way you think about creating—and living."

—**DEBBIE MILLMAN,** host of the podcast *Design Matters* and author of *Why Design Matters*

The Laws of Creativity

Unlock Your Originality and
Awaken Your Creative Genius

Joey Cofone

BARONFIG

BARONFIG CIRCUS BOOKS

An imprint of Baronfig Inc., New York City
baronfig.com

Text © 2022 by Joey Cofone
Design © 2022 by Joey Cofone
All rights reserved. No part of this publication may be reproduced or used via any method (analog or digital) without the prior written consent of the publisher.

Exterior design by Joey Cofone
Interior design by Joey Cofone & *the*BookDesigners
Printed in Taiwan

First Edition - First Print
ISBN: 978-1-943623-38-9 (Hardcover)
ISBN is: 978-1-943623-39-6 (eBook)

To my wife, Ariana

"Once you have tasted flight, you will forever walk the earth with your eyes turned skyward, for there you have been, and there you will always long to return."

—Leonardo Da Vinci

Contents

INTRODUCTION.. 1

PROLOGUE: REMEMBER YOUR POSSIBILITY

The Law of Origin.. 15

PART 1: FOUNDATION
How to Think Creatively

THE LAWS OF MINDSET 21

1. **Be Weird:** Law of Expression........................... 23
2. **Challenge Assumptions:** Law of Disruption 33
3. **Think in Combinations:** Law of Connection 41
4. **Embrace Fear:** Law of the Unknown..................... 49
5. **Welcome Failure:** Law of Continuity 57
6. **Measure Against Yourself:** Law of Competition.......... 65
7. **Have Fun:** Law of Play 77

PART 2: PROCESS
How to Create from Start to Finish

THE LAWS OF ACTION 89

8. **Ask More Questions:** Law of Curiosity. 91

9. **Define the Problem:** Law of Precision 101

10. **Gather Inspiration:** Law of the Muse. 111

11. **Limit Yourself:** Law of Simplicity 123

12. **Jump In:** Law of Beginning 137

13. **Sketch It Out:** Law of Ideation 147

14. **Locate the Anchor:** Law of Grounding 159

15. **Forget the End:** Law of Wandering 169

16. **Focus on Quantity:** Law of Iteration 177

17. **Create for Yourself:** Law of Specificity 187

18. **Don't Discount the Obvious:** Law of Plain Sight. 195

19. **Go Where Others Are Not:** Law of Obscurity 203

20. **Talk Out Your Ideas:** Law of Collaboration 213

21. **Come Back to It:** Law of Stepping Away 227

22. **Wear Your Heart:** Law of Vulnerability. 235

23. **Champion Your Work:** Law of Rebellion. 243

24. **Publish Imperfection:** Law of Good Enough 255

25. **Let It Go:** Law of the Finish Line. 263

PART 3: EXCELLENCE
How to Rise Above the Rest

THE LAWS OF GREATNESS 277

26. **Do the Work:** Law of Showing Up...................... 279

27. **Develop Self-Discipline:** Law of Order 289

28. **Adapt to Circumstance:** Law of Chaos 299

29. **Tailor Your Surroundings:** Law of Habitat............ 309

30. **Engage in Quality Practice:** Law of Intention.......... 319

31. **Push Mental Endurance:** Law of the Will 329

32. **Expose Yourself to New Things:** Law of Adventure.... 339

33. **Never Stop Learning:** Law of Growth.................. 351

34. **Treat Your Body Well:** Law of Symbiosis.............. 361

35. **Locate the Present Moment:** Law of the Now.......... 369

36. **Live the Golden Rule:** Law of Reciprocity.............. 379

37. **Don't Give Up:** Law of Tenacity........................ 389

EPILOGUE: DREAM THE FUTURE

The Law of Vision 401

APPENDIX

The Laws of Creativity at a Glance 409

Common Creative Doubts and How to Overcome Them . . 417

How to Be More Creative at Work 421

How to Be More Creative at Home 423

Index of Original Terms. 425

Acknowledgments 427

Introduction

A worm taught me how to be creative.

My day began like any other, with my mother kissing me on the cheek and gently booting me from the car. My oversized backpack was a vibrant green and teal. I had my pants hiked up above my belly button, and my hair—somewhere between curly and wavy—was unsuccessfully pulled to the side. I was seven years old.

My first-grade teacher met me as I entered the classroom. She had a smile that filled her entire face, and she knew how to handle young kids well. One by one, she handed out an illustration to color and cut out for the bulletin board. Everyone got the same cartoon worm with big eyes and gangly limbs.

The students, myself included, fervently jumped to work as soon as the papers hit the desk. We all wanted to be able to say, "Look at mine!" and have it be different from everyone else's (dare I say better?). I hooked my arm around the worksheet, shielding prying eyes from my soon-to-be masterpiece. My box of sixty-four crayons—the second biggest in the class—sat at the edge of my desk, ready to be called on at a moment's notice.

And call on it I did, scrutinizing each color in hopes of creating something that everyone would absolutely gush over.

When I was done coloring Mr. Worm and cutting him out, I crept up to the bulletin board, holding him flat against my chest so no one would see my magnum opus until I was ready. As I reached the board and looked at the worms already posted, my heart dropped. They were all the same—including mine. Sure, everyone used different colors, some kids even used horizontal lines or dots to color with, but as a collection, all together there, not one of them stood out.

"Joey, do you need help putting yours up?" the teacher asked.

A world of emotions hit me all at once. I couldn't bear to add another worm to the sea of the same. "No, not yet," I said, and sulked back to my desk.

What was I going to do? I thought for sure mine would be different, but I ended up with the same outcome as the rest of the class, just remixed a bit. My eyes scanned my desk, moving from crayons to Mr. Worm, then down to my hands held open in grief, when suddenly I noticed all the pieces of paper left over from cutting.

A bright light ticked on.

Until this point, I played the same game as everyone else, competing with my classmates by trying to color as uniquely as possible—but still inside the same lines. After cutting out Mr. Worm, I had created an untapped resource right in front of me: the small pile of cut paper. I immediately started pulling shards and arranging them around my cutout. I drew accessories for him—a microphone, boombox, and hat—and glued them on. My project became distinct from everyone else's, just by looking at things a bit differently.

I walked back up to the board with infinite confidence. Now, no one's worm was even close to mine. The way I rushed back to the board with a big grin attracted the teacher's attention. She came up behind me and watched as I pushed three thumbtacks into the brown cork board. I turned around, still beaming, and looked at her.

"I've never seen anything like it," she said with her signature smile.

In an instant, the course of my life was forever changed. I realized there was a yet-to-be-discovered river of ideas flowing beneath our feet, just out of sight—and I began my lifelong journey to uncover the laws that teach us how to tap into it.

The Legend of Creativity

Creativity scares people. Most freeze when they're given a blank page and challenged to make something from nothing. Ask the average person if they are creative, and you'll be served up a heaping plate of doubt. Nearly every time I told someone I was working on this book, they said something to the effect of, "Are you going to teach us the magic?"

The answer is a resounding *no*. Not because I can't teach creativity, but because it isn't magic.

Creative thinking—the human mind's unique ability to combine unrelated and abstract ideas—has been harnessed in countless ways since the dawn of humanity. Scientists use it to produce medicine that saves lives as well as weapons—like the atomic bomb—that have the power to wipe out thousands of lives in an instant. Technologists use it to bring to life machines that put people in space, connect individuals across vast distances, and optimize mundane activities, such as you obtaining and reading this book. Writers put pen to paper and weave stories that change the thinking of entire generations or collect and present information that enables entirely new types of industries and ideas to bloom. Visual artists craft messages that excite and persuade, sometimes for personal expression and other times for commercial gain. And every day people in "non-creative" fields take advantage of creative thinking to reach their goals.

There tends to be a belief that creativity is a talent, that it's a magical ability a select few are born with—but even Harry Potter wasn't born with an immutable defense to Voldemort.[1] Being creative isn't a magical power. It isn't a talent. It's a skill—one that can be developed if we stop fearing and start understanding it.

When we look deeper, it makes sense as to why we have such a fear of creativity. For hundreds of thousands of years, the unknown was what got us killed. Primordial humans did not walk into a dark cave if they could help it. It was exploring dark places and walking around unknown corners that got them mauled by a bear or bitten by a poisonous snake. Instincts like these kept us from going extinct. But the world is different now, and our basic programming is lagging behind reality. We are no longer in daily situations that could end in death. Still, we are hardwired to avoid the unknown.

Furthermore, today's education is built upon the bedrock of yesterday's instincts. The methods that we use to educate our youth—while seemingly effective in creating a contributing citizen—go against the very nature of creative thought.

---

[1] That's right, I said his name.

Introduction

Our school system imprints three devastating perspectives on impressionable young minds around the world. The first is that authority—teachers, principals, deans, and other staff—is unquestionable. Second is that man-made rules must be followed to a fault. And the third—perhaps the most damaging of all—is that the end is visible from the start.

These three perspectives are poison to the mindset we need in order to be creative. Authority *should* be questioned; it's how the current authority came to be. Rules *aren't* infallible; they're best guesses, and—if a good authority is in place—they're constantly evolving, allowing us the opportunity to affect and contribute to their evolution. And lastly, the finish line—in the real world—is almost *always* invisible at the start. We are taught at a young age that once we complete our assignments—which have been clearly laid out for us—then all our work is done. This teaches us not only to look outward rather than inward for direction but also to expect to know the end result before we even lift a finger.

Rebellion, then, is an inherent part of the creative act. It's no wonder that some of the most successful innovators have some kind of event in their personal history that society would consider a transgression. Albert Einstein's special relativity was contrary to the understanding of the universe at the time and was ridiculed by critics as "totally impractical and absurd." Marie Curie's lab was described by one fellow chemist as "a cross between a stable and a potato shed." Emily Dickinson wrote for herself, ignoring traditional punctuation rules; Ben Franklin had only two years of formal education; and Oprah Winfrey, Steve Jobs, the Wright Brothers, Lady Gaga, Richard Branson, Miles Davis, Alicia Keys, John Lennon, Tom Hanks,

Tiger Woods, Madonna, and Ralph Lauren were *all* dropouts, just to name a few.[2]

Creativity has long been viewed as a mysterious talent, one you are either born with or not, and something that cannot be developed. I'm here to tell you that this is far from the truth. By the end of this book, you will understand how creativity functions—and how you can make it work for you, every time.

What is Creativity?

In order to understand how creativity works, we must first understand what it *is* as well as what it is *not*. In its purest form, creativity is a force. Just like gravity, whose laws are derived from the mathematics of the universe, creativity's laws are derived from the psychologies of human nature.

Unlike the rules previously mentioned, the Laws of Creativity are not man made.[3] In fact, the Laws of Creativity encourage the kind of rule breaking that Emily Dickinson, Marie Curie, and many other creators practiced. They stir up the troublemaking celebrated in the Law of Rebellion (which advises that rules by humans should be questioned, can often be bent, and even require a little breaking every now and then). The laws contained within this book are explanations of how the force of creativity works. Learning them allows you more control, which increases your skill at harnessing creativity.

The force of creativity is used to solve problems and

---

2 This is *not* a pro-dropout message. Stay in school, kids. Just keep an open mind.

3 I wrote them down, but I did not invent them. Just like Isaac Newton wrote the law of universal gravitation but did not invent gravity.

express concepts. It channels the imagination to combine two or more ideas in order to provide answers to a question. Simply put, mastering these laws will make you more creative. You will be better at solving problems and expressing ideas in nearly every aspect of your life.

Why Creativity Matters

If Warren Buffett—top investor and one of the world's richest people—could invest in skills, creativity would likely be at the top of his list. Why? His approach to allocating capital is called "value investing." Essentially, he looks for undervalued stocks—companies—and goes all in for long periods of time. And creativity is as undervalued as they come.

How can we tell that creativity is undervalued? You're reading this book, so you either have an awareness that there's truth in the claim because of personal experience, or you have an inkling that there's something just outside your domain that could prove to be useful and enlightening.[4] Regardless, you don't have to believe me. Just follow the numbers and decide for yourself.

In the United States, federal funding for arts education is around $250 million, while the sciences get a whopping $5 billion. That's a 2,000 percent higher emphasis on science over art. Yet even Albert Einstein—one of the most famous scientists of the last few hundred years—noted, "Imagination is more important than knowledge. Knowledge is limited. Imagination encircles the world."

---

4 If it's the former, props for being ahead of the curve. If it's the latter, get ready to learn just how right you are.

One NASA study found that 98 percent of kids are at the creative *genius* level at age five, but by fifteen years old only 12 percent rank as high, and by adulthood the number dwindles to a mere 2 percent.[5] Kids who take part in the arts are 400 percent more likely to participate in a science fair, 300 percent more likely to win a school attendance award, and 400 percent more likely to be on the honor roll.

It doesn't end there. Hold onto your hats. On average, students who take four or more years of art education score one hundred points higher on the SAT—a test that was designed to measure an individual's readiness for college across *all* subjects. Another study found that 37 percent of low-income students who are highly engaged in the arts earn a bachelor's degree, compared to just 17 percent of those who aren't. Think about that. These students who are highly engaged in the arts are *twice* as likely to graduate from college.

Creativity is just as important for adults. In the workplace, 72 percent of business leaders say that creativity is the top skill they look for in new hires. The World Economic Forum reviewed two million resumes across eighteen industries, and, despite the clear desire (and need) for creative thinking on the employer side, only 25 percent of candidates listed creativity *anywhere* on their resume. In addition—and perhaps the most to-the-point answer on why creativity should matter to you—Adobe did multiple studies that found creative people earn 13 percent more and are 278 percent happier at work than their non-creative counterparts.

Organizations benefit from creative thinking just as much

---

5 This puts data behind what Picasso intuitively understood when he said, "Every child is an artist, the problem is staying an artist when you grow up."

as individuals. An organization that invests in creativity sees a 78 percent increase in employee productivity and a 76 percent increase in employee satisfaction. Furthermore, creative companies are 350 percent more likely to see notable revenue growth *and* enjoy 150 percent more market share than their non-creative competitors. Still, in the face of overwhelming evidence on the benefits of creativity, only 11 percent of companies studied fall into the category of "highly creative."

As we've proven, creativity isn't just undervalued—it's *severely* undervalued. There comes a reckoning when, at some point, people begin to realize that the demand for something exceeds the supply. That's when the value—and the price—goes up. As a creative individual, you will be able to command more opportunities, attention, money, and, ultimately, more freedom in your everyday life.

You'll also have a lot more fun.

A Life of Creativity

Since that fateful day in first grade, I spent years learning to harness the power of creativity. Every problem I faced, big or small, I tried to come up with a new way to solve it. Over time, I made use of creativity so reliably that I built not only a profession out of it, but a company.

Baronfig started in 2013 with a single product: the Confidant notebook (Law of Beginning[6]). At first, a notebook may seem like a boring product, but so was the sneaker before Phil Knight

---

[6] These references won't mean much to you now, but after reading this book, you will understand how each law plays a part in the creative process.

and Nike got to it (Law of Plain Sight). The notebook is one of the oldest tools known to man—it's just a stack of paper with a stiffer piece of protective paper on the top and bottom—yet it's still one of the most important in living a full, creative life (Law of the Expression). We use them to take notes, brainstorm ideas, doodle or sketch, and as journals that house some of our most private thoughts (Law of Simplicity).

I designed the Confidant notebook over five months (Law of Ideation) after talking to hundreds of thinkers[7] around the world (Law of Collaboration), doing the appropriate market research (Law of Precision), and designing dozens of prototypes (Law of Iteration). We introduced it on Kickstarter with a humble goal of fifteen thousand dollars (Law of Vulnerability), and after a whirlwind thirty-day campaign (Law of Tenacity) that included me personally engaging in thousands of emails, hundreds of phone calls, and countless social media posts around the clock (Law of Showing Up), the campaign finally ended. We ended up raising over eleven times our goal and clocked out with $168,289 from 4,242 supporters in forty-eight countries. In one month, we had sold just shy of ten thousand notebooks.

Today we have over fifty products, ship to more than a hundred countries, and sell our goods in hundreds of stores (Law of Growth). I have the privilege of leading our team as the Founder and CEO, a responsibility I am grateful for and challenged by every day (Law of Reciprocity). The company has evolved since we started, but the mission—originally just

---

[7] A thinker is anyone who has a brain and uses it. Designers, writers, accountants, carpenters, illustrators, developers, entrepreneurs, business folks, chefs, etc.

a few guiding words scrawled on a whiteboard—has always been our guiding light (Law of Vision):

To champion thinkers around the world through inspiration and imagination.

Not only do I get to personally create new products through design, but I also have the honor of working with incredible creators—in-house and from around the globe—who, through example and discussion, have added to my understanding of creativity from start to finish.

What's Inside This Book

The Laws of Creativity is filled with principles that were uncovered over years of research, experimentation, and lessons learned. I personally tested them across a host of disciplines—including design, writing, business, programming, music, drawing, sculpting, cooking, speaking, leading, personal development, and even interpersonal relationships. They were sharpened through observation and conversation with top performers in dozens of fields. Despite the varied applications, the laws hold firm.

There are "creatives" out there who like to make you believe that what they do is a wonder to behold because of its sheer mystery. While creativity's *results* are often magical, there is no reason to believe that the act itself is magic. It is not.

Creativity is a reliable practice, just like accounting, basketball, law, carpentry, medicine, exercise, and so on. Don't take my word for it; think about this: If creativity were not reliable, how would people be hired to do it (and be paid handsomely) day after day? Indeed, they would be discovered as frauds, no?

These laws have proven themselves time after time, both in my life and in the world around us. They will help you think and act under a new paradigm. Take care to absorb the underlying reasoning behind each law, and you will come away with a better grasp on how creativity works and how you can harness it in your day-to-day life. Don't feel like you need to memorize each law, however. This book is designed to get you familiar with the ideas that power creativity so that you can recognize their use in a given situation. Use it as a reference as these laws come in and out of your daily life.

Each law has its own dedicated chapter. Each chapter starts with one or more stories,[8] includes a breakdown of said stories, and ends with additional concepts and explanations of the law being discussed. Chapters are distributed among three distinct parts:

Foundation contains a set of laws that provide the bedrock for approaching any creative act. They put you in a mental state that primes you for the laws that come after.

Process contains a set of core laws that encompass any creative act from start to finish. The laws are arranged in chronological order—from the actions taken at the beginning of a process right through to the end.

Excellence contains laws for those who have begun to apply the first two sets of laws. If employed, they will take you to the next level. I've had the good fortune of being around—and working with—world-class performers in a variety of disciplines, and they all follow the same set of principles that help them rise above the average person.

---

[8] In addition to the primary goal of using these stories to illustrate laws, my goal here is to either tell you a story you've never heard or reveal something about a story you thought you knew.

Introduction

For those who want to learn to be creative, this book will help you become more comfortable with every step of the process. For those who consider themselves creative, this book will serve as a reminder—and you may learn a few things along the way.[9]

Most people think of creativity as wizardry, when, in fact, it's more like gravity. Dig in, enjoy the journey, and by the end you will know how to make the apple hit the ground every time it falls.

---

9 If you're reading this book to address a specific creative issue, flip to the Appendix and take a look at Common Creative Doubts and How to Overcome Them.

PROLOGUE
Remember Your Possibility

The Law of Origin
Everyone, including you, started out creative. Creativity is not something you need to learn, but remember.

You're a Natural

You wake up without a care in the world. The cartoon characters on your bedsheets dance in a tangle as they wrap around your small body. The sun casts bright colors and playful shapes across your room as light passes through the stickers on your window.

Your five-year-old self gets dressed, eats breakfast, and heads off to school. On the bus, you look into other cars and imagine where each person is going. You wonder if, maybe, they're superheroes in disguise. If someone looks in your direction, you wave.

Now in class, the teacher is explaining a math problem. You're at your desk, lightly listening as your imaginary friends jump across the room, chasing one another. They're only a few inches tall, and you watch as a blue duck with human proportions chases a furry brown creature that you saw on a cereal box.

Before you know it, it's lunch time. You hurry out the door (not too fast, though, just in case there's a teacher around) and immediately find your friends. All at once, the playground turns to lava. The cracks in the asphalt are your only lifelines. Careful not to fall in, you race across those thin bridges, tagging and avoiding being tagged.

When the bell rings, you head back inside and spend the rest of the school day intermittently learning and doodling silly characters and goofy robots.

After school, you race home and pull out half a dozen toys. You spend the rest of the afternoon in your own world. What you're up to is a mystery to others, but in your mind you're part of a grand storyline filled with all kinds of interesting characters. You aren't playing with toys but hanging out with heroes and inventors and artists and athletes who are all your best friends.

Together, you go on adventures to all sorts of places, both real and imagined.

Awaken the Genius Within

When we're kids, our default mode of operation is that all things are possible until proven otherwise. Everywhere we go, we're filled with wonder. The world is our oyster and we are the pearl.

For many, however, that approach gradually reverses with age. It's a subtle change. Instead of seeing possibilities, thoughts

PROLOGUE: Remember Your Possibility

of limitations are the first to jump out. Over time, our powerful imaginations are used to adverse effect, thinking up limits that aren't even there. The longer we spend with this mindset, the more rooted it becomes.

Fear not, however: Roots can be pulled. New seeds can be planted.

According to NASA, there's a 98 percent chance that you were a creative *genius* at age five.[10] This is the same institution that builds spaceships, satellites, planet rovers, and sends astronauts into space. Their estimates are accurate, down to the micron, even lightyears away. Which means that they're a particular bunch who chooses their words carefully. When they say you were likely a creative genius, you can take their word for it.

Now that you know you were a creative genius, logic follows that everything contained in this book—the entirety of creative mindset, process, and even excellence—is not something you need to learn. You already know it. You just need to remember.

In picking up this book, you've already started pulling up the roots of your old ways of thinking. Every page you read is a new seed planted. When you finish, you will have grown a mighty tree filled with leaves of creative potential.

Welcome to the forest of possibility.

---

10 Don't be self-defeating and think you must be part of the other 2 percent. What did we say about imagining possibilities first?

PART 1
FOUNDATION

How to Think Creatively

The Laws of Mindset

"I only know that I know nothing." — *Socrates*

———

You weren't born in a box. Your life began under a metaphorical clear blue sky—a child of possibility. But, over time, people put you in that infamous box. Not because they want you in there, but because that's all they know. Every time they told you that pink isn't for boys or artists don't make money or a thousand other this-is-how-it's-done's, they put you in that box. And, because that's how society operates, you eventually learned to climb into that box all by yourself.

Good news: Everything is about to change. Like Neo and the little boy with the spoon in *The Matrix*, I am here to tell you the truth:

There is no box.

There never was. Like money and time, the "box" is just a construct made by man. It's a relic of ancient ways of thinking. From this moment forward, you're going to stop worrying about how to think outside of it because that's a fool's errand—like trying to capture fireflies on a Christmas light display.

The Foundation laws are designed to rewire your thought processes and build a brand-new perspective—one which not only allows you to see your way out of the box but gives you the tools to banish the illusion entirely.

You must first adjust the way you think and tune the machine of the mind before you are able to optimize its output. Think of creativity as a piece of software. To run it, you need the correct operating system. Unfortunately, the operating system installed by society isn't the most efficient platform for creative thinking.

It's time to install your new OS.

1
Be Weird

The Law of Expression

Embrace the parts of you that others call weird. Don't hide what makes you different. Allow those parts to float to the top and be seen by all. Your uniqueness is what makes your creations original, effective, and memorable.

Masked Mask

We put on different masks for different situations. There's a mask for your loved ones, for your lover, for the people at work, and those at school. Having a variety of masks is normal; it's how we navigate society. The part that's often missed, the most important element of all, is making sure each mask you wear is constructed from pieces of who you are underneath.

In the cold Canadian winter of 1962, a boy was born. His father was an accountant; his mother was a homemaker. He was a bright kid with a curious spirit and a fondness for being silly. As soon as he was tall enough to see himself in the bathroom mirror, he spent hours each day contorting his face and making impressions—wearing mask after mask. In the evenings, he stood on the coffee table in the family living room, put on those masks, and performed for his parents.

The boy continued to follow his playfulness, however weird it seemed to others, throughout his teens and into young adulthood. Janitor by day, he worked on being a comedian by night. It wasn't long before his impressions were so entertaining that people flocked to see him perform on stages across Hollywood—a far cry from his parents' living room coffee table.

It was at this point, at the pinnacle of recognition for his skills, that the widely known King of Impressions realized he had a problem. He had spent his life, and become known for, wearing other people's masks—presenting other people's weird—but never his own. Right at the height of his impressionist fame ... he dropped the act entirely. "I just stopped doing impressions. I completely cut them out," the boy-turned-man remembers.

After that, he committed to going on stage every night, cold, without any material. It was a struggle at first. In his words, there were "many nights when I just bit it completely. Where I had people throwing things at me. Nights where I went home and crawled into bed." Still, he stuck to it, determined to figure out what his own masks looked like and how to use them.

In 1990, his hard work paid off. First, he was hired as a full-time cast member on a television show. It was short-lived, but it got his name out there. Then his big break came in 1994 when he was cast as the lead for a movie. Then another. And another. Today, his career sports an impressive twenty-eight leading roles with over $4.8 billion grossed worldwide.

Chances are, you've seen one or more of his movies. You know him better as Jim Carrey, the one-of-a-kind actor who dominated theater marquees for close to two decades. And yes, that includes the movie *The Mask*, where his character is seized by a magical green mask—and eventually learns to embrace and control it to wondrous effect.

Worldwide Shake

With the advent of the internet, there have been brief moments in time when the majority of the planet is united in thought. Sometimes it's because of a discovery, other times a tragedy, and still others for cultural movements. On February 2, 2013, a musician named George Kusunoki Miller, better known as Joji, uploaded a video to YouTube that would ripple across news stations and dinner tables around the world.

The video is a mere thirty-five seconds. It opens with four people, each dressed in a different costume. There's a red Power Ranger, a gray alien, Joji in a big pink suit—aka "Pink Guy"—and what looks to be a ninja. Each of them is gyrating to an electronic beat. The camera angle, music, and dance moves don't change for the first thirteen seconds. At the fourteenth second, the beat drops and the characters go wild. What follows is cut after cut of zany, frenetic dance moves and interactions. Then it ends as abruptly as it began.

That video was the original "Harlem Shake" dance spinoff. It spurred a global response. Imitations were uploaded by people in every country, of every age, in groups large and small. They all followed the same framework: the song "Harlem Shake" plays loudly; either a slight dance or single dancing person is seen before the music changes; then the music enters the second verse and the video cuts to a massive upheaval of both sight and sound.[11]

These videos weren't just a bunch of people shaking their booties double time to energetic music; they were glorious recreations of the original—and every bit as weird.

One of the first "Harlem Shake" imitations involves an entire Norwegian Army unit. It starts with a single soldier grooving among twenty-three serious fellow soldiers standing at attention. Then the music drops and the video cuts to a chaotic scene which includes, in no particular order: a soldier zipped up in a sleeping bag, wiggling frantically on the snowy ground; another soldier with a red bucket on his head, waving a hockey stick; a blue jumpsuit-wearing soldier on skis hopping about; what looks to be a soldier in full scuba gear strapped to the back of another soldier; and a dozen more soldiers in zany outfits, all of them dancing with delightful abandon.

And that's just one video.

What started as a short, quirky spinoff quickly turned into a global phenomenon. By February 11, just nine days after the original was shared, YouTube reported that over four thousand "Harlem Shake" spinoffs were uploaded *per day*. At the thirty-day mark, there were over a hundred thousand videos with nearly a billion total views—and every one of them was full of people letting their weird out.

---

11 If you haven't seen a Harlem Shake spinoff video, stop reading and go to lawsofcreativity.com/harlem-shake. You owe it to yourself.

It's Already There

Jim Carrey's first movie, *Ace Ventura: Pet Detective*, wasn't met with critical success. Roger Ebert, the famous movie critic, gave it just one star, calling it "a long, unfunny slog through an impenetrable plot." Audiences, however, absolutely loved it. Carrey was unabashedly himself. The movie grossed over $200 million, launching his career into the stratosphere.

There is no question that Carrey is what most people would call "weird." His roles and the way he performs them are seemingly caricatures of humanity. They're over the top, almost uncomfortable to watch. But they're also magnetic. We can't help but gravitate towards him; there's no one else like Jim Carrey. He's entirely different from the masses, and that makes us want to see what he'll do next. It also makes us admire him, regardless of whether we want to be like him, because he's created a persona built upon his own image. What's inside is also on the outside. He doesn't hide behind a mask—he *is* the mask.

Carrey managed to maintain, throughout his childhood, the things that kept him unique. As we grow up, society tends to ostracize those who deviate from the norm. Of course, we can't stop being ourselves, so instead we create partitions. We keep our uniqueness on the inside and wear masks that fit the uniforms of each time and place. Jim Carrey is an example of someone who dramatically defied social expectations, choosing to put it all out there and risk everything rather than be someone he isn't.

You have it in you too.

The "Harlem Shake" phenomenon is the single greatest example in the history of humankind that people all around the world, at their core, are *weird*.

"Harlem Shake" gave everyone an excuse to let what's inside, out. For a brief time, societal expectations were subverted, and what was ordinarily shunned, became celebrated. People of all nationalities, ethnicities, and classes shed their false masks to wear ones made from the materials within.

Does being weird require an over-the-top display of extroversion? Absolutely not.

Weird means you're different. Different means you're unique. And unique means you are original. Being weird, then, simply means letting your originality shine through rather than hiding behind a socially prescribed mask. Every person discussed in this book is, without a doubt, weird. They dared to be different, and that difference allowed them to *make a difference.*

When Marie Curie chose to stay in the lab rather than be distracted with awards, she was weird. When Jan Erntz Matzeliger thought machines could do a better job than humans, he was weird. And when Walt Disney decided he was going to produce a feature-length animated movie, he was weird too. Time after time, weirdness—*originality*—proves to be the underlying commonality amongst history's greatest creators. Throughout the rest of this book, you'll read countless stories about people who were weird and who, because of their weirdness, changed the world.

While the "Harlem Shake" phenomenon is gone, the gift it gave us is still here: There's weirdness in all of us. It's up to you to find a mask that represents your inner weirdness, put it on, and join the party.[12]

---

12 ...annnnd the beat drops.

Be the Nail

The word "weird" has been weaponized. With a single utterance, you can dampen a person's spirits and kill their confidence. Like the nail that sticks out and gets hammered, calling someone weird is society's way of banging them into conformity. If you've ever done a carpentry project—or even built Ikea furniture—you know that every now and then a nail won't go down correctly no matter how hard you hit.

You must be the nail that resists the hammer.

Martha Graham, the choreographer whose ideas reshaped dance worldwide, said, "There is only one of you in all time. This expression is unique, and if you block it, it will never exist through any other medium, and it will be lost."

There are a lot of people out there who like the things you like. But as you start to layer your interests, they form a unique imprint that is entirely your own. Considering all the variables that are actually in play—hobbies, personality, experiences, family, culture, skills, location, beliefs, education, knowledge, and more—you are *far* more unique than you give yourself credit for.

For example, there are millions of people out there who love the video game *The Legend of Zelda*. But how many of them have *Dune* as their favorite book? And of that subset, how many of those are utterly obsessed with candles that crackle and smell like a fireplace? With just three variables—game, book, and candle—and, say, one-thousand options for each, there are one billion permutations.[13] If you add just one more variable to that,

---

13 There are a lot more options than one thousand for each of these variables.

the number of unique combinations is one *trillion*. That's more than 128 times the population of Earth.

It's up to you to accept the true version of yourself. No one else has your unique combination of variables—it's time to let them show.

It's difficult to go left when the crowd goes right. You will undoubtedly stick out, and sticking out requires fortitude. You must walk into the headwind of opinions and judgment that will no doubt crop up. But like walking into any strong gust, just put your head down and take one step at a time.

When people call you or something you do weird, embrace it.[14] That's society accidentally helping you zero in on what makes you different. Once you identify your special sauce, that's when you can start cooking up unique dishes that are all your own.

Summary

There are two powerful forces at odds with each other. One is who you are, the other is who the world wants you to be. And you must choose to stand out or fit in. To stand out brings attention, which requires more effort and saps more energy. To fit in allows you to meld into the background, which seems easy on the surface but also saps energy by forcing you to be someone you aren't.

Foster a mindset of self-acceptance, one that goes against the grain, that's willing to stand out in order to stand up and be

---

14 Use common sense here. Not *everything* weird is good—snorting cookies, for example, is probably not a good thing. Also: if it harms someone else, that's not weird, it's wrong.

heard.[15] To do that, you need to celebrate your interests, skills, and idiosyncrasies, not hide them. In doing so, you truly become the only person like you.

The more you lean into the traits that make you *you*, the more unique you allow yourself to be. That's where you have to start operating from. Take those quirks, the ones you may have been keeping to yourself, and put them into everything you create. You may be surprised at how much easier expressing yourself becomes, and just how often others gravitate to you.

---

15 More on this in the Law of Rebellion.

2
Challenge Assumptions

The Law of Disruption
You have every right to challenge, question, and improve upon the ideas that are handed to you. At some point, these ideas evolved from and innovated on what came before them. It follows, then, that they themselves will eventually be replaced.

The Gordian Knot
Legend has it that the people of Phrygia, what is today known as Turkey, were once without a ruler until an oracle proclaimed that the next person to enter the city with an ox cart should be named their new king. As it turned out, that person ended up being a peasant farmer who went by the name Gordias and eventually became father to King Midas.

Midas was so grateful for his father's good fortune that he dedicated the ox cart in Gordias' memory, tying it to a pole with a knot so complex that it was described by Roman historian, Quintus Curtius Rufus,[16] as being made of "several knots

---
16 Say that ten times fast.

so tightly entangled that it was impossible to see how they were fastened."

Kings and kingdoms rose and fell, but the knot held. It was still tied to the pole in 333 BCE—generations after Gordias had first unknowingly rolled into Phrygia. Yet again, an oracle made a prophecy about an ox cart. This time, it was prophesied that any person who could untie the cart from the pole would be destined to rule Asia. People tried and failed, but no one could figure out how to free it from its bounds.

Alexander the Great was leading his army through the Phrygian capital of Gordium when the story of the Gordian Knot reached his ears. Curious, he asked to be brought to the infamous ox cart so he could see this supposedly impossible knot for himself. He poked and prodded under the watchful eyes of those around him, but it appeared he could not loosen the knot in the slightest, let alone untie it. It became apparent that the knot was as strong as the stories claimed.

Suddenly, Alexander stepped back, declaring, "It makes no difference how they are loosed." With those words, he drew his sword and cut the rope, untying the knot with ease.

Breaking Rules

Some historians claim that Alexander the Great may have simply unpinned the cart and sorted the knot from the source, but regardless of whether it was untangled in a sword-swinging flourish or through less exciting—but just as effective—means, the legend has stood the test of time because it teaches a valuable lesson:

Assumptions, which are regularly handed from person to person, oftentimes across generations, can and should be challenged.

In the case of the Gordian Knot, the prophecy was that whoever untangled the knot would conquer Asia. It didn't apply rules or stipulations to the task. Everyone *assumed* that the knot needed to be solved in the same way that we untie our sneakers or, more appropriate for the time, dismantle a fishing net: cleanly, without force, and with the ability to be reassembled.

And so it went, day after day, try after try, no one could solve the puzzle of the legendary Gordian Knot. It isn't that the knot was an immovable force—the rope was ordinary, the knot was made by man—but that the rules by which people operated, in combination with the knot, made it *seem* impossible.

Alexander the Great understood that most limitations require one's own permission to be applied, that many can be rejected or fashioned into new ones. It was this belief that allowed him to disrupt the status quo. Since the knot itself could not be fundamentally altered, it made sense that the only flexible entity in the equation would have to be the rules. Assumptions about how the puzzle could be approached had to change.

According to Alexander, "With the right attitude, self-imposed limitations vanish." The trick is recognizing that most limitations, while seemingly originating from others, ultimately rely on you to give them power.

As for Alexander, he did, in fact, go on to conquer Asia. Whether it was prophesy or coincidence... that's for you to decide.

Smoke and Mirrors

Assumptions about the world are passed down like heirlooms. Often, they are made of time-tested, well-worn materials that only get better with age. Other times, they are fragile, made of the moment, like a firecracker shot in the night: strong, loud, but as fleeting as the puff of smoke that follows.

Before Nicolaus Copernicus proposed his heliocentric model, which put the sun at the center of the universe, people assumed that we—Earth—were the center, and everything revolved around us.[17] He published his radical idea in 1543, disrupting a belief that for millennia had been accepted as truth beyond question. It took another *five decades* before astronomers came around. Today, even a child knows that the earth revolves around the sun.

Like Copernicus, we inherit the assumptions of those who came before us, including ones that have been around for ages. But that doesn't necessitate their truth. It is up to us to keep aware of the impermanent nature of ideas—to appreciate the difference between fact and "fact"—that reverberate through times and cultures, that are delivered by family, friends, authority figures, and mere strangers passing on the sidewalks of life.

When you are faced with a problem, take inventory of the elements and ideas involved. The best path to a solution is found by shaping the clearest question possible, and it's in this question that the strongest assumptions lie. Start by asking:

---

[17] Back then, there was no such thing as the "solar system." It wasn't until the end of the twentieth century, over four hundred years later, that we discovered planetary systems other than our own.

- *What's the goal?*
- *What has been tried?*
- *What hasn't been tried?*
- *What resources are available?*
- *What's blocking the path?*
- *What's allowed?*
- *What's* really *allowed?*[18]

You will often find that, with enough digging, roadblocks deemed impervious are later discovered to be malleable. Perhaps it's through conversation that you are able to shed light on a new thought, or through research that you discover a previously unknown fact. Whether it's a matter of perspective, knowledge, or both, the more fundamental assumptions you put under a magnifying glass, the more chances you have of dropping the dead weight of outdated or unproven ideas.

Do not attempt to enact change for change's sake, however. That's a path of wasted energy and forgettable results. Instead, focus on ideas that move the needle forward in some regard. Like Copernicus' new view of the solar system, a constructive idea opens the door for others to contribute their own ideas.

When you enact positive change—true disruption—you leave the world better than you found it. *That* is progress.

---

[18] The questions don't end here. Ask anything. We'll talk more about this in the Law of Curiosity.

Respectful Examination

As we've learned, it's important to challenge the assumptions of those who came before us. This kind of thinking is the cornerstone of progress. However, it is equally important to recognize that many assumptions—perhaps even the majority—have stood the test of time for a reason: they're correct.

Every day, we are inundated with stories of entrepreneurs disrupting this industry or that, or of exceptions that are touted as rules, to the point where it's easy to get swept up in the excitement, to be convinced that everything, everywhere can be revolutionized. Oftentimes that simply isn't the case. Many rules stay the same despite how much time has passed or how many minds have attempted to change them.

Let's take inventory of just a few of the mundane things that have stayed the same throughout time. Since this could go on for a while, we'll restrict our analysis to the objects we use at mealtime: You sit on a chair at a table; you use a fork or spoon or knife or a combination of the three; your food is laid out on a plate; you wipe your mouth with a swatch of cloth or folded paper; and you drink out of a glass. Every item in that process has been essentially the same for hundreds of years. Why? Because they work. Sure, your plate or cup may be made of plastic, which is a fairly recent invention, but a material change does not constitute a revolution. And it's possible—likely even—that newer, contemporary items will be more stylish in their presentation than their predecessors. But we must recognize that these types of changes often only make the items *different*, not better.

Make sure that the assumptions you challenge are assessed from a neutral mindset. Don't go looking for a revolution where none is necessary because your bias will convince you that you've found one, only to be proven—down the line and through a lot of wasted effort—that your idea is unreasonable. Take your time, judge reality as it is rather than as you wish it were, and you will soon wield the power of rebellion for positive impact.

Summary

In the first law—The Law of Expression—you recognized the importance of being true to yourself, of letting your differences float to the top. Now, in the second—The Law of Disruption—you are reminded that you can bend, and even break, the mold that the world gives you. In this case, however, being different is only the beginning. Your changes must also be *better*. If done correctly, you can contribute to the collective progress by breaking the rules that no longer serve humanity.

It is of paramount importance that you fine-tune your meter for assessing which assumptions are valid, which are flexible or incomplete, and which are outright replaceable. You can do this by starting from zero—throwing out all assumptions—and working your way back to the problem at hand, building your own understandings from scratch.

Keep in mind, however, that many assumptions *are* correct. Do not turn an exercise of validation into a witch hunt that focuses on proving the ideas you *want* to be true. If you aren't careful, you will waste a lot of time and energy in denial before ending back where you started.

Ideas come and go, some last centuries, others last seconds. Stay neutral, assess fairly and without agenda, and build your own framework of assumptions from the ground up. The responsibility for managing your limitations in the world rests squarely on your shoulders.

3
Think in Combinations

The Law of Connection

Base concepts can neither be created nor destroyed, they simply merge to form new combinations. Creativity is not about creating—it is about combining.

What Comes Around

The world's oldest coin is dated over twenty-seven hundred years old. Even before that, ancient civilizations understood the rarity—and therefore the value—of precious metals.[19]

At first, gold and other metals were traded in their from-the-earth forms, eyeballed and haggled over until parties agreed on a value at that particular moment in that distinct context. (On a given day, perhaps a nugget was worth two cows, six chickens, and a bale of hay, for example.) Eventually, currency was formalized. Coins were measured by weight, stamped with images of the rulers in their respective eras, and universal values began to emerge.

---

19 Hence the "precious." Not to be confused with Gollum's ring.

This went on for centuries, until 1704 when Queen Anne adopted a gold standard in the British West Indies, which allowed trade to use certificates that represent gold, rather than gold itself. Value no longer moved directly between hands; it was now the *promise* of value which was exchanged. Great Britain adopted the gold standard by 1821, and the rest of the world soon followed.

These certificates, of course, are better known as money. The system worked so well, in fact, that only a century later the gold standard was dropped altogether. Money had garnered so much inherent value—and was so separate from gold in the minds of those using it—that gold was no longer necessary. And that's the way things stayed for several decades.

Then, on October 21, 2008, in a quiet corner of the internet, an unknown entity named Satoshi Nakamoto posted a white paper to a little-known message board titled *Bitcoin: A Peer-to-Peer Electronic Cash System*. In just nine pages, the paper introduced the concept of the "bitcoin" and outlined its unique method of transferring value. It was built using three technologies: a distributed consensus system for processing transactions, private keys to sign transactions and access the digital wallet, and a shared public ledger to keep the system accurate and accountable.[20] For the first time in thousands of years, since nuggets of metal were used, the system for value transfer was again decentralized—no one controls it.

Like currencies that came before, the value of Bitcoin—a cryptocurrency—rises and falls with the tides of public opinion,

---

20 Don't worry if you don't know what these mean; it's not important for what we're trying to accomplish.

economic climate, political affairs, and a host of other factors. Each currency, whether nugget, coin, or paper, went through their own highs and lows, and now the byte follows in their footsteps.

When I first heard of Bitcoin, in 2010, each was worth $0.09. Since then, the price has skyrocketed into the tens of thousands of dollars.[21]

Carrots and Coins

Currency, regardless of transfer vehicle, permeates every society at all levels. It is inescapable, and, for our purposes, one of the most ubiquitous examples of the combination of ideas.

It's easy to forget that everything, at one time, was regarded as an invention. Money is such a common, basic concept for us today that it's difficult to imagine a time without it. Because it seems so fundamental to our daily lives, breaking it down into simpler concepts can be a challenge. But that's exactly what we're going to do.

Desire is one of the core aspects of human psychology. Whether it's a want or a need, we regularly yearn for things that we do not have. It can be an object, experience, whatever. In order to acquire that thing, we must go out and get it, usually from someone else.

Bartering was the first type of value exchange. For example, one person has a carrot farm and wants to cook their carrots, the other has wood but no food to heat—boom, a perfect trade. But what happens when a third person has pelts that both need,

---

[21] Depending on when you read this, Bitcoin could be more valuable, a fraction of this, or replaced by another cryptocurrency altogether. Like currencies before it, crypto will go through evolutions.

but they themselves don't need carrots or wood? You could get a fourth person that has something the pelt owner needs, who can then do a secondary trade to the original two people. Everyone's happy, in theory. But in practice, it doesn't work. The trades get too convoluted, and perceived values may differ between parties—especially as the group grows larger.[22]

At some point, far before recorded history (and at *least* twenty-seven hundred years ago), someone invented currency. They combined two fundamental concepts—desire and value via rarity—and started using precious metals to trade from person to person. No longer did the carrot farmer need trade partners that had a desire for carrots; they could trade carrots for metals and, later, trade those metals for pelts or whatever else was needed.

Fast forward nearly three millennia and currency is *still* evolving. The fundamental concepts that combined to enable metal nugget trading have given way to more nuanced concepts that together form cryptocurrency. What's even more on-the-nose is that the ideas—the technologies—that combine to form Bitcoin, while as a single unit are entirely fresh and exciting, separately have been around for years.

Satoshi Nakamoto took shared distributed consensus, private keys, and public ledgers—none of which were new in concept or practice—and synthesized them in a new way. The combination itself was the innovation, not the things being combined.

A modern-day alchemist of sorts, Nakamoto figured out how to turn abstract ideas into honest-to-goodness digital gold bars.

---

22 It's difficult enough reading about the trade, imagine arranging it.

The Sum of Parts

The word "creativity" is a misnomer. It does an unfortunate disservice, leading you to believe that creating is at the heart of being creative. It isn't.[23] *Combining*, rather, is the actual act of creativity—while creating is, if anything, a byproduct of the act (and still a poorly named one at that).

Steve Jobs, whom some have called one of the greatest innovators of his time, and, regardless of whether you agree, whose ideas founded and developed one of the most valuable companies on the planet, said this: "Creativity is just connecting things. When you ask creative people how they did something, they feel a little guilty because they didn't really do it, they just saw something. It seemed obvious to them after a while."

The additional nugget of wisdom here, besides that creativity is simply connections, is that it requires us to pay attention. It requires us to not only look, but *see*. As a designer, when I look at a graphic illustration, I see thirty-seven separate components that comprise the whole, while your average person sees the illustration as a single entity. Everyone does this with their respective interests.

Once you realize you have this ability, you're able to start applying it to more things. The trick, if we can call it that, is twofold:

First, start to be aware of what you're already breaking down by component. If you're a watchmaker, for example, you see a watch as multiple time-keeping elements. You are aware of the high-level sections of the movement (the engine)—crown, mainspring, gear train, escapement, balance wheel, dial train,

---

23 Just reading that sounds counterintuitive. But that's why the word "misnomer" exists—sometimes things are named just plain incorrectly.

and jewels—and understand the set of low-level components that make them all work. A carpenter understands materials, fabrication, safety; a businessperson understands finance, corporate structure, management; a writer understands language, tone, setting; and so on.

Second, now that you're aware of your proficiencies, the areas you are able to break down, it's time to start applying that thinking to different contexts. If you're a carpenter and you only focus on carpentry, it's much more difficult to innovate than if you exposed yourself to, say, candy making or digital display manufacturing. I can't tell you why I chose those or what their outcomes would be—that's where curiosity and exploration enter—but I can tell you that a carpenter would look at those two things differently from a businessperson or a writer.

We all know the adage "Jack of all trades, master of none," but the true insight lies in the oft-abandoned second half: "...but oftentimes better than a master of one." To wield a few perspectives, even though they may not be masterful, gives you more varied information to work with.

Now that you appreciate the importance of training yourself to recognize fundamental concepts—be they components of a whole, independent ideas, or parts of a cluster—it's time to take that input and turn it into output.

The ideal number of concepts to combine is two or three. Any more than three and the person on the other end, the one trying to understand you, isn't going to make all the necessary connections for your new concept to hit. Any less and, well, you just have one thing—that's called copying.[24]

---

24 Take a look at the Law of the Muse for more on inspiration vs. plagiarism.

Like money, everything in our lives, mundane or otherwise, is composed of fundamental concepts. Ludwig Wittgenstein, an Austrian-British philosopher of the late 1800s, reminded his readers that when you talk about a broom, you're not making a statement about a stick and a brush. Together, they form something entirely different.

We now have the basic recipe for connecting: paying attention to components and combining two or three concepts. Let's look at a few mainstream hits and see how the Law of Connection applies. The following is a short list of combined concepts that have struck so strongly the chords of culture that their music was heard far and wide.

- The iPhone combines a **computer** and a **phone.**
- The Avengers combine **the allure of the gods** and **the relatability of everyday people.**
- Pokémon combines **our love of pets** and **our fascination with fantasy worlds.**
- Survivor combines **documentary film** and **the magnetism of unplanned reality.**
- Slack combines **chatrooms** and **the workplace.**
- Tesla combines **cars** and **batteries.**
- Instagram combines **photography** and **messaging.**

Of course, all of the above are made of more than the concepts listed. There's depth in execution. But they are, at a high level, combining these basic ideas, and far better than anyone else.

Tesla, for example, is much more than cars and batteries.

The company employs machine learning, always-connected hardware, computer-controlled driving software, and dozens of other traits and features that someone far more knowledgeable on the subject could tell you about. But ask a grandparent what Tesla is, and you will undoubtedly be answered with, "That's those cars that run on batteries."[25] The combination of concepts is a starting point. It's an answer that serves up more questions, those of which are further answered, which is how depth is inherently added.

Summary

Creativity is about making unexpected connections. Whether you are combining fundamental concepts or more complex ones, the method is the same:

Pay attention—*see* rather than look—and use your specific perspective to investigate the world around you. Follow your interests as per the Law of Expression, and you will naturally go down a path that is all your own.

Take two or three of those curiosities—the ideas that develop from the things you know and learn—and combine them to form a new concept. Don't force it, but find existing overlaps and nooks and crannies that help them naturally fit together.

Above all, remember: don't worry about making anything "new." All concepts are simply a combination of those that came before.

---

25 "Phone a grandparent." The ultimate simplicity filter.

4
Embrace Fear

The Law of the Unknown

Fear is necessary to all creative acts. Your goal is not to eradicate fear, but to acknowledge it and continue in defiance of your mind's backward tugs. When you are afraid, you are on the right path.

Mighty Douser

Fear. It's the enemy of progress, the foil to growth, the villain in the back of our minds that tells us we can't be the hero of our goals—and it's completely normal. If Lonnie Johnson, mechanical and nuclear engineer, gave into his fears, many of us would have had less enjoyable childhoods.

Johnson worked at NASA's Jet Propulsion Lab but tinkered with side projects in his spare time. In 1982, he was working on a pump that would replace freon with water and air pressure for a more environmentally friendly cooling technique. With one hand on the nozzle and the other holding the opposite side of the contraption up to the bathroom faucet, he pulled the trigger.

Kswessshhhhhh! A burst of water shot across the room and into the tub.

Johnson was shocked by the power of the stream and the distance it traveled. He shot again and again, enjoying his new contraption more with each burst. As he put it, the simple act of pumping and blasting water was "very gratifying." With a smile on his face, he began to imagine ways to turn it into a toy. Over the next few days, he pieced together several PVC pipes and an empty two-liter Coca-Cola bottle to form a self-contained water gun.

Prototype in hand, Johnson went to a picnic and told people about his idea. They were skeptical, and few showed interest. Then he pulled the trigger. Soon they were all laughing as they scrambled for cover, passing the water gun around so everyone could try it.

Johnson was convinced he was on to something. He went from company to company, pitching his idea until finally one agreed to make it. With a toy deal in place, he quit his day job and went all in on the water gun project, committing himself full time. His joy was short lived, however. Plans didn't go as expected, and the deal fell through.

All this time, there were zero paychecks coming in. Confident that the water gun would one day be a success, the Johnsons—himself, his wife, and four children—made the difficult decision to move out of their home and into a small apartment. Johnson was "angry and scared," but he believed in his idea.

By day he pitched companies and investors, by night he refined prototype after prototype. Six years went by before he got the phone call that would put him back on track. It was from a company in Philadelphia. They called with mild interest but told him not to come by unless he happened to be in the area.

Despite being asked not to make a special trip, that's exactly what he did. Johnson boarded a plane right away, and the next morning walked into the meeting carrying his wife's suitcase. He opened it to reveal the latest prototype (still powered by a Coke bottle), pumped it up, and shot a blast of water across the room. They were instantly sold.

This time the deal didn't fall through.

Originally dubbed the "Power Drencher" and released in 1990, the water gun was renamed to "Super Soaker" shortly afterwards. In 1992—seven years and one less home later—Lonnie Johnson's Super Soaker was the top selling toy *in the world.*

Leaping and Landing

Every time you avoid a challenge, whether you realize it or not, it's fear that's stopping you. Fear is borne from the unfamiliar, and to overcome it is to grow. Fear, then, is the compass by which areas of personal growth are revealed.

Facing your fear isn't a one-time event. Fear pops up throughout the creative process, sometimes at every step, other times when you least expect it; you don't conquer it once and then sprint to the finish line home free. Like an actual hurdler, one must overcome fear-hurdle after fear-hurdle. For unless you jump past your fear, there is no way to reach the rewards on the other side.

Johnson's journey was littered with instances when he could've surrendered to fear. Rather than give up his home and soldier forward, deeper into the unknown, it would've been significantly easier to call it quits, go back to his old job, and reactivate a much-appreciated income. Instead, Johnson kept going, confident that his idea was worth the trouble—and the risk.

- **Hurdle:** Before that moment in the bathroom, Johnson had never thought about making a toy, let alone professionally working on one. He knew there were reams of industry knowledge he was entirely unaware of. Yet he decided to do it regardless.

- **Hurdle:** Bringing that early prototype to a picnic with friends and coworkers required some serious vulnerability. It's scary to present ideas, especially when they're in a rough state. But Johnson did it anyway. By doing so, he learned that people couldn't resist having fun with the toy he'd made.

- **Hurdle:** With confidence that his water gun was, indeed, enjoyable to use, Johnson pitched his idea to countless companies. He took meetings, explained the product, and, despite rejections, kept going until he landed a deal.

- **Hurdle:** Johnson had quit his job to work on his endeavor full-time when the first deal fell through. Suddenly, he found himself without current or expected income. It's at this point that most people would call it quits and attempt to resume the safe structure of a previous life. Instead, Johnson doubled down by moving his entire family into a small apartment.

- **Hurdle:** With the future of his career, his family, and his project shrouded in uncertainty, he took yet another plunge. Despite a lack of financial security, Johnson bought a plane ticket and booked a hotel room—expenses that he couldn't afford to take lightly—and traveled to yet another meeting. This time, finally, he got a deal that stuck.

Can you imagine starting a project in an unfamiliar industry? Or presenting that idea to people close to you? How would you handle getting turned down repeatedly? What would you do if you took a big leap—and didn't land it? Would you keep going?

Every creation requires us to face our fears. Sometimes the fear is centered around creating the thing itself. Other times it's about what happens after you create it. For Lonnie Johnson and the Super Soaker, it was a little of both.

Years later, Johnson summed up his experience: "You will always face pushback. You will always face naysayers. You will always face difficulties. If you can make it real, you can make it happen. And by far the most important thing you can do is persevere."

Munching Numbers

Mark Twain once said, "Courage is not the lack of fear. It is acting in spite of it." Every creative act, at some point, demands that its creator face their fear. And every successful creative act means that the person or people involved were able to overcome it.

There are no exceptions.

I've been designing for over twenty years at the time of writing. At this point, I've created more than I can remember. If you name something, I've probably made a thing that's similar or in a related category. Yet I still feel fear *every single time* I start something new. Every time![26] I can't help but think, "This might be the problem I finally don't solve." But somehow it manages to work out—every time.

---

26 This is not hyperbole. I really do question myself. Same goes for countless creators I've discussed this with. Over time, the fear doesn't necessarily go away—we just get better at handling it.

How do I do it? I stop thinking and start doing. We'll talk about this more in the Law of Beginning, but for now the only thing you need to know is that there are three basic techniques to get past the fear.

- **Commit to tiny bites.** Creative projects are often intimidating. When you start to think about all the work involved, it can be difficult to even begin. That's called analysis paralysis. To get past it, do your best to forget about the larger project and instead focus on a small portion, usually the next task. When I'm having trouble designing, I commit to drawing, say, twenty sketches or designing for just ten minutes. By the time I hit my number or the time's up, nine times out of ten I'm past my hesitation, the fear is behind me, and I keep on going.[27]

- **Quantify the challenge.** Most fear results from not fully understanding what lies ahead. That's what makes creative endeavors particularly frightening: The very nature of the act necessitates the unknown—like Johnson quitting his job without the certainty of what would happen—otherwise it isn't truly creative. While you can't predict how it'll end, you can control how you get there. For example, if you write just two hundred words a day—less than what you send in a day's worth of text messages—you'll have a sixty-thousand-word manuscript in less than a year. Double it to four hundred and you'll be done with the first draft in just five months. You may not be able to guarantee you'll

---

27 Isn't this a form of self-trickery? You bet. But it still works.

have a *good* book, but you *will* have a book. And that's a great place to start.

- **Rationalize the risk.** Most people overestimate how risky a given endeavor is. The biggest risk—which isn't big at all—is usually just looking silly in front of others. It's the ego that most often stops us from trying. Put into perspective the actual damage you'd incur from failing, and you'll realize that your fears are frequently unfounded.

You alone must make the decision to face your fears. Know that you are not being judged—most people are too concerned with how others' view *them* to worry about what you're up to—but even if you do face resistance, it won't last long.

Anaïs Nin, the French-Cuban writer, said, "Life shrinks or expands in proportion to one's courage." How big or small your world is—and the life you lead—is wholly up to you.

Summary

To succeed creatively, you must walk towards your fear. Use it as a guide to show you the things in your life that are worth doing. If you aren't afraid, it must be familiar; if it's familiar, then it isn't fully creative.

Fear can occur at several points in the creative process. Most often, it strikes right after thoughts of beginning. It tries to stop you, to pull you back into the world of the well-known. Other times it happens during the creation, as you repeatedly toil away and come up empty-handed, taking the form of self-doubt. Even after creation, when you're faced with the prospect of sharing your work with others, you may feel fear of judgment.

Regardless of when your fear turns up or how frequently it knocks on your door, be prepared by wielding the knowledge that it happens to everyone—and this isn't the first time it's happened to you.

Remember: Commit to tiny bites by focusing on just the next step. Quantify the challenge by letting go of the unknown and controlling what you can. And rationalize the risk by putting things into perspective.

One foot in front of the other. You can do this.

5
Welcome Failure

The Law of Continuity

Failure and success are directly proportional. The more you fail, the more likely you are to succeed. A failure is not a true end, but a lesson to apply going forward.

Gliding and Gilding

It was Christmas in New York City. The year was 1957. A girl and her father were walking through Central Park, fresh snow crunching under their feet as they went. They stopped at the edge of a frozen lake. It was covered with people zooming left and right, their red and green scarves billowing behind them. Holiday music played from an unknown source.

The father bent down to eye level with his eight-year-old daughter. She was holding a brand-new pair of ice skates. Watching the skaters enjoy themselves, her eyes were filled with both excitement and apprehension. It would be her first time ice skating, and she wasn't quite sure she could pull it off.

With no other choice but to give it a shot, the girl slid her feet into the skates, and, with help from her father, laced them up. She held his hand as she wobbled onto the ice. Her knees buckled and gave way, but her father held tight. She took another step, this time falling to her knees. Not to be deterred, she jumped up with newfound determination and pushed forward. The moment the blades slid onward, she let go of her father and effortlessly glided across the lake.

It was as if she was born to skate.

That night, with visions of becoming an Olympic figure skater, the girl begged her parents for ice-skating lessons. This went on for days. No matter what her parents said, she wouldn't let up. Finally, they gave in.

Within just a few months, she outgrew the abilities of her ice-skating coach. Then she outgrew another coach. And another. At that point, her parents realized their daughter had a passion for skating that propelled her beyond all expectations. They hired a coach who specialized in working with Olympic-level athletes.

The girl and her father commuted to New Jersey—every night—to practice in a public skating rink. In addition to her training, she took up ballet to better understand dance and movement, applying what she learned back to her figure skating.

A few short years later, at the age of twelve, the girl won the figure skating regional championships and began competing at the national level. Experts agreed, she had all the markings of a success story waiting to happen. The next logical step was to train for the Winter Olympics.

So that's what she did.

Night after night, year after year, the girl trained as hard as she could. Opportunity finally reared its head at age eighteen.

Now a promising pair skater, she and her partner, James Stuart, entered a competition to qualify for the 1968 Winter Olympics.

When their names were called, they skated onto the ice, hand-in-hand. Their hearts beat out of their chests, but from the outside they were serene. The music started. Immediately, they were in motion, skating as if their lives depended on it. Several toe loops, Axels, and Lutz jumps later, they struck their final pose and eased off the ice. Both of their faces were wide with ear-to-ear grins.

The judges concluded their assessments and submitted their individual scores. The girl's breath hung in the air. Time moved at a snail's pace. One by one, the scores were revealed. Giant numbers appeared across the score plates. Then, as abruptly as they started, they stopped. The final tally was in.

The girl and her partner placed fifth.

They didn't qualify for the Olympics. Both skaters were devastated. Just like that, it was over.

Realizing she didn't have what it took to reach the Olympics, the girl quit figure skating altogether. In an effort to separate herself from the only lifestyle she'd known, the girl signed up for a semester abroad, in France.

Unbeknownst to her, it would be yet another life-changing experience.

In Paris, the girl discovered her second passion: fashion. She got a job at *Vogue* and became the youngest senior fashion editor at the age of twenty-three. She prospered there for years before moving on to Ralph Lauren, where she worked as a design director. And when she couldn't find a wedding dress she liked, she decided to design her own. The dress was such a hit that it was featured in fashion magazines around the world, and before long fashion-forward individuals flocked to her for bespoke dresses.

That girl who discovered her first passion with her father on Christmas, the young woman who endured a trying defeat and redirected her passion, is the legendary fashion designer Vera Wang. Since then, Wang has designed clothing for movies, television, celebrities, and more. In 2013, Wang was awarded the Lifetime Achievement Award by the Council of Fashion Designers of America—an achievement akin to a gold medal in the world of fashion.

To Be Continued

If there's one thing that's guaranteed in the creative process, it's failure.[28] It comes in all sizes, from minuscule minute-long hiccups to enormous life-changing disappointments. The challenge is not to avoid failure—that's impossible—but to learn what to do once you encounter it.

Even as a little girl, Vera Wang displayed the valuable ability of trying *one more time*. For many kids, falling on ice is game over. But not for Wang. She brushed herself off and chose to use failure as fuel for her next attempt rather than an excuse to call it quits. It was because of those following attempts that she discovered her passion for figure skating. All the joy skating gave her for years can be traced back to that single decision to keep trying.

In retrospect, it's easy to say that Wang's failure to qualify for the Olympics may have been one of the best things to happen to her. But in the moment, when the future she imagined

---

28 If you haven't failed, you haven't tried.

seemingly disappeared in an instant, it was as far from a positive experience as one can be.

What happened in the skating arena that night put an end to a goal she had spent most of her life working towards. "I was devastated," Wang recalls, "I was completely lost. I needed to find something else that I could love as much. It turned out to be fashion."

Instead of abandoning hope, Wang took everything she had learned from figure skating and funneled it into fashion. "Skating was a chance for me to express myself in a creative way. It was the blend of all worlds—music, dance, athletics, choreography, and, of course, costumes," Wang explained. "From an early age, I really fell in love with what a body could look like, what it could do, what you could express, and how you could look."

Wang's life finally came full circle when she was asked to design costumes for Olympic figure skaters. It was a task she didn't take lightly. "I know, as a skater, the responsibility it is," Wang said in an interview. "If there is any wardrobe malfunction, you can ruin someone's Olympic championship. When you stop and think about it, the responsibility is staggering."

Despite the fear of costing a skater their Olympic medal—and in defiance of her own traumatic experience—Wang went ahead and designed some of her most technically challenging outfits to-date. While Wang never personally made it to the Olympics, her creations did.

In fact, the costume she designed for Evan Lysacek saw him through to winning a gold medal for men's free skating at the Vancouver 2010 Winter Olympics. On top of that, in recognition for her commitment to figure skating both as a participant and costume designer, Vera Wang was inducted into the U.S. Figure Skating Hall of Fame in 2009.

To Do or Not to Do

Failure is often provoked by fear. It's a circular disaster because the fear of failure often *causes* failure. Whether the source is within or without, because of something done or not done, fear is the cornerstone of unmet potential.

There are two types of creative failures: those that happen *by* you—via action—and those that happen *to* you—via inaction.

FAILURE BY ACTION

When we talk of failure, we're usually referring to failure by action. For example, if you attempt to write a book and quit, it's by your own hand that the failure emerges. It is characterized by giving up after getting an unwanted result. The source of the fear stems from self-judgment:

- *I am terrible at this.*
- *I'm never going to succeed.*
- *It's pointless to keep trying.*
- *My skills and abilities are not good enough.*

A mistake isn't a mistake if you don't allow it to be. Instead, look at your journey as a process of elimination. Every time an attempt doesn't work, you didn't fail, you learned a lesson.

After every new endeavor, whether it's a failure or a success, the Baronfig team always stops to ask ourselves the same two questions: "What did we learn?" and "What can we do better next time?"

FAILURE BY INACTION

This one is harder to spot. Human beings are skilled at hiding their fears. Because it is marked by a lack of action, failure by inaction renders a failure effectively invisible.[29] It's characterized by never starting or not restarting. In this case, it's fear of judgment by others that halts progress and growth.

- *What will they think of me?*
- *How do I explain it to them if I don't succeed?*
- *Are they laughing at me?*
- *Will they cast me out if I don't measure up?*

Outside of your close friends and family, the world isn't rooting for your success. It isn't against it, either. In fact, the world, generally speaking, doesn't care about the majority of us, myself included. People care mostly about themselves. Such is human nature. But, of course, it's difficult to put things into perspective under duress.

Because of this, you *will* feel tossed aside at some point in your life. Most likely, it will happen more than once. On those occasions, it's easy to think others are out to get us, that they're conspiring behind closed doors to climb up our backs, step on our heads, and leave us in the dirt below as they launch themselves skyward, happy and free.

If that sounds ridiculous, you're correct. We've all had moments like these, however. Being rational is challenging when you feel like you're at the center of some kind of judgment storm. Unfortunately, these thoughts create social fear, which, in turn, causes a paralysis that leads to inaction.

To combat these fears, you need to face them head on.

---

29 Since it's invisible, failure by inaction is a lot easier to fall victim to. Most people prefer to never try (and remain invisible) rather than to try and fail in front of others.

When you find yourself asking a question like the ones listed above, follow that thought through to completion. Yes, it can be scary. Facing truth often is. But it's also empowering. Ask yourself, *What will* really *happen if I don't succeed?* Frequently, the answer is: *Not much.* Failure can be a huge hit emotionally, but more often than not it is just a small hit to reality.

You have endured failures in the past, and you will endure them in the future. As long as you learn from them, you *will* make progress.

Summary

Failure must not be viewed as a setback, but an opportunity. Within every misfire is a lesson to be learned. Change your perspective from what failure seems to be to what it actually is: a normal, necessary part of the process.

We all agree that it makes no sense to expect someone to succeed on the first try, yet when we turn to look at our own lives, we forget to apply the same expectations.

Whether it is failure by action or inaction, you must actively choose to push past your fears to reap the rewards that lie beyond the unknown. If you make a mistake, learn from it. If you face adversity, forget what others are saying (or what you think they're saying) and focus on yourself. Ultimately, a failure isn't a failure if you pick yourself up and try again.

Thomas Edison said it well: "Our greatest weakness lies in giving up. The most certain way to succeed is always to try just one more time."

6
Measure Against Yourself

The Law of Competition

Do not compare yourself to others, but rather compare today's you to yesterday's. Strive to be incrementally better and you will reach new heights, untethered by the unreasonable expectations derived from comparisons to an infinite supply of others.

What Are the Odds

Most incredible feats happen on days that start out like any other. On a warm morning in 1939, a young man raced across the college campus of UC Berkeley. His name was George Dantzig, and he was late for statistics class.

Huffing and puffing, he pulled open the door and walked into a class underway. His professor was deep into the day's lecture and his fellow students were fervently taking notes. Dantzig found a seat in the back and pulled out his books, doing his best not to make any noise. Up on the board were two statistics problems, which he assumed were that week's homework. He carefully rewrote them in his notebook. Class ended not long after, and, to avoid being chastised, he slipped out ahead of everyone else.

Dantzig went home and subsequently got to work. Unlike most assignments, the latest proved to be more challenging than usual. Still, he persisted, and after a couple of days he had functional proofs written for each of the two statistics problems, solving them both.

Finally having the solutions, he went to his professor's office, head down, to personally apologize not only for being late to class, but for taking so long to complete his homework. The professor acknowledged Dantzig's apology with a wave of his hand and told him to leave the work on his desk.

For the next six weeks, Dantzig continued on with his life. The incident was all but forgotten ... until one Sunday morning when someone banged on his front door. He groggily opened it, not sure who to expect, but least of all thinking he'd see his statistics professor standing before him.

Like Dantzig had been the day he was late to class, the professor was breathing heavily from running across campus. The professor's eyes were wide as he tripped over his words, all the while waving something in the air. Dantzig soon realized that the professor was waving the math proofs he'd turned in weeks earlier. As it turned out, the two homework assignments that were written on the board were not assignments at all, but examples of famous unsolved statistics problems. And George Dantzig had solved them both.

Luck of the Will

How was George Dantzig able to solve the problems when no one else could? Was there something special about him that allowed the answers to emerge?

Perhaps we could point to the fact that both of Dantzig's parents were linguists, and that his father was also a mathematician. Maybe we could claim his success was because he had grown up with a quality education and a fascination for geometry and math. It could be argued that he was uniquely equipped to produce such a fantastic revelation. But when we look at the rest of the graduate-level students in his class, we discover they were *all* top performers—Dantzig didn't stand out in the least.[30]

Instead of having a special advantage, Dantzig accidentally put himself in an advantageous position.[31] He missed the beginning of class, the critical part when his professor unintentionally perpetuated the impossibility of the two statistics problems. Before he arrived, the professor explained to his students how mathematicians had tried and failed for years to come up with the correct answers, which painted a bleak possibility that they themselves could figure it out. The tone was set, and not one of the other students even attempted to give the problems a shot. Dantzig, however, had no idea.

Thinking they were homework assignments, he took them home like any other night and started chipping away. There were no pre-filled notions of impenetrability, no suggestions of failure, and because of this, Dantzig was free to work without the shackles of expectation.

---

30 At least they showed up on time, though.

31 In other words, he got lucky.

He even admitted it himself: "If I had known that the problems were not homework but were in fact two famous unsolved problems in statistics, I probably would not have thought positively, would have become discouraged, and would never have solved them."

Dantzig went on to publish two papers, one on each of the proofs. He worked a full career, contributing to the field of linear algebra more than anyone else during his time.

The story of that fateful morning was so powerful, so memorable, that fifty-eight years later two young writers fashioned a version of Dantzig's tale to begin their movie, *Good Will Hunting*. In it, actor Matt Damon plays the part of the titular character, Will Hunting, who figures out a solution to an "unsolvable" problem and unknowingly launches himself on a journey of self-discovery.

It's no wonder that Dantzig's story resonated with Matt Damon, who co-wrote the movie: When Damon was younger, friends and family ardently petitioned him against acting. If he were to measure his progress or self-worth against others' estimation of him, Damon certainly wouldn't have continued down that path. Of course, we know that wasn't the case. In fact, Damon was so committed that he dropped out of Harvard to pursue his dream.

When things are tough, Damon remembers the words his college acting teacher constantly recited, "Just do your work, kid." All these years later, he still uses those words to measure against himself: "If everything on the movie is going wrong, I'll make sure that my work is tight and go from there."

Now that Damon is successful, other people ask him if *they* should become an actor, and his answer is always a strong "no."[32] His reason is that acting is so difficult and full of rejection, that if you persevere through your peers and loved ones (and Matt Damon) telling you it's a bad idea, then you just might have what it takes.

As for *Good Will Hunting?* It won Damon and his co-writer, Ben Affleck, the Oscar for Best Screenplay.

You Versus You

There's roughly eight billion people on earth. For a given skill, there's only one person who can be the "best" and one who can be the "worst" because to be either signifies they alone top the charts (or bottom them out) in a particular category. That means the odds of you holding one of those titles are approximately one in eight billion—which is effectively zero.

Why does that matter? Because by comparing yourself to others, you are giving yourself zero chance to overcome the feeling of being lesser than. There will always be someone better than you, and there will always be someone worse. It's a statistical guarantee. Therefore, instead of focusing on others, compare yourself to—you guessed it—yourself.

Part of having a healthy outlook on life is being able to discern the difference between what you can control and what you can't. Trying to beat others falls into the latter category. You can't control who you're exposed to, what they can do, the way they perform, or how you stack up. You can, however, control how you stack up against your own performance.

To measure your progress, you must first identify the

---

32 Surprised? Me too.

elements in play. There's a variable that doesn't change (static) and one or more that do (dynamic).[33] In this case, the static variable is your past self. Once the present becomes the past, it can't be changed; the now morphs from a moment of possibility into a memory, the data of days gone. Take that data, the unchanging facts of your personal history, and use them to compare against how things are going right now—today's dynamic self.

When you measure against yourself and operate at your own pace, a few things happen. First, your progress becomes apparent and trackable. Second, you are more relaxed, having finally stepped off the hamster wheel. And third, you become more original; no longer being tugged by others, you start to drift into your own lane, paving new roads without concern for the highways of the masses.

Let yourself travel at a natural speed. Don't force progress. While getting better as fast as possible sounds great, you will come to realize that when you get to the distant point you imagined a few months or years ago, you will already be aiming for another point, yet again in the distance. You will never get anywhere satisfying with this approach—instead, you'll forever be on your way.

The true challenge is being satisfied with the moment while simultaneously working towards growth. To try to rush is to live in a future that never becomes the present, with success always just out of reach.

Society inundates us with stories of young achievement. People love the idea of quick success, and the very few who are

---

33 In science it's called the *control*, in mathematics it's called the *constant*—regardless of field, the approach is always the same.

independently successful at an early age are hoisted up above the rest. Oftentimes they're even presented as the norm, suggesting that if you haven't found massive success by the time you're in your late twenties, then you're a failure. Just look at how popular the Forbes 30 Under 30 list is—to be named there is much more prestigious than on the 40 Under 40 list.[34] Take a look at those who made the former list a few years back, however, and you'll see that the majority have fallen into obscurity, while those on the latter list have much more enduring success.

If the tortoise and the hare teach us anything, it's that going slow and steady wins the race. Many of the people you admire achieved success under this philosophy, by measuring against themselves and not worrying about how fast they arrive at their destination.

There are countless examples throughout history of great success at all ages. Vera Wang started in fashion design when she was forty. Samuel L. Jackson hit it big with his role in *Pulp Fiction*, which didn't premier until he was forty-six. Charles Darwin published his revolutionary *On the Origin of Species* at age fifty. Momofuku Ando was forty-eight when he invented instant ramen. Ray Croc spent most of his career as a milkshake machine salesman until he bought into McDonald's at age fifty-two and made it what it is today. Laura Ingalls Wilder was sixty-five when she published the stories that became *Little House on the Prairie*. Henry Ford was forty-five when he finally got it right with the Model T. Sam Walton opened the first Wal-Mart when he was forty-four. Julia Child wrote her first cookbook at age fifty. And Harlan Sanders, aka Colonel Sanders, franchised his first

---

34 Have you even heard of it?

Kentucky Fried Chicken when he was sixty-two years old.

If any of these people worried about what others thought of them or how they compared, they'd never have made it even half the distance to their goals.

Sweets and Drumbeats

Epictetus, the Greek philosopher, once said, "When someone is properly grounded in life, they shouldn't have to look outside themselves for approval." Hundreds of years later and thousands of miles away, Wang Anshi, the Chinese emperor, similarly advised, "The one who remained grounded is the one who reached heights."

The proof is in the philosophical pudding. For an idea to still be important centuries later, to be thought worthy enough to record, it must hold validity. It would be wise to heed their advice. Of course, it's easy to claim a belief but another thing entirely to live it.

How do you march to the beat of your own drum? Everywhere you go, people are constantly beating theirs. The more people that gather, the stronger the beat. It spreads, becoming so loud that it is almost deafening. Yet to be original and happy, you must find a way to tune it out.

In today's world, it is both easy and tremendously difficult to distance yourself from the common beat. At the click of a button or a few taps on a screen, you can be sucked right back in. Very few people do what it takes to achieve separation and inner peace.

Here are a few things you can do that will go a long way towards centering your life and mind around yourself:

- **Use social media responsibly.** Know how you pop open

Facebook or Instagram or Twitter in an idle moment and check out what's going on in the world? Try to minimize thoughtless use. Don't scroll forever. Delete the apps, delete your accounts—whatever it takes. In today's world, social media is the primary driver of insecurity and unhealthy comparison.

- **Watch thought-provoking media.** You probably understand that reality TV isn't actually reality, that you're just watching it for entertainment. It still affects you. Like a placebo that works even when people know it's a placebo, this kind of media hurts you even when you're aware of the dangers.[35] Instead, watch movies that explore curious concepts or human nature; choose shows that challenge your thinking.

- **Focus on healthy relationships.** It has been said that great minds discuss ideas, average ones talk about events, and poor minds speak about people. Prioritize the people in your life that do more of the former. Minimize or cut out those that do the latter.

- **Rethink your self-applied labels.** Do not pigeonhole your identity. You are not what you do, you are who you *are*. For example, if you think of yourself as a writer, then you're going to start comparing yourself to other writers. If you

---

35 This includes shows that bring you into the lives of the "rich and famous." Would I like a yacht out back and a swimming pool in my basement? Sure, why not—but not at the expense of my happiness and personal freedom.

think of yourself as a person who writes, there's no one else like you—and no one to accidentally compare to.[36]

As with physical health and nutrition, you are what you eat. If you fill your mind with empty information, you will become an empty vessel. The suggestions listed above are enjoyable *and* healthy to consume, participate in, or apply. Think of the opposites like candy: It's okay to have a bite every now and then, but if that's all you eat, then your psychological health will quickly take a turn for the worse. Conversely, if you consume inspiring information, then you will get inspiring results.

Summary

Limits are most often self-applied. Comparing yourself to others quickly leads to expectations and parameters that otherwise may not be necessary. You are not in a race against anyone but yourself.

If you do compare, you will find there is always someone who is better than you. This leads to constant self-doubt and dissatisfaction because you will never surpass the ideal you've set up. There's an endless supply of people to surpass, ultimately creating for yourself a struggle that has no conclusion.

Focus on competing with yourself rather than others. Who you were and what you did yesterday will no longer change—it's

---

36 When someone asks you what you do, it's better to say "I write" rather than "I'm a writer," but don't take it too hard if you slip now and then. Sometimes we just need to communicate with others in the clearest way possible. The important part is how you talk about you to *yourself*.

a data point now. Use that data to drive your improvement today. If you continuously outperform yourself on a regular basis, even if only by a small margin, you will go great distances over time.

Remember that your mind reflects what it consumes. Fill your head with ideas and thoughts that expand your universe rather than collapse it.

7
Have Fun

The Law of Play

When you are having fun, you are doing something of your own free will. In this state, you go further, longer, and harder with less overall effort. Identify the things you enjoy and put them at the heart of your creations—then you will find true freedom.

Un-Spread the Jam

Hedy Lamarr was one of the most playful women of the nineteenth century. She ran her life not according to the things she needed to do, but according to those she *wanted* to do.

Lamarr was born in Austria in 1914. As a child, she spent countless evenings exploring Vienna with her father. He was a bank director during work hours and a technology enthusiast after. Lamarr hung on his every word as he explained how technologies and society intermingled. For every technological invention, he told her, there was tremendous potential for sociological innovation.

She showed early interest in acting, eventually turning it into a well-honed skill, and finally a profession. While in London, when she was twenty-three, she met the head of Metro-Goldwyn-Mayer film studio, whom she convinced on the spot that she was the next big actress. He brought Lamarr to America, where she became an instant hit after starring in *Algiers* the very next year.

For most actors, that would be the dream: To star in a Hollywood blockbuster, have your face plastered on billboards and posters in every major city, for your name and work to be casually discussed at dinner tables around the nation. At that point, an actor would most likely either come out with more hits and leverage their fame or release a few duds and fall into obscurity. But neither of these was for Hedy Lamarr.

Lamarr continued to star in movies, but her heart was in inventing. Despite dropping out of school at age fifteen to chase a career in acting, her passion for creating enabled her to overcome any lack of formal training. When she wasn't on a Hollywood set, she could be found head down, tinkering in a small workshop inside her home.

She was famously friends with the aviation magnate Howard Hughes. "I thought the airplanes were too slow, so I decided that's not right," she recalled. "They shouldn't be square, the wings. So I bought a book of fish and I bought a book of birds, and then used the fastest bird, connected it with the fastest fish. I drew it together and showed it to Howard Hughes and he said, 'You're a genius.'" Hughes was so impressed with Lamarr that he allocated resources and employees to her without explicit parameters, save for one: Do whatever she says and help her with whatever she needs.

When World War II began, Lamarr felt guilty being so safe and making so much money at home while soldiers were losing their lives. Soon after, she learned that the Germans were jamming British torpedoes, rendering them useless the moment they left the ships' hulls. If there was a way to prevent the jamming, she thought, then the playing field would be leveled.

So she began to work on it.

If she could figure out how to skip frequencies at irregular intervals and sync the channel on the receiving end with the source on a ship, then the signal would be secure. There would be no way to jam it. The missiles would begin hitting their marks again.

Within just a few months, Lamarr came up with the solution: frequency hopping.

Along with George Antheil, a pianist and fellow tinkerer, it wasn't long before she had a working prototype followed by a successful patent in 1942. They handed their idea, fully functional and completely proven, to the U.S. Navy, who went on to integrate their technology in future ships.

Hedy Lamarr's frequency-hopping approach is still in use today as a key part of spread spectrum technology, the technique that enables Wi-Fi and Bluetooth to function.

Culmination of Mindset

How is Hedy Lamarr an example of having fun when she applied her inventing skills to a very serious and practical problem of war? Can you have fun *and* solve important problems?

The answer is a resounding yes.

You will discover that most chapters in this book feature a

story in which a person or people solve a real problem. At the same time, nearly all of them were indulging their curiosities—having fun—while doing it.

Having fun and solving problems aren't mutually exclusive. You can do both. In Lamarr's case, it just so happened that the activity she found enjoyable—inventing—overlapped with a need. And she took advantage of it.

Every law of Mindset is integral to allowing yourself to play. Lamarr was billed by Hollywood as "the world's most beautiful woman." She recalled society's perception of her, telling one interviewer, "People have the idea I'm sort of a stupid thing." She went on to remind him that, "The brains of people are more interesting than the looks," challenging assumptions about beauty and intelligence (Law of Disruption).

It was critical to her self-expression that she didn't fashion her life around the goal of meeting the expectations of others, but of her own self (Law of Expression). When she left school to act, those close to her were disappointed in the decision (Law of Continuity), yet she traveled alone across the Atlantic and reached phenomenal heights (Law of the Unknown). When she gave up acting opportunities to spend more time in her studio (Law of Play) to focus on inventing (Law of Connection), those around her (and celebrity armchair critics everywhere) disparaged her choice—but again, she was met with wonderful success (Law of Competition).

Hedy Lamarr embodied the Laws of Mindset. She stayed true to herself, challenged expectations, faced confrontation, took chances, and measured against herself. Combined, she was able to play, have fun, and ultimately shed the shackles of expectation to be truly free.

Full-Time Hobbyist

In our family, whenever we're about to face a challenge, we always remind each other to "have fun." It's a family motto of sorts. Regardless of how important the obstacle is that we're coming up against—a speech, interview, experiment, whatever—we know that our best work emerges in a state of play.

Finding the fun in things—especially important ones like our work—isn't easy. But it *is* worth the effort. When we enjoy ourselves, time falls by the wayside. We tackle problems with more energy and depth. And we go at it longer than if we were doing something we didn't enjoy.

Play brings freedom. No longer will you worry about the end result or how much time and effort something takes. When you're having fun, those things matter less. The joy becomes a reward in itself.

Think about one of your hobbies. How many hours do you spend on just that activity? Perhaps you like to garden or watch movies or cycle. Whatever it is, you almost certainly don't track how long you do it or watch the clock waiting for that session to end. Why? Because it's enjoyable. That's the feeling you must find in the creative things you do.

Even for people who absolutely love their work (myself included), there are still aspects that they don't enjoy (also myself included). They just focus on the parts they love. As difficult as it may be, you must do the same. We can't love everything about our jobs or the project at hand, but we can do our best to find the pieces that make us happy or get us excited—and use them to energize our work as a whole.

As sad as it may sound, the truth is clear: society values

money over happiness. In practice, that translates to people doing things they don't like because the pay is better.[37] To make happiness your priority is to *go directly against society*. This is one of the most challenging things to do. Every day, people all around us fail to do it.

To succeed, to put your happiness at the top of the totem pole, you must embody the Laws of Mindset in their entirety.

- **The Law of Expression:** Be honest with yourself about what makes you happy and gets you excited. Let that show through. Ignore the naysayers.

- **The Law of Disruption:** All our lives, we are served up "truths." Peel back the layers of what you were told to believe to discover what you truly believe.

- **The Law of Connection:** Ideas are made up of fundamental concepts. Creativity is a misnomer—you don't actually create, you *connect*.

- **The Law of the Unknown:** Let fear pass over you, acknowledge it, and thank it for showing you the path towards growth. Accept the possibility of confrontation.

- **The Law of Continuity:** Failure is part of the process. It teaches you lessons and helps you grow. Welcome it and keep going.

- **The Law of Competition:** Stop comparing yourself to

---

[37] I understand it's a privilege *not* to have to prioritize money. There are people out there who have no choice, and I respect that. There are also people out there, many of them, who do have a choice and still choose money over happiness.

others and start using your own journey as a measuring stick. Be better than you were yesterday.

- **The Law of Play:** At the end of the day, you must strive to be happy. You achieve this by filling your time with activities you enjoy. As a bonus, you also perform at a higher level.

Once all of these are in place, remind yourself that the time you have here on Earth is short—you might as well enjoy it. Whenever possible, play as if you were a kid again. It's not always possible to find work that's fun, but you *can* find fun in your work.

Summary

Those who enjoy what they're doing will always outshine those who don't.[38] Their passion turns work into play. When you have a fiery enthusiasm for the task at hand, you have the best chance of success in bringing your creation to life.

Think of the ability to have fun as if it were a superpower. With it, you can stop clocks, think clearer, and last longer. As with all superheroes, it takes time and practice before you reach your true potential. Don't fret if, in the beginning, you find yourself disheartened. The mind is a powerful tool, you must put in the work if you want to wield it with effect.

Use the Laws of Mindset to help you overcome the obstacles

---

[38] Think about that photograph of Einstein—the most iconic genius of our time—with the goofy grin, wide eyes, and tongue sticking out so far it almost touches his chin.

of the intellect and of society. You will be pulled in all directions from the things that bring you joy. The journey may be difficult; at times you will question yourself or feel like the only person in the world—but persevere and you will reap the rewards.

PART 2
PROCESS

How to Create from Start to Finish

The Laws of Action

"Sometimes we make the process more complicated than we need to. We will never make a journey of a thousand miles by fretting about how long it will take or how hard it will be. We make the journey by taking each day step by step and then repeating it again and again until we reach our destination."
—Joseph B. Wirthlin

When traveling, the places you go may have different societies, cultures, architecture, faux pas, people, and languages, but regardless of how different the destinations are—and there's a whole planet full of them—each one is reached in similar fashion: you travel on roads, follow signs, and perform a combination of riding in vehicles and walking on foot.

Creativity is like traveling. The end results—the destinations—can be wildly different, mysterious even. But the process by which you arrive is fundamentally the same. This section takes those roads, signs, and transportation methods and outlines them so that you'll get to your destination, every time.

The Laws of Action are arranged in chronological order, from the beginning of the creative process right to the end. You can use them as a resource for understanding, as well as a step-by-step guide to the process of creativity.

You have no doubt heard this before. Perhaps you understand it already, maybe you don't, but by the end of this section, and with a sprinkle of real-world application, you will:

Trust the process.

8
Ask More Questions

The Law of Curiosity

The only way to know what is not known is by asking. Do not fear answers, for they hold no power over you. Questions are journeys: the ones worth going on hold unknown destinations.

Know Thyself

The evening sun casts low rays of light across a gravel path. A short, balding man with bulging eyes moves one foot after the other, in no rush, rustling up small clouds of dust as he walks. His hands are lightly clasped just below his lower back. There's an oily shine to his hair that seems to have rubbed off on the neck of his battered tunic, which looks as if it was once white, many years ago. His eyes are out of focus, until—

A young man appears from behind him, slightly out of breath. His hair is cut in clean lines, his tunic is bright and spotless. Unlike the short man, he represents the refined Athenian standards of the time.

"Excuse me, sir?" the young man says.

The balding man's eyes snap back to the present, then to the young man. He says nothing and keeps walking.

"I'm sorry to bother you. Are you Socrates?" the young man asks.

"Am I?" the man says.

"You have the look ... from the stories. You look just like him."

"What does he look like?"

"Like you," the young man says as he waves his arm up and down the balding man's torso. "And you talk like him." He claps a single strike of recognition. "You *are* him!"

This scene, or a version of it, played out day after day for the man that was called Socrates. People young and old (but mostly young) went to great lengths to find and speak with him. According to the records of his students, Plato and Xenophon, Socrates was obsessed with the concept of self-knowledge.[39]

For most of his life, Socrates was relatively unknown. He was a stonemason, like his father, and served in the military during three campaigns. It wasn't until he retired that he stumbled upon teaching, unintentionally gaining the renown that still carries his name to our ears today.

It is said that the Oracle at Delphi was asked who the wisest person was. Without hesitation, she named Socrates, a man most had never heard of. Word finally reached Socrates himself, and, determined to better understand true wisdom, he began questioning influential and important public figures in Athens.

Using what would later be called the Socratic method—essentially a series of questioning that gets to the heart of

---

[39] Socrates, despite being one of the greatest teachers and philosophers in history, has no official writings of his own.

knowledge—Socrates discovered that those whom most people think are wise don't know much more than the average citizen. The difference is that they *claim* to know. This disgusted Socrates because he knew that praise of unqualified persons frequently had ill consequences.

Socrates ultimately realized that he, too, knew very little. And, equally important, *he did not know what he did not know.* Ignorance was a guarantee. Thus, the Socratic paradox was born:

"I know that I know nothing."

A Truth, Examined

Nearly everyone has heard of Socrates. Most know that he was a philosopher. Many have heard of the Socratic method. Some know what it is. But few are aware that Socrates was one of the first martyrs for truth.

Socrates was born in Athens, Greece in 470 BCE. Most of his life is unknown. However, we do know that he fought in the Peloponnesian War, which allowed him to travel far and wide. That experience—all the life, death, and people along the way—shaped him into the great mind whose thoughts have rippled across centuries and cultures.

It was Socrates who famously stated, "The unexamined life is not worth living." Of course, he was not saying that life is not worth the effort, but rather that without the effort to self-analyze, little benefit could come from it. He focused on the concepts of virtue and good and used the Socratic method to break down ideas and arguments to their core.

For the first time, someone was teaching that everything should be questioned. The youth of Athens were particularly drawn to his perspective. As time went on, more people heard of the man called Socrates and the revolutionary philosophy he was spreading.

As with most radically new ideas (whether good or bad), Socrates' ideas began to garner opposition. Socrates slowly gained the attention of the ruling class. It wasn't long before he was arrested for supposedly corrupting the minds of the youth. Soon after, he was tried and sentenced to death.

In ancient Greece, citizens who were found guilty of a grave crime had the option to choose exile rather than execution. But Socrates told Plato and his other students that he couldn't possibly run away, that to do so would be admitting he was afraid of death—that his ideas weren't worth dying for. So, on that fateful day in 399 BCE, Socrates willingly drank poison hemlock, voluntarily ending his own life.

Today we remember Socrates as one of the first western philosophers. He taught us that wisdom is admitting there are many things (most things, in fact) that we do not know. With that position, how can one possibly make a claim of any kind? The only words that can be uttered, under this pretense, are ones of questioning.

Questions, then, are the path to truth.

Innies and Outies

The best way to have a creation resonate with others is to speak to truths. Imagine that each nugget of truth is a fossil buried deep below the earth. The only way to get to them is to grab a shovel and start digging. Every question you ask is another sweep of dirt tossed aside.

There are two types of questions: external and internal. A few poor souls out there never learn to employ either, but most of us have a tendency towards one or the other. If you are extroverted, chances are you're an external questioner; if you're introverted, then you're most likely an internal questioner.

Perhaps you know the type. The external questioner is one who is bold—brash, even—in the face of confrontation, who doesn't stand down and has no problem letting their thoughts be heard or raising their hand and asking a question. They are also most likely to have trouble with self-reflection or looking within for knowledge and truth rather than without. While they may be professionally successful in the world, they are also more likely to feel disconnected from it.

Conversely, there's the quiet type. The internal questioner is one who avoids social pressure, who opts out of raising their hand, preferring instead to let the current flow around them rather than divert it. They are more aware of themselves and how they feel than the bold type because their thoughts and feelings are their primary world—it's the only safe place. While they tend to be less traditionally successful, they also tend to be more self-aware.

Keep in mind that no one is only external or only internal. Extroverts have introverted qualities and introverts have extroverted ones. Nothing is black and white. So while tendencies do exist, and there are probabilities one can bet on, they aren't the rule for everyone.

While there is profound power in both types, there is also immense weakness. To make the best of your creative adventures, you must be well versed in both. You must ever endeavor to know the world as well as yourself. The benefits are tremendous:

External Questions: Ask questions about the world and borrow expertise from everything and everyone around you. Learn from knowledge and experiences that you would otherwise not be exposed to. For example:

- *What is the burning point of olive oil?*
- *How do reptiles grow their limbs back?*
- *Who is the most technically skilled drummer in history?*
- *Why does the fire alarm beep at such a high pitch?*
- *When did the first human tell a lie?*
- *Where does plutonium come from?*

Internal Questions: Ask questions about yourself to better understand others, as well as your relationships with them. Distractions are everywhere; it's easy to forget to take the time to be still and look inward. The only way to put a piece of yourself into your creations is by knowing yourself. Examples:

- *What patterns do I see that no one else can?*
- *Who truly challenges me?*
- *When do I give up and when do I persevere?*
- *Do I genuinely care about the things I give my attention to?*
- *How can I be a better person? parent? sibling? partner? etc.*
- *Why do I feel this way about this thing?*

Explore the world to gather knowledge. Using that knowledge, investigate yourself to assemble opinions and ideas. Take those opinions and ideas and put them back out into the world. Ask questions about them. Explore the world to gather knowledge—rinse and repeat.

We agree that questions are critical, but are answers as well? Does every question *need* an answer?

The answer is no. Not just no, but a resounding no. If every question we ever asked didn't get answered, sure, that would be a hell unlike any other. But if they *all* had answers, then one of the most important subjects in the history of humankind wouldn't exist: philosophy.

Philosophizing is the practice of asking questions without answers. *What is the meaning of life? Do we have free will?*[40] *Does true objectivity exist? Is there such a thing as a selfless act?* And so on. Philosophy doesn't exist to provide answers, but to provide questions. In turn, its questions help us think abstractly about ourselves and the universe we live in.

When you learn to get comfortable with questions that don't have answers—when you feel at ease soaring through the clouds and mists and sunlight of abstract thought—*that's* when you expand the bounds by which your mind operates. And that's when your creativity becomes endless.

Sometimes a question is all you need. It's an impetus to explore for exploration's sake. No one is called curious when they find answers, they're called curious because they ask questions. Curiosity is the desire for knowledge without a reason. Isaac Asimov, the Golden Age science fiction author, said it best: "The true delight is in the finding out rather than the knowing." This idea hearkens back to childhood, when every other question was *"Why?"* until we'd finally had enough or (more likely) the adult being questioned had had enough.

There's a reason that "childlike curiosity" is a phrase. As

---

40 My personal favorite.

children, before society hooks us with its leash, we are curious about everything. There is no question too silly or too ignorant or too obvious. Anything goes. And, because we are only children, our lack of knowledge is accepted. But then we grow up and all that goes out the window.

Remember this fact from the Introduction: One NASA study found that 98 percent of kids are at the creative *genius* level at age five, but by fifteen years old, only 12 percent rank as high—and by adulthood the number dwindles to a mere 2 percent.

Adults who act like curious children are frowned upon. Actions that are pardoned by society at a young age are deemed foolish at an older age. Playfulness and curiosity are no longer positive, encouraged traits. Because of this, 96 percent of children lose their creative genius. Are you one of them? Think about how you act when someone around you does or says something that's out of the ordinary, albeit totally innocent. How you treat others is how you also treat yourself.

Do not be afraid to look stupid. The only way to learn is to ask, and not every question you ask will be perfect or sensible. Why would they be? Unless you know the answer before asking a question, how can you possibly know if a question will deliver?

You can't.

Communal Beacon

Fair warning: All the questions, answers, and knowledge in the world are useless if you don't do something with them. It's fine if you disagree with an insight, but make sure to understand why, and what position you *do* support instead.

That's not to say you should simply accept all answers as

truth. Not at all. You must verify them by comparing your answers to those of others. The truth is like a lighthouse. It stands tall in the dark and gives you an unmoving reference point. When your boat is thrashing in the wind, when the ocean waters are spraying in your face, you can look to your lighthouse for guidance. But a lighthouse isn't built by one person—it's built by a collective.

Share your answers *and* your questions. Overlap your reality with those of others. And you will always find your way back to what is real and true.

Summary

Questions are powerful tools that excavate truth. Truth is the means by which a creation connects with others. It draws others in, whether you are making a slide presentation or the next great bridge.

Use external questions to explore the world around you. They will give you the fuel you need to create things worth creating. Use internal questions to better understand yourself. In doing so, you will better understand humanity. Together they will bring you closer to the truth.

Don't be afraid to let your curious inner child surface. Ignore what others may think. Exploring the world (and being smart) does not necessitate that you look or sound like you know what you're talking about.

Be at peace with questions that don't have answers. Often, it's not the answer that enlightens, but finding the right question.

Allow yourself to be playful and you will not only find the truth—the truth will find *you*. Like Socrates said, "Wonder is the beginning of wisdom."

9
Define the Problem

The Law of Precision

Sharpen your understanding of a problem through investigation. Peel back the layers until you are left with a single question that, when answered, resolves the heart of the matter.

A Lasting Invention

In 2008, a 5,500-year-old shoe was discovered in Armenia. It was dubbed Areni-1 after the cave it was found in. Made of a single piece of cowhide, the shoe was preserved for thousands of years thanks to a healthy covering of sheep droppings, which created a seal that protected the shoe against the elements. Finding Areni-1 proved that human beings searched for ways to protect their feet as far back as 3,500 BCE.

For most of modern history, shoes were not as common as we might expect. Some Ancient Egyptians wore sandals but not many and not often. In Ancient Rome, wealthy citizens identified clothing with power, starting a shift that resulted in the upper class being the only ones who wore foot protection, which became the status quo for centuries.

That is, until Jan Ernst Matzeliger came along in the nineteenth century and changed everything.

Matzeliger, originally from Dutch Guiana, started working with his father in a machine shop at the age of ten. He traveled the world as a mechanic on an East Indies merchant ship, and subsequently settled in Philadelphia, Pennsylvania, where he was first introduced to the shoe trade. Despite not having much money, any friends, or the ability to speak English, Matzeliger leveraged his technical skills to earn an apprenticeship with a cobbler and quickly learned the ins and outs of shoemaking.

Every human being needed shoes, but only a few were able to get them. He was fascinated with the industry, determined to figure out why shoes were relegated to the rich. Why did they cost so much? Was it one particularly problematic step or the entire process as a whole? Could anything be done to make them more affordable?

Matzeliger soon moved to Lynn, Massachusetts, a small town north of Boston and the center of shoe manufacturing in the United States, and got a job at a shoe factory. It was there that he uncovered the part of the process that caused prices to rise: lasting.

"Lasting" is the term used to describe the method of attaching the top of the shoe to the sole, and "hand laster" is the title of the person who performs it. Lasting was a delicate process, requiring years of training and practice to ensure a shoe's durability. Hand lasters were few in number and only able to produce a limited quantity of shoes per day. While the rest of the shoe could be made by the hundreds, the final step—putting everything together—created a massive bottleneck that caused shoes to be scarce, thus raising prices and relegating them to the wealthy.

After carefully watching hand lasters sew shoes, Matzeliger taught himself how to do it through trial and error, and, having a thorough understanding of how to build a shoe, he had a fully working lasting machine within six months.

When the hand lasters got wind of it, they bashed the idea, laughing at all the energy spent on a project they said would go nowhere. Still, Matzeliger persisted, eventually selling rights to two-thirds of his findings to raise enough money to make the second and third models, which led to the submission and acceptance of his patent in 1883.

Hand lasters could only make fifty pairs of shoes per day, but Jan Ernst Matzeliger's invention made a staggering seven hundred—one machine did the work of fourteen human beings. Shoe prices were driven down so that anyone who wanted to protect their feet could finally afford to, forever improving the lives of the general public around the world.

Inverse Proportions

They say necessity is the mother of invention. In this case, the necessity came from Matzeliger's actual mother, an enslaved person, who gave birth not only to the solver, but the problem in the solver's eyes. Because of her, he witnessed firsthand what the earth could do to exposed feet. Matzeliger watched his mother work barefoot despite injuries that often left her limping and bloodied. This led to chronic pain and infection, which was significantly more dangerous in his time before the invention of antibiotics.

Jan Ernst Matzeliger picked up on the fact that there was a problem in the shoe industry causing high prices, but he didn't know exactly what part of the shoemaking process was causing it. From the outside, one could point to any number of factors and wonder if they were the source. Was it the inherent nature of bespoke customization? Could it be that artisans were in short supply? Was it just the raw amount of time it took to fashion a shoe?

Making shoes was a complex process that involved several dozen people and a multitude of materials before a single pair could be made. It included salespeople who met with customers to measure their feet; tanners who fashioned animal hides into usable leather; tradespeople to take those measurements and cut various elements of the top and sole of a shoe; lasters who fastened both parts together with enough precision and strength to endure the beating our bipedal species gave shoes on a daily basis; and a myriad of finishers who would scrape, smooth, and burnish the shoe into near perfection.

There was a problem to solve, but Matzeliger was helpless without first understanding the industry to identify the problem—so that's exactly what he did.

Starting at the bottom rung, he repaired shoes with a local cobbler and worked through the process step by step until he encountered the bottleneck that was the hand laster's contribution. It became evident that every step before and after the lasters could produce significant results per day. Leather could be cut en masse, the individual pieces could be fitted together relatively quickly, but everything came to a crawl when it hit the laster's station.

Matzeliger, by elimination, defined the problem by locating its source. It evolved from *How do I make shoe production cheaper?* to *How do I make the lasting process faster?* Through experience and investigation, he concluded that the faster his machine, the lower the price. With his technical experience, that was a challenge he was certainly capable of overcoming.

Within five years, Jan Ernst Matzeliger built three lasting machines, each one better than the previous, patented the method, and revolutionized the shoe industry—all because he had a clear goal to work towards.[41]

Peel the Onion

In the Law of Curiosity, we learned the importance of asking questions—that while necessity is the mother of invention, curiosity is the father of discovery. Once you have uncovered a problem, whether through necessity or curiosity, that problem must then be sharpened to a point.

An idea doesn't just materialize; it's the effect of some cause. There are two ingredients: (1) A particular set of events, knowledges, and experiences—the cause that triggers (2) an idea—the effect. These are also commonly referred to as the problem and the solution, respectively.[42]

In 1908, Henry Ford brought the Model T into the world. It was the first universal vehicle that could be employed in a variety of ways, answering his question: *How can we make travel easier?*

---

41 In other words, each lasting machine was better than the last, until, at last, the last lasting machine replaced hand lasters for good.

42 We explore the importance of and methods for defining problems in the Law of Precision.

Before the Model T, the average American used a horse and buggy to get around. Unlike cars, horses need to be fed, housed, and looked after. They require regular maintenance: horseshoes need to be replaced, harnesses and saddles require repair, and when horses fall ill or sustain injury, they're out of commission until they get well. It's as if your car doubled as a one-ton pet.

For a time, cars were a vast improvement, and people were happy. But as the years drew on, newer generations had nothing to compare them to. They either didn't live during horse-and-buggy times or were too young to remember. When the golden age of science fiction introduced us to flying cars, robots, and computers, the question emerged again: *How can we make travel easier?*

It took a few decades, but eventually computing evolved enough to take self-driving cars from the pages of sci-fi, right out of our imaginations, and drop them onto our real-world roads. The new question became: *How can we make cars drive themselves?*

Every car company from Audi to Volkswagen has, at some point, attempted to solve the problem. Every year, one of them got closer, and every year they discovered several more hurdles. Finally, in 2003, Elon Musk, engineer and entrepreneur, founded a company called Tesla to scrutinize a host of assumptions about cars, including those regarding self-driving.

Josh Kaufman, author of *The Personal MBA*, said, "Whoever best describes the problem is the one most likely to solve it." It's no wonder, then, that Tesla has gotten so far. In less than two decades, Musk and Tesla repeatedly evolved and defined the problem that would help them achieve self-driving success:

- For a car to drive itself meant that it would need to be able to parse situations on the fly rather than follow a given directive. It had to see and react, not simply follow a line from A to B. They took the initial question: *How can we make cars drive themselves?* and instead asked: *How can we help cars read the road?*

- When they achieved that—a car could parse the road using their Neural Network—they realized that they couldn't just program it to handle the road, they'd have to send the car out into the world to parse scenarios as they came, learning from them and performing better the next time. The new question became: *How can we help cars learn?*

- Then it became a machine learning problem, which they also figured out, but, despite being able to learn, a single car couldn't absorb enough data to prepare for the almost limitless number of scenarios it'd find itself in. They needed more data. It dawned on them that while one car alone couldn't learn fast enough, the entire "fleet"—all the Tesla cars on the road—could bring in enough data to make headway. They began asking: *How can we help cars learn from each other?*

Tesla connected all their cars to the internet, and together they began to share and learn at an exponential rate, successfully achieving self-driving capabilities.[43] In addition, this continues to improve the effectiveness—and safety—of vehicular travel

---

43 Now cars can drive themselves like horses did over a century ago.

with each passing year. By the end of 2020, the company had sold over 1.4 million cars.

The Problem Method

Many describe creativity as "problem solving," when in fact it only accounts for one third of the general process. To get to a true point of satisfaction—to give birth to solutions that matter—you must first ask *questions* that matter. The Problem Method has three separate stages that happen in sequence:

1. **Problem Seeking:**[44] First, a worthwhile problem must be uncovered. This can happen through necessity—there's a pain point in everyday life. Or curiosity—an inefficiency is discovered through inquiry.

2. **Problem Sharpening:** When a problem is identified, the source must be tracked down through patient investigation and experimentation. Once you diagnose the issue and outline a precise objective, *then* you are ready to begin solving.

3. **Problem Solving:** With a clear objective—a question or specific result—active work begins. Through a process of trial and error, continue to zero in on the resolution you're looking for.

Throughout the process, you will often answer one problem and uncover several more. Fear not; that's normal. If it happens, start

---

[44] Credit goes to Brian Collins for this term.

from step one or two, and repeat the process. Eventually you will find yourself with an answer that will alleviate the core problem.

Summary

Problems are served up from two general sources: necessity and curiosity. Necessity is when they come to us; curiosity is when we find them of our own accord. Regardless of a problem's source or size, before any work can begin, you must first understand the foundation on which it lies.

Study the problem—the question you're trying to answer—from all sides. Learn about the history of the subject or the future an answer could provide. Talk with people who know more than you. Fill your cup with the waters of knowledge that come from action and discussion.

Using alternatingly broad and deep insights along with experimentation, repeatedly sharpen the question you're asking, often writing and rewriting it until the problem you end up with addresses the heart of the issue. Oftentimes this may not even resemble the initial question.

Once the dagger of inquiry is sharpened to a fine point, then—and only then—strike down the wall behind which your solution is hiding.

10
Gather Inspiration

The Law of the Muse

Do not start from zero. Do the necessary research to collect relevant ideas. Use these as inspiration, plucking the best parts of each to combine into something of your own. Don't wait for the muse to strike—reach out and strike it yourself.

A Hike to Remember

George de Mestral took his dog for a hike in the Swiss Alps on a beautiful morning in 1941. The sun was just peeking over the horizon as they began their peaceful journey on a quiet path through the woods.

As they made their way between the trees and up the mountain, Mestral and his dog encountered a portion of the path that was overgrown with shrubbery. With no other way around, Mestral grabbed the leash with a firm grip and waded through the brush.

They came out on the other side unscathed thanks to Mestral's long sleeves and pants and his dog's thick coat, but both of them were covered in small burrs from the burdock plant. If a porcupine turned into a spherical seed, they'd look a lot like burdock burrs. Mestral found a resting spot on a nearby log to rid him and his dog of the prickly balls.

After a few minutes of methodical removal, Mestral and his canine pal were on their way again, all thought of burrs left behind with the burrs themselves. The rest of the day was pleasant as the two enjoyed a leisurely walk up the mountain. But, as they say, what goes up must come down.

With sunlight waning, Mestral packed up his things and the two began their descent. Again, they were faced with the overgrown portion of the path, and again they were covered in burrs when they emerged from the other side. This time, however, Mestral's mind was clear and fresh from the day of solitude. The burrs drew his attention. Curious as to how they worked, he pocketed a few and headed home.

Mestral was an electrical engineer, and he just happened to have a microscope in his home workshop. He carefully removed a burr from his pouch and placed it under the lens. A few knob-twists later and the burr was in focus, magnified several times over. What he saw led him down a path that would inspire him, challenge his perseverance, and ultimately find its way into the homes of millions of people around the world.

The burrs were made up of countless spikes packed closely and pointing straight out from the center. Under the microscope, Mestral noticed there was a tiny hook at the tip of each spike, similar to the curve at the end of a crochet needle. When the hooks rubbed up against fabric or fur, they inevitably caught, creating a natural binding that could be undone with a gentle, but firm tug. Mestral couldn't help but be curious, pondering the potential uses if he could reproduce the effect.

Over the next eight years, Mestral developed the mechanical process to artificially reproduce the burdock burr's natural form. He eventually succeeded, and in 1955 his patent was accepted in Switzerland. By 1960, he had patents in close to a dozen countries, including Canada, Germany, Italy, the United Kingdom, and the United States.

George de Mestral named his invention—the hook-and-loop—by combining the French words *velour* (velvet) and *crochet* (hook) to form "Velcro." Because it is durable, waterproof, corrosion proof, and flexible, NASA used Velcro extensively during the space race, and by Apollo 7, over five hundred applications of Velcro were used inside and outside the spacecraft. Today, Velcro, with all its varied uses, can be found in just about every home and workplace around the world.

Concept Collector

There are opportunities for inspiration happening around us every day if we only tune our minds to be open to them. Even for George de Mestral, it took multiple burdock-burr run-ins before his curiosity kicked in. That now-famous incident didn't occur on his first ever expedition into the woods (he was an avid hunter), but, for some reason, on that day, a certain series of events and thoughts allowed him to see what was right in front of him.

Inspiration can strike of its own accord or it can be sought after. For Mestral, it was the former. Even though he had all the right components for the burdock burr to incite his curiosity, it still took innumerable run-ins before inspiration actually struck. This is why being open to experiences and putting oneself in the right scenarios is so important. It may take several—if not dozens—of interactions before a tipping point is reached. But when you do reach it, your subconscious awareness overflows into your consciousness, pulls your attention, and inspires new thinking.

As we learned in the Law of Connection, "Base concepts can neither be created nor destroyed; they simply merge to form new combinations." The more you pay attention to the world around you—the more concepts you collect—the more ideas you are bound to produce. Remember, creativity isn't about creating, it's about combining. With a vast collection of inspiration, you will inevitably combine ideas in the same way Mestral did on his hike.

The moment of curiosity (picking up a burr to take home) and the moment of epiphany (putting it under a microscope) were—critically—the genesis of everything that came after. While Mestral's discovery makes for a good story, what occurred over the following fourteen years is equally important. Determined to solve the problem of the hook-and-loop, Mestral kept at it year after year.

Society often gives massive credence to ideas, but little attention to determination and hard work, which is why the phrase "ideas are cheap" is thrown around so often. People assign brilliance to the idea portion of creating, when in reality the execution phase deserves just as much credit.

You will find time and again that ideas are celebrated so thoroughly that merely having an interesting idea on the business front allows you to raise millions of dollars from venture capitalists to launch a startup. The lack of scrutiny on execution is exactly why these same startups have a failure rate of over 90 percent—roughly eleven out of twelve will not succeed.[45]

Execution is what takes a good idea and makes it real, but inspiration is necessary for an effective outcome. If George de Mestral spent fourteen years working without a guiding light, an idea to drive him day after day, he wouldn't have gotten very far. Understand that being inspired is a key component to bringing ideas to life, and equally important is everything that happens afterward.

Furthermore, like inspiration, execution itself is subject to the one doing the executing. Mestral wasn't just in the right place at the right time, he was also *the right person*. His background in electrical engineering made him more likely to investigate the burdock burr—and considerably more likely to solve the mystery. It was Mestral's years of training and his in-depth background knowledge that fortified his persistence.

In order to be the right person, you must be realistic about your own knowledge. Do not attempt to innovate in a field or on a subject you know nothing about, but rather in those that you have experience with. You do not need to become a master of said subjects, however (that would actually lean on the side of counterproductive). You just need to have an awareness and fundamental understanding of the general variables in play, which is why gathering inspiration—doing your research—helps increase your likelihood of discovering an idea worth chasing.

Of course, in the end, you must still put in the work.[46]

---

[45] Venture capitalists only need one startup to succeed to cover the risk they took on all the rest. You as a creator are effectively turned into a dice roll in which snake eyes is the only way to win.

[46] More on this in the Law of Showing Up.

Strike the Muse

Look around you. No matter where you are, there's *something* to observe, and if you let your mind wander and your inner child tickle, you will start to appreciate beauty in the mundane. American writer Henry David Thoreau understood this well: "It's not what you look at that matters, it's what you see."

There are things right in front of us that most people don't see at all. For example, did you know that hot and cold water sound different when they come out of the faucet? It's true—go try it. Why does it matter? Because curiosity about how water produces various pitches at high and low temperatures is the same curiosity that led George de Mestral to pick up a burdock burr and bring it home.

When you're working on a creative project, however, you don't have the luxury of waiting for inspiration to happen *to* you—you must go out and find it. Most people believe that we have to wait around for the muse to strike, when, in fact, it is we who must reach out and strike the muse. What you're looking for is called **Active Inspiration**; what happened to Mestral is **Passive Inspiration**.[47]

How do we best go about gathering Active Inspiration? The key component is keeping your senses alert. Examine things: touch them, break them down in your mind, smell the smells, taste if it's appropriate, listen for depth and time. Crank up your curiosity, then follow these steps.

---

[47] If you've been struck by Passive Inspiration, chronologically this chapter better flows if you read it before Define the Problem. If you are looking for Active Inspiration, it flows better after. Since most people are trying to solve problems they've already found—projects for work, personal endeavors, etc.—I put this chapter after.

STEP ONE: COLLECT

Before you begin to create, you must first do your research. Engineers don't build an airplane without first studying existing ones. Gather your findings using whatever receptacle makes sense: a notebook, spreadsheet, text document, computer folder, physical box, etc. This collection will serve as inspiration for your own creation.

If you're making a spreadsheet, search the web for example sheets to see how others are arranging the data. Pick and choose the parts you like from various approaches to make your own. If you're writing a song, make a log of inspiring tracks and time stamps, or swipe open your phone and use the audio recorder to make low-fi clips of all your favorite parts. If you're designing a book cover, go to the bookstore and take pictures of covers that get you excited, or go online and look through listings of e-books, screenshotting as you scroll.

However it makes sense, begin to amass a targeted library for the task at hand. As you do so, keep in mind the following principles:

- **Volume:** Gather *a lot*. Don't find two examples and move on. Instead, grab dozens. The more you find, the better (as long as it is, in the literal sense, inspiring).

- **Contrast:** Make sure that you don't just gather many things, but many *different* things. The more unrelated and varied, the better.

STEP TWO: ASSIMILATE

Once you collect inspiration, you must do something with it. Like a library of books, it isn't enough to simply have shelves packed with all sorts of bound tales and essays, you must actually read them—they need to become a part of you.

Start by taking the pieces of inspiration that speak to you the most. (If something gets you excited or gives you a positive gut reaction, go with it.) Now you must spend time *reproducing* them, piece by piece.[48]

In college, I spent a lot of time designing movie posters. I love movies, and posters are a great microcosm of branding, typography, illustration, composition, and all the other design elements. When I saw a poster in a book, I'd design it from scratch myself. Oftentimes I'd be drawing, sculpting letters, and taking photos in order to get the desired effect.

I never used the posters for anything outside of my dorm room (they've long since been lost to time), but by tracing the steps of other creators I was able to digest their processes and absorb their thinking. I have done this thousands of times in my design career, always learning and assimilating new building blocks to manipulate as I see fit.

Once you can play a song without needing the sheet music, move on to the next piece of inspiration. Over time, the songs meld together and emerge anew.

STEP THREE: COMBINE

The next step is to take what you've learned—the ideas that, if assimilated correctly, have begun to fade into the background—and begin to integrate it.

---

[48] Beginners should go all the way, taking the reproduction as close to completion as possible. Veterans can stop earlier. Once they learn what they can, the final stretch is execution, which is no longer productive since it's not knowledge, but ability, that brings them to the end.

Look at your collection of inspiration as if each piece was a building block of information. Each bit of research is made up of many blocks that form a whole. Your job is to break down the wholes, identify those blocks, and understand how they contribute and why their creators likely chose to build in the manner they did. The more you learn, the better equipped you become to build your own creation.

For example, let's say I am tasked with designing an athletics facility, something akin to a gym, that has an old school look. First, I'd collect inspiration (step one) from limited, but targeted subjects: gym brands, athletics brands, and vintage brands. Then I'd assimilate each (step two): break them down by recreating various elements, note the consistencies as well as the variables, and reorder the blocks not by original source but by subject and expression. Then I'd combine those blocks through iteration (step three). As I continue to create, the blocks shed their source identities and come into their own as something new and unique: a contemporary athletics brand with a vintage look that merges state-of-the-art equipment with the look and feel of a high school gym class.

Active Inspiration, in short, is the proactive process of gathering, understanding, and using relevant research.

Inspiration vs. Plagiarism

Pablo Picasso, the legendary Spanish artist, famously said, "Good artists borrow. Great artists steal."[49] Upon initial read,

---

49 Fun fact about Picasso: His full name is Pablo Diego José Francisco de Paula Juan Nepomuceno Crispín Crispiniano María Remedios de la Santísima Trinidad Ruiz Picasso.

it seems like he's condoning the act of copying others. Surely there must be more than meets the eye—but what is it?

It wasn't until my thirtieth year on planet Earth that I finally figured it out.

So what did Picasso mean? Was he saying that it's okay to take from others?[50] That's what the vast majority of people get from the quote, unfortunately. I've seen it used to defend copyright infringement and plagiarism on more than one occasion, and all over the internet there are articles that skim the surface with a whole lot of words that don't amount to much.

I remember when the true meaning clicked. It was a winter morning in New York City. I was on the subway looking up at the latest advertisements. There was one ad with a unique illustration style that was clearly based on another brand, but as a whole the ad was put together more effectively than its spiritual predecessor. For a moment, I was angry at what I initially perceived to be copying, but as I continued to take in the artwork, I realized that it was pulling from a number of styles. Someone on the other end had grabbed the best parts of several brands and made something fresh and, dare I say, better.

The thought behind Picasso's words is simple: When you borrow, you're taking something that is still someone else's; even if you use it, it's still clearly theirs. When you steal, you make it your own. In making it your own, it changes to fit who you are and how you use it. What was stolen is no longer

---

50 This is one of the few times I'm going to suggest that you put this book down and ponder the quote. If you're in a reading mood, then drop a bookmark or bend the corner of the page and go to the next chapter. I discuss the truth behind the quote in a few sentences, and when I do it will seem so obvious that you will laugh in disbelief that it took so long to arrive at it.

theirs—not because it's with you, but because now it's *part of you*.

When you heed Picasso's words, remember to take elements of a whole, not the whole itself, and combine it with other elements from other wholes to create a whole that's wholly yours.

Summary

Inspiration can be found everywhere. Passive Inspiration happens when the muse strikes, even though you aren't looking for it. Active Inspiration happens when you are searching for ideas to help bolster a project or endeavor.

To strike the muse, you first need to collect inspiration in volume and contrast. Then you must assimilate by breaking down a variety of pieces and reconstructing them from scratch. Finally, you are ready to combine what you have learned.

Above all, understand that gathering inspiration does not mean you take from others to use as your own. Never put your name on another's creation, but instead learn from their ideas in order to create unique, better ones.

Stay curious, keep your senses engaged—and the universe will provide you with more ideas than you can ever possibly bring to life.

11
Limit Yourself

The Law of Simplicity
While counterintuitive, the more options you have, the less likely you are to make progress. Keep your parameters tight, your path narrow—and you will find that innovative thinking appears faster and more reliably.

Builders of Blocks

In 1932, a Danish carpenter named Ole Christiansen fashioned a small duck out of wood and showed it to his young sons. They were overjoyed with the toy. Inspired, he switched from making ladders and ironing boards to full-on toy production.

The toys gained in popularity, and Ole realized he needed to name his new toy company. Without a name, it was hard for people to spread the word of his incredible work. He decided to combine the Danish words *leg* and *godt*, which means "play well," into a single word: Lego.[51]

---

[51] Little did Ole know that in Latin, *lego* also means "I put together." It would be years before he discovered this, much to his satisfaction.

Ole's son, Gotdfred, began working with his father after school every day. He had a way with numbers, and together they prospered. Gotdfred continued his work into adulthood and is responsible for the catalyst that would transform his father's company.

In 1954, on a business trip to England, Gotdfred met a fellow businessman who enjoyed hearing about their family's work. In an offhand remark, the man complained that toys don't have a system. The thought stuck in his head, and in 1958 they created the small plastic bricks that we know today, calling it the LEGO System.

For many years, the LEGO System was only comprised of simple, interlocking blocks, which they originally called "automatic binding bricks." The system was sold in kits, each including the various pieces required to assemble a particular model, such as a house or a train. Kids quickly began to build more than what was prescribed. As their block collections grew, they gave way to endless results.

What started in the hills of Denmark as an unknown father-and-son business has grown into a worldwide household name. Today LEGO employs close to twenty thousand people and has sold upwards of 400 billion pieces since Ole and Gotdfred Christensen first started making them.

Pinnacle of Puzzles

Imagine a puzzle made up of cubes arranged in a few repeating formations. Each arrangement passes in front of you, one by one, as you solve sequential mini rounds by fitting them together. It's similar to a jigsaw puzzle, but the pieces contain straight lines and right angles rather than bulbous curves and dips.

Your job is to arrange cube-sets together so that they form a long enough alignment to get wiped off the board, almost as if you were crossing them off, like three lined-up Xs or Os in Tic-Tac-Toe.[52] If you fail and too many arrangements are placed in front of you, you lose. But if you manage to keep going, the cube-sets get passed to you at increasing speeds.

There's only one core shape, the aforementioned cube, which appears in sets of four and has exactly seven different arrangements. The rules never change. The only way to win is to keep going until you can't think or move as fast as the arrangements are placed in front of you, which means that losing is inevitable. You are essentially doomed from the start.

Does that sound fun to you? Does it sound interesting? Can you imagine yourself playing this game?

Chances are, you already have, or at the very least you've heard of it. It was designed by Russian game designer Alexy Pajitnov in 1984. Since then, it has sold over 495 million copies worldwide, earning the title of bestselling puzzle video game of all time. If you haven't already guessed, the game is *Tetris*.

Craftiest of Cubes

If you happened to be walking down the street in Stockholm, Sweden in 2011, without even knowing it you may have passed by Mojang, one of the most culturally impactful video game studios in history.[53] They're the company responsible for *Minecraft*, the iconic sandbox-style video game. At the time, all they had to

---

52 In some places it's called "noughts and crosses."
53 In Swedish, mojang means "gadget."

identify themselves was a small piece of paper with their name scribbled on it taped to the front door.

Markus "Notch" Persson, who started programming at age eight, created the first version of *Minecraft* entirely on his own in early 2009, thinking it would be a six- to twelve-month hobby project. Originally, *Minecraft* was called Cave Game even though there were no caves involved at the time. It consisted solely of a large grassy platform floating in empty game space. Players had access to three blocks—dirt, stone, and wood (aka "planks")—to build whatever they could imagine.

And build they did. Despite zero marketing or advertising, *Minecraft*'s audience grew by thousands of downloads per day on word of mouth alone. *PC Gamer*, the top computer gaming media outlet, named it Game of the Year while it was still in alpha. The millionth copy of *Minecraft* was sold in January 2011, less than two years after Persson began. What started as a side project turned into not only a full-time endeavor, but a full-fledged company.

Since then, players around the world continue to build all sorts of impressive structures and models within the game, including a to-scale model of the Titanic with all of its floors and rooms; a massive recreation of Middle-earth from *The Lord of the Rings*; the entirety of Disneyland, complete with working rides; the Eiffel Tower, Palace of Versailles, the *city* of Los Angeles, the *Enterprise* from *Star Trek*, and pretty much anything else you can think of.

Today *Minecraft* is available on over half a dozen platforms, from phones that fit in your pocket all the way up to super-powerful desktop computers. There are in excess of a thousand different blocks available in-game, and more than 120 million people of all ages create to their heart's content in the world of *Minecraft* every *month*.

Two-Third Triplets

LEGO, *Tetris*, and *Minecraft* are derived from the same two fundamental concepts: **creating** and **blocks**. However, they each add a third fundamental concept that brings them into their own. LEGO adds **building**, delivered in physical form. *Tetris* adds **puzzling** and *Minecraft* adds **crafting**, both in digital forms. They each appeal to the inherent nature of human beings—mainly that we love to create (especially as children). With LEGO, you build things using predetermined plastic shapes. With *Tetris*, you solve puzzles by arranging simple cube formations. And in *Minecraft*, you craft and stack blocks in a near-infinite digital realm.

How is it that all three of these can be so similar—two thirds of their fundamental concepts are identical—yet so different and simultaneously successful? One might presume that with 66.7 percent of the final idea derived from the same concepts, they would be more alike in final form, but that's not the case at all. As we can see, limiting just one element—only 33.3 percent of the idea—to a different fundamental concept is enough to create something entirely distinct.

Nature provides proof of how sensible this is when we take a look at humans and chimpanzees. The DNA between the two species is 98.8 percent identical, yet aside from having generally similar physical layouts—hands, feet, head, and such—we lead massively contrasting existences. That tiny 1.2 percent difference is enough to put human beings in space while chimpanzees are still in trees.[54]

Limitations aren't prisons, but boundaries that invite you to think vertically (building on what's already there) rather than horizontally (adding more to the mix). When they're applied correctly and the process is given enough time to work, limits produce expressions of profound simplicity.

Do not confuse simplicity for similarity. Even an identical idea can be expressed in endless ways. Take the idea of a car, for example. We have small cars, large cars, round ones, square ones, cars that are bright or dull or multicolored, those that run on fossil fuels and those that are powered by electricity. The fundamental concept of **personal locomotion** persists, but the manner in which it manifests regularly evolves.

Fundamental concepts continuously develop as a result of emerging technologies and discoveries. When LEGO came up with their snapping blocks, it was an inevitability of the times; plastics were just emerging as a new technology. When *Tetris* was created, the game pushed computing to its limits. And when *Minecraft* was programmed it, too, was a result of opportunities—in this case, affordable personal development tools, accessible software-sharing platforms, the rise of social media to carry the idea around the world and back, and enough time to have someone who grew up building with LEGO blocks reach adulthood to make it happen.

New ideas do not emerge from adding complexity, but from the ripple effect of new developments in related or unrelated fields that trigger fresh applications elsewhere. There's a

---

54 Technically, chimpanzees were in space before humans. Ham the "astrochimp" spent six and a half minutes in weightlessness on January 31, 1961. Since humans sent him there, I still put that in our list of successes.

constant wave of innovation hurling itself onto the shores of our consciousness. It starts far back in the waters, out of sight, and slowly gains momentum as it creeps towards us, only at the last moment cresting into view as if the ideas were created in an instant. But we know better.

We understand that new ideas breed more new ideas, a constant cause-and-effect with no starting point. Like the universe itself, they are an *always-was*. It's because of this that we can confidently predict that a new idea will come along at some point that combines **creating**, **blocks**, and **virtual reality** (or augmented/mixed reality—all of which I'm a fan of) in some fresh and exciting way, and people will start all over again building wonderful creations from the depths of their imaginations.

Be One With the Pastry

Growing up, we are taught to think that *more, bigger,* and *faster* is always better. This kind of thinking puts people in a never-ending cycle of yearning and buying, always looking for the next thing to surpass the existing ones.

There is a place for this, but in creativity the opposite is often more beneficial. Limitation breeds innovation. In most cases, it's smarter (and harder) to do less; more communicable to take massive ideas and make them small and palatable; and advantageous to stop flying from one thing to the next and slow down, paying attention to what's right in front of you. The combination of these three approaches—limiting the variables in play—contributes to what we refer to as simplicity.

In the case of ideas, simplicity is the way to go. Charles Mingus, the American jazz musician, said it well: "Making the simple complicated is commonplace; making the complicated simple, awesomely simple—that's creativity."

There are two primary methods for successfully managing limitations to put something simple into the world. The first deals with how you make it; the second deals with how you talk about it.

THE ATTENTION PIE

Imagine that a person's attention span—the amount of information that they can grasp in a given moment—takes the form of a pie chart. No matter what, there are only one hundred slices to the pie, and it can't be expanded in any way. This is what you have to work with.

THE ATTENTION PIE

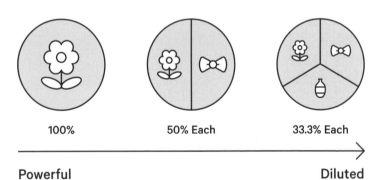

The power of simplicity in action: Here is a person's attention span as depicted by the Attention Pie. There is a maxium of 100 attention points (AP). To find the communicability of each element, divid the total AP by the total elements. The more elements added, the less attention—and the less effective—each one has.

Let's say you give that person a daisy. It's a single thing, nothing added or special beyond the beauty of the flower itself. In relation to their Attention Pie, it takes up all one hundred slices, the maximum amount of attention that one can give. For a brief moment, it's their entire world.

Next, let's tie a purple ribbon around the daisy's stem. Because there are now two elements to perceive, the flower and the ribbon get fifty slices each. From the first to the second scenario, the flower is devalued by half in the eyes of the person receiving it.

When LEGO is presented—with core concepts of creating, blocks, and building—each part of that idea gets thirty-three and one-third Attention Pie slices. If we were to add just one more concept for a total of four, each would be reduced to twenty-five slices, a reduction of 25 percent effectiveness per element. With each added element, the time necessary to process the cumulative idea exponentially increases. This is why highly complex ideas are often overlooked. Most people don't have the patience, desire, or reason to do the work to parse them, even if the concepts are true and effective in their own right.

The more elements you add, the less value each one has in the eyes of the viewer.

THE GROK THRESHOLD

Taking a simple idea and creating it is only half the battle. Afterwards, if it's something that you plan on putting out into the world, the next challenge is communicating it. Again, simplicity reigns supreme.

When you present ideas, you want people to grok them. To "grok" something is to understand it "profoundly and intuitively," according to Merriam-Webster. The difference between knowing something and grokking it is seemingly slight, but immensely powerful. To know is merely to be aware of knowledge; to grok is to understand how the knowledge comes together and fits in the grand scheme of things.

Why does it matter if your idea is grokkable? For two reasons. First, your audience understands better and is more capable of doing whatever it is you're looking for, such as joining your cause or trying your service or buying your product. Second, and arguably even more important, if they can understand it, they can share it. That's how ideas spread—when they're so simple and palatable that others can explain them in an instant.

How do we achieve grokkable ideas, then? Like many things having to do with creativity: through trial and error. You must practice communicating them to person after person. Try various approaches, emphasize a certain aspect in one test, a different aspect in another, and so on. In business, this is often called an "elevator pitch," which essentially challenges you to deliver the entirety of your idea in a short elevator ride. If the other person doesn't understand what you're saying by the time the doors open, try again.

The Grok Threshold can't be directly measured. It's a combination of abstract components. However, you can indirectly observe their effectiveness by paying attention to the body language of those you're speaking to. You'll know you've passed the Grok Threshold when their eyes light up, they lean in, and a smile stretches across their face. When you see these responses, isolate what's making them happen and experiment to maximize their intensity and frequency.

When people can grok your ideas, they will more readily

subscribe to whatever thoughts you're presenting, and they have a higher probability of spreading the word.

Figment of Fundamental Facets

Oftentimes, the thing you're looking to create has a fundamental limiter baked in. To build upon an earlier example, for something to be a car, an element of the greater idea must include **personal locomotion.** Without this core concept, no matter what you create, it can't be a car.

When we started Baronfig, we knew that the first product would be a notebook. Our company and the brand we wanted to make was going to focus on the power of imagination and creativity—on ideas. And the blank page is the cornerstone of ideation.

In order to create a notebook, we had to adhere to the fundamental limiter of what a notebook is: a stack of paper with harder pieces of paper on the top and bottom. The problem we faced was not *How do we make a new notebook?*, but *How do we make a better notebook?*[55]

As long as we stayed within the limits, pretty much anything we made could technically be regarded as a notebook.

After months of prototyping, we eventually had our answer. Our notebook, the Confidant, opened completely flat using a patented design, contained archive-grade paper that was off-white to reduce eye strain, had a high-quality bookmark that would stand the test of time, and used microweave book cloth on the cover for enhanced protection (and style).[56]

---

55 For more on defining problems, read the Law of Precision.

56 "Confidant" because a notebook is like a close friend—holding and protecting important thoughts or valued work.

Now, when people see our Confidant, the Attention Pie is refined so they understand what it is, and the message is simple enough that they pass the Grok Threshold and grasp the possibilities of this new take on notebooks. Today, people in all corners of the world use them to make every kind of creative expression possible.

Page by page, our notebooks help people push the limits of their ideas.

Summary

Limitations provide direction. If you were dropped off at the entrance of a large field and told to find the other exit, there would be a lot of wasted energy spent going in directions that wouldn't prove fruitful. If you were dropped off at the beginning of a road, however, and told to find the end, your only option is to move forward.

Strong limits give you a focus on simplicity. You leverage the benefits of *less*, *slower*, and *smaller*. Doing less makes your ideas easier to understand; approaching them slower invites a strong attention to detail and quality; and making them smaller allows them to be easily communicated.

When making a creation, be sure to weigh it against the Attention Pie. If it's too complex, it won't be understandable no matter how accurate or useful it may be. And when communicating it, strive to reach the Grok Threshold where people begin to light up with understanding; if you hit that, they'll not only participate with more depth, but it'll also be easy for them to spread your idea to others.

Creating something simple is a complex endeavor. If you do it right, you will see that less is more, slow moves fast, and small gets big—all on their own.

12
Jump In

The Law of Beginning

By its very nature, your creative destination cannot be perfectly predicted or precisely planned for. Do not waste time wondering about what could happen. Instead, take sensible precautions and simply begin.

Energy Rocks

Imagine a rock—or the mineral potassium uranyl sulfate, to be precise—that could help you see through matter. If you put your hand over it, along with a special type of black paper, you could take a snapshot of the bones within. Before 1895, that sounded impossible. Then the x-ray was invented by W.C. Röntgen.[57] And, just like that, reality got a little bit stranger.

When Marie Curie learned of the x-ray, she was fascinated not only with what Röntgen and his team did, but how they did it. Somehow, matter was being looked right through. She

---

57 Or, perhaps better said: it was *discovered*.

couldn't help but study the phenomenon.

Curie and her husband, Pierre, took rocks that were rich in uranium and began extracting just that element. They needed a lab, so the university offered them an abandoned shed to work in, which was formerly the dissection room for the school of medicine. Regardless, Curie looked fondly upon her time there, saying "It was in this miserable old shed that we passed the best and happiest years of our lives."

Eventually, they distilled enough uranium from the ore to create what is known as pitchblende, a compound that's 50–80 percent uranium. While impressive, it wasn't groundbreaking, and it certainly wasn't the end of the road for the Curies.

What came after was a realization that fueled their next several discoveries. The Curies continued to extract uranium, now from the pitchblende, until they had isolated an entirely pure sample. It took great effort and was exactly what they were working towards. But then something curious happened.[58] The Curies noticed that the remaining ore, free of uranium, had *more* energy than the pure element they had distilled. It came as a surprise—and a complete mystery.

As any good scientist would, they explored the components of the remaining ore. One after the other, they compared the energetic parts to all the known elements, coming up negative each time. There was nothing like it on the periodic table, yet there it was, right in front of them. With no other possibility in sight, there was only one thought left for their hypothesis: the Curies had discovered a new element.

Again, they worked to isolate whatever was throwing off so

---

58 The Curies' curious curiosity.

much energy. And again, they were eventually left with a pure version void of all other minerals. Their hypothesis turned out to be correct. They named the new element "polonium," after Poland.

Then, unbelievably, it happened again.

Now free of uranium and the newly discovered polonium, the leftover ore *still* had more energy than the two pure elements. The Curies hypothesized that there must be something hidden in the ore in trace amounts that was causing their electrometer to go wild. So they searched.

It took three years and several tons of ore, but they finally isolated one tenth of a gram (not quite pure) of *yet another new element*. They named it "radium" after the Latin word "ray."

As it turned out, radium was significantly more energetic than uranium and the newly discovered polonium. According to their calculations, radium was a *million* times more radioactive than uranium. The element was so active that it had a soft, blue glow. It sat in beakers scattered around the lab, which Curie described as looking like "faint fairy lights." Radium was discharging large amounts of energy through some mysterious mechanism, which they named "radioactivity."

At the time, it was thought that the atom was the smallest particle of matter. But following their discoveries, Curie hypothesized that there must be more going on in an atom than previously believed. She wrote up their findings in her PhD thesis, titled *Radio-Active Substances*. The committee in charge of reviewing called it, "The greatest scientific contribution ever made in a doctoral thesis."

In addition to discovering two elements and pioneering our understanding of radioactivity, her thesis turned the science world upside down by setting forth a plausible—and later proven—case that the atom was not the smallest particle of matter.

In 1903 Curie was awarded the Nobel Prize in Physics for her work on radiation, and in 1911 she was awarded the Nobel Prize in Chemistry for discovering polonium and radium. She is only one of four people—and the only woman—to be awarded two Nobel Prizes.

Bliss and Risk

If you find yourself having difficulty beginning—if you fear the unknown—don't be hard on yourself. That fear is hardwired into our human instincts. For millennia, avoiding the unknown was what kept our species alive. Back in prehistoric times, one wouldn't put themselves in any precarious situation that could be avoided. Risk was only worthy of the necessary.

Today, risk-taking is an inherent part of many hobbies. Skydiving and spelunking and bungee jumping are all obvious examples, but even hiking or swimming as recreational activities are fairly recent phenomena. The advent of physical safety through advancing treatments and more effective medicine has allowed humanity to push the bounds of what is considered safe. The level of risk relevant to a given activity has lowered over time.

While physical risk is lower than ever, mental risk is still very much an omnipresent threat. The world is more connected than ever before. In many ways, social pressures are at an all-time high. Just by making a post on social media, you open your life—and your identity—to judgment by tens or hundreds or even thousands of virtual followers.[59] Because of this, the fear of "doing something wrong" is stronger than ever. It's the reason we often have difficulty getting started on a new project.

The fear of judgment—from ourselves and others—exponentially magnifies the actual mental risk involved in a creative act, which, in reality, is almost zero.

In this regard, Marie Curie was primed for discovery. She was incredibly open to receiving—and reacting to—developments as they occurred. Curie was more concerned with exploring her work rather than evaluating its immediate value, whether in her eyes or anyone else's. This openness allowed her to engage in several new beginnings as the process repeatedly forced her to start over. In fact, she was so focused and unconcerned with outsider judgment that when she won a Nobel for her discoveries, she refused to travel to accept the award because it would interfere with her progress.

Like Curie, you must let go of trying to predict or control the creative outcome. Instead, simply begin and adjust course as necessary. You will find that you save more time jumping in and figuring things out as you go—even if that leads to multiple mistakes—rather than trying to prepare for every potential outcome before you even begin (and still making mistakes anyway).

When in doubt, ask yourself: *What's the worst that could happen?* Then follow that question through to an answer. As you learned in the Law of Continuity, answers to questions like this are rarely as scary as the questions themselves.

---

59 Not to mention the entire network if you post to a public profile.

Paper Pyramids

When you put a blank sheet of paper in front of someone and ask them to fill it with anything, most get anxious. "What should I do?" and "Where should I begin?" they often ask. The empty piece of paper represents near-infinite possibility.[60] When anything is possible, almost everything is unknown. Before you can jump in, however, you must manage your logical and emotional selves.

The logical self wants you to learn as much as you can, to prepare in every which way, so you can make something great right out of the gate. But that's not possible because your logical self, separately, also knows that no one gets things right on the first try. For some reason, unfortunately, the logical self illogically separates the knowledge it has, and becomes disappointed when you don't come out with something perfect on the first try.

The emotional self has a natural inclination to treat everything you do as precious. It gets caught up in the moment-to-moment work, alternating between foolish pride and unnecessary fear. It distracts from the simple truth that your creative work develops best when you allow a healthy detachment from it. You are not the things you create. You are *you*. The emotional self conflates the two, often intertwining your identity with your inventions.

To combat the tendencies of your logical and emotional selves, you must proactively prepare yourself for what's to come. You can do this by adopting two mantras. Say the first one before you begin, and the second as you continue iterating.

---

60 The very first page of a notebook can be intimidating, as if it's precious or represents all that comes after it. Years ago, I started putting a big slash across the first page to get past this feeling, and I've been doing it ever since.

- **For your logical self:** "It is unreasonable to expect to get things right on the first try. I will not wait until I feel ready, for that feeling will never come. Instead, I will begin with the understanding that failure is a part of the process. I am always and never ready."

- **For your emotional self:** "I am not my creations. However important they are to me, ultimately my creativity—and the things I create—is just one aspect of my identity. My failures, and my successes, do not define me."

These mantras will give you the steadiness needed to answer the two questions presented at the beginning of this section:

WHAT DO I DO?

Imagine that you're sitting in front of that blank piece of paper. If you were asked to write your name, how would you respond? Probably without any fear at all. You'd jump right in, write your first and last names, and put the pen down. What if you were asked to write a short story or draw up the layout of your home or sketch a bowl of fruit? Out of those three, does one incite more fear than the others? If so, then that's the one you should do.

As discussed in the Law of the Unknown, fear is an incredible tool. It shows you your boundaries. Like being in prison, there's so much more outside the walls of your cell and even more outside the walls of the facility. Fear points you in the direction of things you *should* do because those are the things that will expand your boundaries. Facing those fears will make your world bigger.

When you're working on a particular project, whether it's at work, school, or for personal purposes, the same thinking applies.

Countless times I've had design ideas that were so complex or challenging that they genuinely scared me away, so much so that I had to drag myself back to give them a try.

One of the earliest moments like this that I can remember was having to design a poster for a 1950s murder mystery movie and coming up with the idea of showing a couple dozen potential murder weapons, such as poison and rope. At the time, I couldn't envision the idea clear enough before beginning to tell whether it would be worth the effort. The only way to find out was to do it. So I spent three days illustrating all these different potential murder weapons before finally laying them out on the poster. In the end I decided I didn't like the result and went in a different direction. But I never would've known without setting aside my concerns about being right or being willing to let it all go.

WHERE DO I START?

Think of any project as if it's a pyramid. Or better yet, use the food pyramid, but throw out the food. There's a big, bottom layer that makes up the foundation, then successive layers that get smaller as the pyramid rises to a point. The top can't exist without the layer below it, which, in turn, can't exist without the one it's sitting on, and so on.

A perfect, efficient execution of your project would have you start at the bottom and work your way up. There would be little, if any, excess. You'd follow a wonderfully linear path right to the tippy top. Seems great, right?

It's also a fairy tale.

The vast majority of creations never follow a linear path. They often have so much excess—effort that doesn't directly contribute to the finished product, or things that get outright thrown away or replaced—that it can outweigh what does make it to the end.

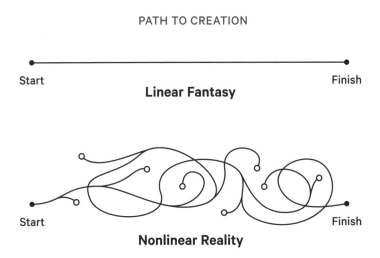

From the outside, creation appears to be a linear process: there's a clear beginning and a clear ending, and what happens in the middle is most often shielded from view. However, this idea that creation is linear is false. In reality, there are many starts and stops in-between the beginning and the end. In finding the right path, many paths may prove to be ineffective; the only way to determine which is which is by exploring.

In one of the many discussions for this book, I was speaking to an author who said their bestselling book was over ninety thousand words at the end of the first draft, but the final product had just sixty thousand. An entire third of their work was thrown out—but it was also necessary to find the two thirds that were worth keeping. And the chapters from the first draft weren't necessarily in the same order by the final manuscript, either.[61]

The answer is simple: start *anywhere*. You can only figure out how your pyramid will be built by starting to lay the bricks.

Summary

The unknown surrounds us. To uncover its mysteries, we must enter the cave and explore its tunnels. Do not concern yourself with a map or the most efficient way through to the other side. Before you begin, it's impossible to know how to optimize your journey for success. As the celebrated author Ray Bradbury said, you must "Jump off cliffs and build your wings on the way down."

Learn to manage your logical and emotional selves. Logically, remember that it's not only unlikely you will succeed on your first try, it's almost a certainty you won't; accept the inevitable falls and rises of iteration. Emotionally, be careful not to merge who you are with what you're creating; for in creativity's realm of inescapable experimentation, it's easy to mistakenly identify with failure as a descriptor for yourself.

When trying to figure out what to create or where to start, look to your fears to point you in the direction of your boundaries. Find the limits worth pushing—and jump in.

---

61 After writing the first draft, I tried to go back and give an attribute to the author who said this to me. I asked several if it was them, and they all said yes. Which is further proof of the necessity of excess in creating something worthwhile.

13
Sketch It Out

The Law of Ideation

Take your idea and make it real, no matter how rough. The final step is only attainable by taking the first step. Once you have something to look at and adjust, you can begin the journey towards completion.

Several Snaps Later

No creation goes from nonexistence to perfection in the snap of a finger. Rather, there are stages of development that help it blossom from the seed of an idea to a strong, towering tree. One of the most formative moments in the creative process is when you take an idea out of your head for the very first time and, no matter how rough, you make it real.

Sara Blakely had just left another sales meeting in which potential clients ripped up her business card in her face. She was a fax machine salesperson, the year was 1996, and the reliance on faxes was starting to dwindle as other technologies became more prevalent.

It wasn't the first time security escorted Blakely out of a building, but something was different on this particular day. Despite being her company's top salesperson, she felt unfulfilled. There was a yearning inside for something more, but she couldn't quite figure out what that was.

Blakely pulled over to the side of the road, deep in thought. She questioned the state of her existence, feeling as if her life had brought her to this point without her permission, like it all happened in the blink of an eye. All at once, she was overcome with determination. "I'm in the wrong movie," she remembers thinking as she drove home with a newfound resolve.

She threw her keys on the table, grabbed a notebook, and sat down on her couch. One at a time, Blakely snatched each of the thoughts swirling around in her head and put them on paper. As she wrote, all her strengths and desires poured out. She filled page after page.

Mentally exhausted from the journey, she put the pen down and held the notebook firmly in both hands. Written in black and white, clear as day, she had her mission: "I want to invent a product that I can sell to millions of people that will make them feel better."

That thought lodged in her mind, and two years later an opportunity finally revealed itself.[62] Blakely was getting ready for a party when she noticed her black pantyhose were visible below the bottom cuffs of her brand-new pair of white pants. They eliminated the problem of panty lines but caused an unsightly fashion faux pas at her feet. With no other option,

---

62 An example of Passive Inspiration, as discussed in the Law of The Muse.

she resorted to solving the problem herself—and cut the feet off her pantyhose.

By the end of the night, Blakely came to the conclusion that this was the idea. Her moment had come. "I looked fabulous, I felt great, and I had no panty lines," she recalls. The next day she was off to the races visiting craft stores, researching yarns, and calling textile mills.

Dozens of prototypes later, Sara Blakely released the first Spanx product—a pair of pantyhose that stopped at the calf. The seed of an idea that was first planted in her notebook has since grown into a company with more than $400 million in annual sales.

Tagline Wisdom

For those who have an idea they'd like to see created, the most common deterrent is not knowing where to start. The answer is straightforward and, like many things having to do with creativity, entirely open-ended: start *anywhere.*

Unglue your eyes from the end goal and look down at what's in front of you. If there's nothing, then make something—anything at all. It doesn't matter how rough, vague, or distant it is compared to what's in your head. The important part is that you make it *real.* There's a reason Nike's tagline "Just do it" resonates. It's incredibly easy to forget that the journey of a thousand miles must start with a single step.

Sara Blakely sketched out her idea when she sat on that couch and wouldn't get up until the scramble of thoughts floating in her noggin was written, organized, and simplified into a unifying concept. It's important to note that sketching requires no drawing whatsoever—to sketch is to explore a thought or thoughts in any way that brings them into the physical world. At the end of her notebook session, it was words, not pictures, that guided her next move.

When Blakely cut the legs off her pantyhose she was, in fact, sketching. She faced a problem and found a solution, regardless of scalability or "perfection." Anyone who has worn pantyhose could predict that, without elastics at the cuffs, they'd roll right up, which is precisely what they did that night. But the imperfect execution didn't matter because the ultimate problem was solved: she wore the white pants and her pantyhose didn't show.

Once you have your idea in front of you, something you can point at, then you can truly begin to develop it. Even though it may not look like much, you're already on your way. Blakely didn't know her impromptu creation would take her down the path of starting a multi-million-dollar company, but she sure wouldn't have gotten there without first making a rough example.

Sara Blakely wanted to create a product she could sell, one that would improve lives—and that's exactly what she did.

Birth of a Notebook

In 2012, I started an entrepreneur's group with three other problems-obsessed people. We committed to spending a year together working on each other's ideas. The trio was composed of Adam Kornfield, a progressive thinker with extensive knowledge in finance; Scott Robertson, a creative thinker and highly skilled developer; and myself, a designer with a passion for making things.[63] We met for several hours every Thursday night and called ourselves Rock & Co., an amalgamation of our last names.[64]

For four months at a time, each of us had all the resources and skills of the other two at our disposal. When it was my turn, I presented an idea to create a notebook for thinkers. There wasn't any judgment, but Adam and Scott weren't enthusiastic. They didn't yet understand why I cared about notebooks or what I had envisioned. I went home knowing I needed to *show* them what was in my head, not just tell them.

That same night, I pulled a notebook from my shelf, measured and cut a swatch of cream-colored painting canvas, and used masking tape to wrap the existing cover of the book. The next week I tossed it on the table and said to them, "Hold it."

The notebook was a mess. There were stains, cuts that went too far over the edge, and masking tape stuck out at the edges—but it was enough to give them an impression of what I was imagining. And it worked. Electricity flowed through our conversation that night, idea after idea flew between the three of us, and by the end of the meeting Baronfig had been shaped in all but name.

Intent on keeping the momentum, I again went home and immediately got to work. This time I wrote down the various features and qualities the product should have. List in hand, I spent a few days running around New York City buying various elements at specialty stores.[65]

---

63 Adam would eventually go on to co-found Baronfig with me.

64 (Ro)bertson, (C)ofone, (K)ornfield.

65 I still remember my jaw dropping when I walked into the store devoted entirely to ribbons. They were presented in rolls from floor to thirty-foot ceiling everywhere I looked.

I woke up early that Saturday morning and sat down at the kitchen table. In front of me were all the things I'd bought—ribbon, fabric, paper, glue, string, and more—and behind them rested my laptop with a "How to Bind a Book" YouTube video playing.[66] By lunch, I was holding the first Confidant notebook prototype, made entirely from scratch.[67]

When I showed the notebook at the next Rock & Co. meeting, what I was going for solidified in their minds. We released the final product the following year. Since then, Baronfig has sold hundreds of thousands of Confidants—all thanks to those first physical sketches.

Make It Real

As stated earlier, to sketch is to explore a thought or thoughts in any way that brings them into the physical world. You need to make them real. You *do not* need to make them good, however. Quality and improvement come later.

There are three fundamental methods you can use: drawing (visual), writing (verbal), and crafting (physical). Which you use depends on how you like to think, as well as what the idea or project is best suited for. At the core of each, the goal remains the same: take what's in your head and pull it out, regardless of how rough.

---

66 As it turned out, I forgot to buy card stock for the notebook cover. I did, however, have an empty Cheerios box that worked well as an improvised replacement.

67 At Baronfig we still have both notebooks—the masking tape one and the from-scratch version.

DRAWING

When I collaborate with someone on anything—a book or event or video, for example—the first step I take is pulling out a notebook or stepping up to a whiteboard to make pictures. Fear not, they don't have to be beautiful. In practice, it's better if they aren't.

I may be *able* to draw photorealistically, but the idea phase isn't the time or place for that. We're looking for speed, to turn on the spigot and let the thoughts flow. At this stage, my drawings are little more than squiggly lines with a few arrows and labels. They're so poorly representative of the final outcome that it's often difficult to decipher what they mean the following day. That's fine. They're meant to facilitate ideation and conversation, and in that regard they perform brilliantly.

Tips for Drawing Ideas

- **Work as small as you can.** This forces you to keep the image simple. It also saves time and space: shorter lines are quicker to create, and you can create several small drawings on a single page before erasing or turning to the next one.

- **Use a fat marker or a thick pen.** Similar to the previous tip, using a wide line forces you to stay high level. You can't add details because there literally isn't the room or fine maneuverability to do it.

- **Use no more than three colors.** The fewer colors the better. The only time to use two or three is when you're looking to distinguish portions of your idea, such as arrows or labels separate from the thing itself. You're not here to make something pretty (yet).

- **Put down only what's necessary.** We humans have a tendency to overexplain. Draw only what's essential to getting the idea across, and no more. This will help you move quicker through your thoughts and iterations.

- **Use the correct medium.** If you're working with more than one other person, use a whiteboard. If it's just you and another person, use sheets of paper or a notebook and sit next to each other rather than across.[68]

WRITING

They say a picture is worth a thousand words. Considering that a thousand words really isn't that much, they must be pretty powerful to piece together an entire picture. Of course, we know they are because people buy millions of books each year without a picture in sight. Drawing isn't the only powerful way to convey ideas, then. You can go right to the source: the written word.

I use words generously in all my creative endeavors. When I'm working on a new project, it doesn't matter how many drawings I make; until I give the project a written name and a thesis statement, I feel like I'm floating without a precise concept to develop.[69]

---

68 Using pen and paper is critical, there's no way around it. It's so important, and I'm so passionate about ideas, that I started a company with that at the heart of it.

69 The Law of Grounding in action.

Tips for Writing Ideas

- **Write a whole lot.** If you're working on a project alone and trying to wrangle a surplus of hazy ideas, then freewrite. Similar to what Sara Blakely did, just put pen to paper and start letting thoughts flow. Don't try to control what comes out, just write until you stop naturally. Then go back and read and see where that takes you next.

- **Create lists.** Without filtering upfront, write down everything that could apply to your idea. Once you can't go any further, start to organize your list into several sub-lists. You could include necessary parts, nice-to-haves, and wastes. Or you could sort by cost or feasibility or expectations. Let it all out and begin to establish a framework that can help you sharpen the images in your mind.

- **Use adjectives.** Is your idea big or small, green or brown, smooth or rough, dynamic or static, mechanical or natural, and so on. Dozens of companies sell shirts—the differentiator is the *kind* they sell. Paint a picture that can give you a foundation to build on.

CRAFTING

Sometimes a drawing or a page full of words isn't enough. In these cases, you have to whip up your idea in three dimensions. Again, the faster the better. Your goal is not to create something that represents the final idea, but a reflection of the idea.

Sara Blakely cut the feet off a pair of pantyhose and I taped canvas to a notebook. Both processes were rough, and would certainly never sell, but they got the idea into the world—and it took less than five minutes to do it.

Tips for Crafting Ideas

- **Make it rough.** Similar to avoiding details when drawing, the rougher you create something, the faster you can put it together. Which means the faster you can look at it, think more, and go from there. Avoid making something beautiful—a precious creation—at all costs when starting the ideation process. Because of how much care was put into it, you'll be more attached and less likely to change it or throw it away to make room for something better.

- **Make it cheap.** You're not here to impress anyone. Don't concern yourself with fancy materials or specialized processes. If you spend a lot, then you're not going to be inclined to make another version that will add more costs to the project.

- **Create several versions.** Ideating while drawing is easy; there's no barrier between making version after version. But creating physical objects is different. They take time, materials, and usually at least a small amount of patience. Remember to put in the effort to express more than one idea or version in physical form.

Whether by drawing, writing, or crafting—take your ideas out of your head and make them real as early as possible. Don't concern yourself with how beautiful or accurate they are. The sooner you can materialize your ideas, the faster you can bring them to life.

Summary

Sketching is more than just visual image-making. It's the expression of a thought or thoughts through a medium that brings it into the world. For an idea to develop, it has to be able to evolve and be communicated. You must take it out of your head and make it real in a way that's suited to your skills and the project at hand.

When real, you are able to look at an idea as a tangible thing with separate elements, no matter how rough they are. You can add to them, remove them, and upgrade them. Once a problem can be pointed to, discussed, and passed around, it can be explored to a greater depth—and with more people—than if it were to exist only in your head.

The quickest way to give birth to an idea is to either draw, write, or craft it. Drawings ought not be beautiful, but minimal and functional in the moment. Writing does not entail full-length prose, but bits and pieces that together paint a picture, however incomplete. Crafts are counter-productive if you make them too detailed. Rather, they should be ugly, made swiftly, and barely function.

A sketch of an idea is not the idea itself, but a whisper of it. If done right, it's just enough to tell the secret that's stored in your head so that the next person—either someone else or yourself in the following moment—can catch it, twist it, and pass it on in a single breath.

14
Locate the Anchor

The Law of Grounding

Find a problem or concept to anchor your idea. If a problem is your anchor, experiment with concepts to solve it. If a concept is your anchor, use different questions to express it.

Crunchy Crunchies

In 1853, Moon's Lake House, located on picturesque Saratoga Lake in upstate New York, was the place to dine. By today's standards, it looked less like a restaurant and more like a small Victorian mansion. The restaurant attracted wealthy customers who had, perhaps, a refined palette … but who also may have had a refined sense of self-importance.

One day, a particularly special customer ordered Moon's Fried Potatoes, commonly referred to as "potatoes served in the French manner." Today we know them as the wonderful, if unhealthy, sidekick to burgers, steaks, and more: French fries. At the time, however, fried potatoes were an imported delicacy. They comprised the entire meal rather than a side dish and were eaten with a fork and knife.

George Speck was Moon's head chef, and happened to be the one to cook fries for this particular customer that day. As usual, he cut the fries in wedges, gently fried them to a golden brown, and tossed just a pinch of salt on top. Out the kitchen door they went ... and within a few minutes they came right back.

The waiter passed on the customer's complaint: "They're not crunchy enough."

Since Moon's Lake House attracted such a fine clientele, it wasn't uncommon for a dish to be returned because it didn't meet a customer's expectations. Speck was a professional; he didn't take it personally. Within a few minutes, he had a second batch whipped up and sent back to the table, along with his apologies.

Yet again, the waiter reappeared with the same dish. The waiter, uncomfortable this time, told Speck they still weren't crunchy enough. The customer wouldn't eat them. Miffed, but still professional, Speck put together another dish from scratch and sent them to the table.

Only a few moments had passed when the waiter cautiously opened the door to the kitchen. He revealed the third dish in his hands, turned back with still the same complaint. Speck was livid.

Speck squeezed his favorite knife, slammed a hearty potato onto the cutting board, and cut the thinnest slices he could manage. He threw them in the fryer until they were downright stiff, rained a colossal amount of salt on top, and sent them back out the door. A minute went by, but no waiter came back. Then another minute. And another. Surely by now the customer would be causing a ruckus, for he had made the potatoes so rigid they cracked like glass when bitten.

The kitchen door squeezed open, but only a crack. This time it was Speck looking out. He peeked into the dining hall, scanning the room for an angry customer or the house manager trying to convince someone not to leave. Instead, he spotted a crowd surrounding a table in the far corner. Diners waved their hands in the air, calling others over. The fourth dish was being passed from person to person, each grabbing a handful and munching wide-eyed.

They were a hit.

Within days, people were traveling up from New York City to taste George Speck's "potato crunches." Soon after, they were packaged up as Saratoga Chips and sold across New England. Eventually the name "potato chip" emerged, and that's what they've been called ever since.

Opposing Forces

George Speck didn't *try* to invent the potato chip. He was trying to get back at a persnickety customer, but the creative process doesn't need to be consciously engaged for it to work.

Back in the 1800s, it was considered lowbrow to eat with your hands. So not only did Speck deliver a dish that was ridiculously uncharacteristic of what one would expect French fries to be, he also delivered a searing insult. The ultra-fried potatoes forced the customer to use their hands rather than a fork.[70]

Every creative process must have an anchor: a core concept being expressed or problem being solved. In this instance, Speck

---

70 If there's anyone out there who eats potato chips with a fork and knife, more power to you.

was repeatedly asked to make the French fries crunchier. With **crunchy** being the anchor, he steadily iterated version after version until a tipping point came along—the third returned dish—that kicked him into an entirely new frame of mind.

Being a professional chef, Speck couldn't avoid doing a good job. He may have thought that thinly sliced fried potatoes was a bad idea, but he still pulled it off with a chef's touch. And by keeping the anchor in place, he unintentionally gave birth to the potato chip.

What's equally curious is how the customer responded. Their reaction is an expression of the ancient Chinese philosophy of yin and yang. In a nutshell, it puts forth the idea that what appear to be opposing forces may actually be complimentary. In this case, Speck created the dish in anger, but the customer received it in joy.

In most cases, it's the opposite. A creator makes something they're excited about and confident in, presents it to the world, and then gets shot down by family, friends, colleagues, and just about everyone else. I can't say that I have personally experienced George Speck's version, but I have certainly encountered the reverse, as have others in this book.

Unintended creation is what makes this story compelling: the creative process is so reliable and effective, even when one isn't intentionally engaging it, it still delivers results.

More to Moor

Without an anchor, it's almost impossible to make steady progress. You may accidentally stumble upon a positive outcome, but that'd be a case of, as my high school geometry teacher Mr.

Allen used to say, "Right answer, wrong solution." The solution is the process that gets you to the answer, that's the part we're focusing on in this book. A right solution is what will deliver reliable results.

I was reminded of this lesson while art directing a limited edition pen alongside a senior designer who had chosen to explore a history-packed concept: luck. She collected symbols from all around the world—the rabbit's foot, four-leaf clover, lady bugs, and a cornicello, among others—but we kept coming up short on bringing them together. We reviewed dozens of versions over several months, but none felt right. Finally, we realized that while we were using themes and symbols of luck, we weren't unifying them with a visual language.

Our core question then became: *What's a universally recognized language of luck?*

As it turns out, most countries have a national lottery. And they all have similar graphic formats: thin semi-translucent paper (like receipts), unique elongated barcodes, digits that look like computer code, etc. After that realization, it took just a couple of weeks to nail down the entire edition.[71]

The end product featured a box that looked like a lottery ticket from the front, but upon closer inspection had a series of luck symbols and notations in place of standard lottery icons and text. There was even a scratch-off card inside that revealed a quote when fully scratched. And the pen itself was beautifully engraved with all the symbols from the package.

How did we manage to turn a project that should've only

---

71 It went on to become one of our best-selling limited editions to date and sold out in a fraction of the time it took us to create it.

taken six weeks into one that took six months? We forgot about the anchor. Looking back, the solution seems obvious (as it usually does in hindsight), but we were scratching our heads when we were in the thick of it. Only after countless versions and a host of conversations did we arrive at the correct solution, but once we got there the project was over before we knew it.[72]

An anchor is the spike in the ground that keeps the kite from flying away. The kite can skuttle in the wind or calmly float among the backdrop of the clouds, but the stake never moves. If you feel so inclined, you can even tie another kite to the stake. Regardless of what everything around it does, the stake holds firm.

Anchors generally appear in two forms: a problem or a concept.

- **Problem Anchors:** Creativity often includes problem-oriented thinking: you seek, sharpen, and solve. Problem Anchors put the sharpened question at the center of your creative endeavor and you build around it.

- **Concept Anchors:** A problem isn't always the focus. Oftentimes, a concept emerges that addresses your goals. In our case with the limited edition, we worked to solve a construct—a type of statement rather than a question.[73]

How do you know if your anchor should be a problem or a concept? Typically, a project naturally dictates the type of anchor required.

---

72 More on the importance of conversation in the Law of Collaboration.

73 The statement you're aiming for may still use sharpened questions to express it.

George Speck's potato chip is a great example of a Problem Anchor. He had a problem—*How do I make potatoes crunchier?*—and, four versions later, had reached the pinnacle of crunchiness. The solution was derived from a question.

Our luck-based limited edition pen used a Concept Anchor. We weren't trying to solve a particular problem, we simply wanted to express luck in a creative, multi-layered experience by combining history, symbology, society, and culture. The solution was born from a construct.

In addition, problem and concept are another expression of yin and yang: If the problem is static, the concept is variable; if the concept is static, the problem is variable.

PROBLEM & CONCEPT ANCHORS

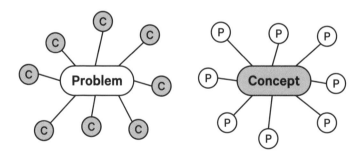

Anchor a creation to a problem or concept. If the problem is the anchor, use concepts to solve it. If a concept is the anchor, use problems to express it.

The potato chip Problem Anchor didn't change, but the concepts evolved. For the first three dishes, Speck made small tweaks to the French fry construct, resulting in more fried but still recognizable dishes. On the fourth try, he engaged an entirely new construct—thin potatoes, extra frying time, loads of salt—to solve it.

With the luck pen, the Concept Anchor stayed the same throughout the project. We researched numerous origins of the idea of luck, played with dozens of symbols, studied expressions of luck in cultures today, and what we learned helped us address a myriad of problems, such as: *What represents luck in the simplest form? What is the difference between good and bad luck? What does luck look like to everyone? What does it look like to individual cultures?*

At the end of the day, problem and concept are two essential parts of a whole. Like the chicken and the egg, it's easy to argue which should come first. However, unlike the chicken and the egg, the answer is both *can*—it just depends on the project.

Summary

For a house to last it must be built on a solid foundation. The same goes for creative endeavors. To create something worth using or sharing or enjoying, it must be anchored with a problem or concept.

A Problem Anchor requires that all ideation works to solve for a singular question. Ideas take shape around it in the form of concepts, like hypotheses, that combine to build its solution.

A Concept Anchor aims to explore a hypothetical construct. It poses an idea as a statement, rather than a question, and demands that problems be built up and addressed, one by one, to establish the truest expression possible.

Locate the Anchor

The anchor you employ becomes the static element. The other anchor type is expressed as a variable. Together they chip in to create—with a bit of luck—something wonderful.

15
Forget the End

The Law of Wandering
To create something new, you must allow the process to lead—inviting serendipity to work in your favor—rather than force expectations of the final result. If you do not wander, then you will only encounter what has already been created.

Pilot's Pilot Pilot

In late 2004, a story gripped the world. It happened on an unassuming Wednesday, much like any other. One would've just been sitting down for the evening before finding themselves glued to the television. Only moments before, it was revealed that a plane had crashed on a remote island somewhere in the Pacific. The passengers who didn't die on impact were now in a struggle for their lives. That story, thankfully, wasn't real—it was the plot of the new hit show *Lost*.

The first one or two episodes of a new television series are called the pilot(s) because, like an actual pilot, they guide the story into what could be if the show is picked up by whatever network airs it. In the case of *Lost*, rather than give the first couple of episodes proper names like most shows do, they simply called them "Pilot: Part 1" and "Pilot: Part 2." Considering that an airplane crash was a major part of the story, it was doubly appropriate. It also attracted a record-breaking 18.6 million viewers.

By the end of the first episode, viewers were left with more questions than answers. What caused Oceanic Flight 815 to crash? Where was the tail section and everyone in it? Who or what was the smoke monster? Why did the radio malfunction? What was Charlie doing in the bathroom? The second episode provided one or two answers, but then tossed twice as many more questions into the mix.

Viewers everywhere were hooked. Episode after episode, they couldn't get enough. Every Thursday morning, water cooler talk was alight with the latest happenings of Jack, Kate, and the rest of the survivors. For those who didn't watch the show—the few that there were—listening in on a conversation sounded like gibberish. People talked about a random polar bear, a hatch, something about unexpected dynamite, and mysterious repeating numbers. It didn't make any sense ... except it did.

On top of the already-confusing narrative, *Lost* also played with variable time. Most storytellers agree that if you want to keep your reader or viewer's attention, you shouldn't include alternating time jumps. Instead, keep the story linear to avoid confusion. Yet *Lost* was full of flashbacks (and, later on, flash forwards) of characters pre-crash, with each one telling a different story. Not only was it jarring as it pulled you out of the island struggle and back into civilization, but the backstories were a lot to remember for a dozen-plus characters. It shouldn't have worked ... yet it did.

The two-part pilot was so well received that the network signed on for another twelve episodes before the initial twelve finished airing. After a brief hiatus, the show came back with a vengeance and ended the first season on a massive, mysterious cliffhanger.

If you told someone in early 2004 that a show would string along its viewers, constantly change direction, and introduce the ridiculous, they'd probably tell you it didn't have a chance. But, after the first season, and as a surprise to absolutely no one, *Lost* went on to win the Emmy for Outstanding Drama Series.

Real-Time Hatch-ing

How did the creators of *Lost* craft such a compelling show? What were they doing that other writing teams weren't? And how had they come up with such an intricate mythology?

J.R.R. Tolkien is famous for crafting the incredible world of *The Lord of The Rings*. He built an elaborate world, called Middle-earth, filled with elves, dwarves, wizards, monsters, and magic. And he did it all before writing a single world. The writers of *Lost*, however, did nothing of the sort.

Unlike Tolkien, the writers of *Lost* planned very little. In fact, they didn't expect their show to get approved for more episodes beyond the initial twelve because ... well ... they didn't really have a show. There was no plan. The pilot itself was only finalized three months before they pitched it.

Carlton Cuse, co-showrunner and one of *Lost*'s head writers, recalled their season one strategy (or lack thereof) as: "Come up with an interesting question and worry about the answer later."

Cuse and Damon Lindelof, co-creator of *Lost*, gathered the team every week to write the next episode.

They turned into a positive what many would see as a negative: having no plan. Outsiders to creativity often believe that creations are premeditated, that creators know where they're going before they get there. In reality, it's the exact opposite: If you know where you're heading before you begin, then you aren't heading anywhere new.

Lost was so refreshing because the writers took an entirely new approach to television storytelling. They stopped worrying about confusing their viewers, trusting that people were smart enough to handle what came their way, and instead focused on writing episodes they themselves wanted to see. Cuse recalls the early days, saying they agreed to "Just make the twelve best episodes of television, ones that are just cool to us."

Instead of planning ahead, they relied on each other to figure it out as they went. They didn't know what the smoke monster was when they wrote it, or why there was a single polar bear alone on a tropical island. But they enjoyed weaving those questions into the mystery of the story in a way that still made sense. And because they were having fun, so were the viewers.

Lost continued to grip audiences for six years. It was named by multiple publications as one of the top television shows of all time. After the first season, in addition to their Emmy, the Writers Guild of America awarded Cuse, Lindelof, and team with their highest award: an Outstanding Achievement in Writing.

And when season one ended on a cliffhanger with the discovery of a mysterious buried hatch that wouldn't open? The writers didn't know what was in there either.

THE POWER OF PROCESS

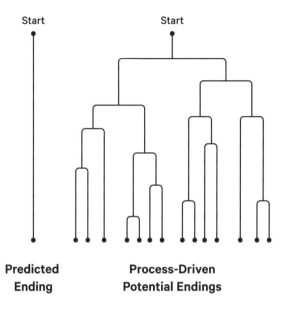

Predicted Ending   **Process-Driven Potential Endings**

When the ending is decided at the beginning, it limits the potential endings to a single, predicted outcome. It also invites frustration as the desired reality clashes with actual reality. When the ending is deemphasized in favor of focusing on the process, the number of potential endings exponentiall increase. This allows for more innovation and less frustration.

Set Your Sights

Looking forward and looking down both have their benefits. When you look forward, you're taking an estimate of what lies ahead. It's great for strategizing and planning. When you look down, you tune out the future and tune into the task at hand. Human nature has a funny way of making us do one when we should be doing the other.

If there's something important that we need to plan for, such as giving an important presentation or preparing to write a book, it's amazing how many petty tasks get done (finally organizing that messy desk, for example). Similarly, when there's something important that needs to get done now, such as compiling detailed feedback on a project, all of a sudden we find ourselves exploring the next idea or figuring out how to optimize the settings in our task list software.

Productive procrastination is an all-too-common fallback mode that allows one to get unimportant things done at the expense of actual, essential progress. Being aware of this tendency is the first step towards controlling it. You must learn when to look down and when to look forward. Because while a forward-thinking mindset is helpful for figuring out *what* to do, it's terrible for actually doing it. Similarly, if you don't plan at all, then you're going to waste significant energy with mediocre results.

With the activity of creating, you have to forget about the end—the future goal—and force yourself to be concerned only with what's in front of you. When it's time to actively explore ideas, you must let go of what may come next. Trust that the process will guide you.

How do you create without an end in mind? Is it even possible to perform any action without thinking about an end goal?

Yes, you can do things that don't necessarily focus on the end goal. Like breathing underwater with SCUBA gear, it's easy to do, but it feels unnatural at first. There are two fundamental techniques to help you succeed:

1. **See everything as an experiment.** Approach the process of creating as an experiment. Think of your work, and all

the little things you do within it, as a hypothesis (guess) rather than a theory (fact). This allows you to downplay the ending because it no longer matters what happens during any single attempt. If your hypothesis turns out to be incorrect, just try another.

2. **Take small steps.** Break things down and focus on the immediate task. There's an end to it, but it's small and, in a vacuum, fairly inconsequential. This puts further distance between you and the ultimate ending because there are dozens of smaller ones before you can even get to it.

For example: Once you decide to write a book, draft your table of contents, and prepare any other research you need—it's time to stop looking forward and start looking down. It's time to write. You must accept that one doesn't write a book. They don't even write a chapter—just a single section. Then another. And another, each one being a small step forward. In addition, those sections are each an experiment unto themselves. The author has the ability to write and rewrite to their heart's content. Once one piece is satisfactory, they can move on to the next.[74]

The more skilled you are at looking down on command, the more creative you will be. If you only look forward, you can only see what has already been seen. There is nothing new in the future that isn't created in the present. The end, the creative goal of the task at hand, is unknowable. If it were known, then it would not be new. You must let the process carry you through

---

74 Just as you are aiming to forget the future, this is a good time to forget the past. Step away from what you've made, for the time being, and move on. There will be a time for revision.

the darkness—through the unknown—to come out on the other side with something truly creative.

Learn to enjoy the process. The end will come of its own accord.

Summary

It's the goal of every creative endeavor to come up with something that has never been seen before. To try to see the end before you start, before exploring, means you will only end up with what has already been discovered.

Instead, trust the process and let it carry you where it may. At the beginning of the journey, even the most successful creators can't tell you what they will end up with at the end. The results of creativity, by its very nature, are unpredictable.

Focus on the task at hand. Consider each attempt a micro experiment. And break up your project into small steps. Don't worry about filling the glass. If the water is running, it will inevitably fill.

16
Focus on Quantity

The Law of Iteration

Do not concern yourself with quality. Rather, prioritize quantity through iteration—even at the expense of quality. Over time, quality will emerge. The more versions you make, the better the results.

Ten Thousand Light Bulbs

Thomas Edison, nineteenth century American inventor and businessman, has 1,093 patented innovations, making him one of the most prolific inventors of all time. One of those patents includes the electric light bulb, which revolutionized society in just a few short decades.

Renowned for putting on a spectacle in addition to being a successful inventor and businessperson, Edison made it publicly known that he was working on the electric light bulb. Early on, when asked about his scores of failed attempts and inability to produce results, Edison famously said, "Results! Why, man, I have gotten a lot of results! I know several thousand things that won't work."

In the late 1870s, when Edison began his experiments, scientists didn't believe an electrical revolution was possible. Gas lights had existed for years by that point. They lit public spaces, factories, and pretty much any location where people gathered in large numbers. As far as everyone was concerned, there was no need for change. Edison was determined, however, because gas was costly, generated loads of heat, and was rather dangerous.

Generating light inside of a bulb, Edison discovered, was a straightforward affair. One simply had to pass electricity through a thin piece of material, called the filament, with sufficient intensity to heat it up and cause it to glow. The challenge was not how to make it work, but how to *keep* it working. So far, no one had figured out how to create a filament that would burn bright enough and long enough. Filaments that burned brightly fizzled out quickly, and ones that lasted long were too dim to be useful.

To invent a functional light bulb, then, was to solve the problem of the filament.[75]

He used copper, platinum, and other metals in his first experiments, which glowed bright but fell apart after a short time. They were also expensive, and therefore unsustainable for businesses and unattractive to customers. Instead of using metal, he looked to a material category that was significantly cheaper: plants.

Treated plant materials were affordable and abundant. Edison and his team tested anything they could get their hands on, including boxwood, cedar, cork, coconut hairs, flax, hickory, and even the hair from the beard of a gentleman on his research team.

---

75 A perfect example of a Problem Anchor.

The first big success occurred in October of 1879. A light bulb using a carbonized cotton filament burned brightly for fourteen and a half hours. Energized[76] by their breakthrough, Edison and his team continued exploring filament options. They soon found that carbonized bamboo could burn for forty-five hours in an airtight glass bulb. He immediately sent his team to Japan in search of the perfect bamboo for his light bulb, which they eventually found.

By 1780, Edison's light bulb could burn for upwards of twelve hundred hours. Combined with the electrical infrastructure he'd built, New York City was the first city in the world to have a power station and widespread electric lighting. Despite gas magnates trying to bury his discovery, Edison prevailed—and to this day we still use his incandescent bulbs to light our lives.

Universal Superpower

"The electric light has caused me the greatest amount of study and has required the most elaborate experiments," Edison wrote. "I was never myself discouraged or inclined to be hopeless of success. I cannot say the same for all my associates."

When you ask people if it's fair to presume success on a first try, nearly everyone agrees that it's an unreasonable expectation. As we learned in the Law of the Unknown, despite rationally understanding that failure is natural at the early stages of any creative endeavor, people still let the idea of failure prevent them from moving past poor initial results.

For *every single creative success*, not stopping when the

---

76 Pun intended.

journey gets tough is a requirement. From the high-tech phone in your pocket to the radio waves and battery technologies that power it, the creator of every component failed before they succeeded. This loop, the process of starting and failing in succession, is called iteration—and it's the underlying superpower behind creativity.

"Before I got through," Edison recalled, "I tested no fewer than six thousand vegetable growths and ransacked the world for the most suitable filament material." He and his team uncovered *at least* 5,999 unsuitable answers before they found that bamboo would resolve his core problem.[77]

It's no surprise that Edison famously claimed, "Genius is 1 percent inspiration and 99 percent perspiration." Everyone has ideas. As he was repeatedly reminded, the difference between those who bring them to life and those who don't isn't intelligence or money or luck, but persistence.[78]

Thomas Edison's incandescent electric light bulb is an example of iteration at a micro scale. He experimented with all kinds of materials and methods before inventing it. But it's also an example of iteration at the macro scale. There were twenty-three light bulbs created by others before Edison's—and many more after, each an iteration of the ones before.

Today we have light-emitting diode (LED) light bulbs that last up to fifty thousand hours—nearly fifty times as long as an incandescent bulb. But we couldn't have gotten to LED bulbs without first having Edison's.

---

77 And that's just plants. They tried all kinds of materials before moving to carbonized plant materials for cost efficiency.

78 The other three things can contribute, but history has shown that world-changing inventions come from all walks of life.

Self-Imposed Limits

The power of iteration is not a secret. Your ability to wield it isn't held behind lock and key. There's no class or age or any other restrictions that prevent you from iterating to your heart's content. All you have to do is follow the Law of Beginning—jump in—and brush yourself off *when* you fall.[79]

If there's one obstacle between yourself and iteration, it's the ego. When we fail and quit, or don't start at all, it's because we're protecting our ego. Preventing failure maintains the positive outlook we have of ourselves. But it also prevents any kind of creative success. You must invite your ego to be vulnerable, to endure failure after failure, before your creativity can blossom into wonderful creations.

The lack of self-consciousness when we're children is exactly why we're so creative at a young age. We don't worry about how we'll look if we don't succeed. Unfortunately, as we grow older, we become insecure, we compare ourselves to others, we begin to concern ourselves not just with what we do but how the things we do appear to others. And then we lose our ability to play, which is at the center of creativity.

As we learned in the very first chapter of this book, we're all eccentric beneath the surface and behind closed doors. Think about all the "weird" things you do that you wouldn't do in public. Eccentricity in itself isn't a marker of creativity; it's the *willingness to let your eccentricity show* that denotes a healthy relationship with the ego. Those who allow their oddities to be on display don't care what others think about them, and, in turn,

---

[79] Remember, falling is inevitable. Grab your knee pads, throw down pillows and a yoga mat, and—knowing it's coming—you'll land as light as a bird on a branch.

are better suited to creative endeavors because failure—specifically public failure—doesn't faze them.

Harnessing the power of iteration requires acceptance of a few fundamental ideas:

- **You are not your failures.** A failure is not a failure unless you quit.[80] When you keep going, a failure becomes a lesson. You learn what didn't work, and why. You shrink the pool of possible options, or you exhaust your perceived options and force yourself to expand your perspective.

- **Quantity is more important than quality.** Do not aim to get it "right," aim to get it out. Continually take what's inside your head and make it real. Each iteration brings new awareness and understanding. Over time, quality naturally emerges.

- **There is a time for output and a time for review.** When you're iterating, don't think too hard about each attempt. To avoid paralysis by analysis, don't analyze. Let your ideas and your efforts pour forth free from judgment. Remember, you aren't aiming for quality, merely for quantity. Success is largely a matter of volume. Once you are done with the iteration sequence at hand, *then* you can review. Even better if you can step away for a while before looking over your work.

- **Most ideas and most work will be thrown out.** If one in ten thousand versions of Edison's light bulb worked, that means that 99.99 percent of his attempts were

---

[80] Keep in mind that there are times when moving on is the right choice. We discuss this more in the Law of Tenacity.

unsuccessful. Not only is that okay, it's necessary in order to find the 0.01 percent that solves the problem. Do not get attached to your ideas or the products of your labor, for then it will be much more difficult to make more.

- **The end comes when it comes.** You can't predict when the creative process will bear fruit. Instead of concerning yourself with what you cannot control, pay mind to what you can: the iterative process. Trust that, with enough effort and patience, you will eventually find the answer you're looking for.[81]

Frontiers of Iteration

The process of iteration is like a Russian nesting doll, but with an indeterminate number of inner dolls. Sometimes it only takes a few twists to discover the final doll; other times it feels like you're opening doll after doll with no end in sight.

As we have discussed, mastery over this process requires mastery over oneself. How you achieve that is entirely up to you—it's different for everyone—but how you go about iteration itself is fairly systematic no matter who you are.

There are three fundamental phases to the creative process: brainstorm, production, and review. As a sequential trio, they form a single high-level iteration. Each phase is also composed of multiple low-level iterations.

For example, on the surface, Thomas Edison decided to make an electricity-powered, filament-based incandescent light

---

81 The end is often not a destination but a choice. You must voluntarily make the decision to stop. The Law of The Finish Line explores this idea in depth.

bulb (brainstorm), went ahead and made a version (production), and then assessed how he could improve it (review). With a deeper look, however, we quickly realize that each phase had many sub-phases.

Edison didn't immediately land on the type of bulb he eventually decided to build. He worked on several variations before deciding which would be most practical for his intentions. Then he had to make many versions of the leading variation to discover which could perform best and be produced with reasonable costs. After that, he assessed the performance of his creation, plucking several lessons from the results of his efforts, and started the process over again.

The next brainstorm wasn't necessarily what type to make, but what materials to use. This process repeated itself until he could no longer produce improved results.

A SHORT BUT LIVELY BEGINNER'S GUIDE TO ITERATION
Iterative Brainstorming: Quantity is your only goal. If you're working with a Problem Anchor (Law of Grounding), make a list of a hundred solutions to address the problem. If you're working with a Concept Anchor, list a hundred ways to express that concept. *Do not judge your ideas, just write whatever comes to mind.*

- Example: I want to make a bath toy, so I list a floating cow, a dolphin with eagle wings, a phone booth on its side that opens with a sail and acts like a tiny boat, a teddy bear in a wetsuit, along with ninety-six other ideas.

Iterative Production: At this point, you have chosen one or a select few of your ideas to run with. Speed is your next goal.

Get a version out of your head or off the paper and into reality as fast as possible, no matter how rough (Law of Ideation). Quickly assess and produce another. And another. *Do not concern yourself with perfection or finality.*

- Example: I decide to experiment with the teddy bear idea. I go down to the local convenience store and purchase several plush turtles (close enough). Then I go home, wrap a turtle in duct tape, and throw it in the tub. It's cute, but I want to see the turtle. So I wrap the next one in clear plastic. The next version comes out better. And so on.

Iterative Review: You've done the work, now it's time to step back and take it in. Is it ready? Does it feel like you could share it? Can it be better? Is the idea totally off? Depending on your answers you may jump back to brainstorming or try your hand at producing one or more new versions. With enough repetition (and patience) you will eventually land on a creation you're satisfied with.

Summary

Do not expect to find the right solution on the first try. Instead, expect to find the wrong ones. With the correct mindset, you will no longer view an unsuccessful iteration as a failure, but as an opportunity to learn.

Keep your focus on quantity, not quality. We've all heard the phrase "Quality over quantity," which claims that it's better to have a small amount of something highly refined than a large amount of something unpolished. The axiom is true, but also deeply flawed. While it does tell us *what* to achieve, it lacks the explanation on *how* to achieve it. The full phrase should be: "Quality over quantity, but quantity begets quality."

Whether you're brainstorming, producing, or reviewing, the more you do, the better you get. Make sure to keep each phase of iteration separate. When brainstorming, don't begin producing or start reviewing until you've gone through a series of repetitions. When you're producing, don't begin reviewing before you've completed the build. And when you're reviewing, be careful to assess what you've learned before you begin ideating again.

It's time to stop iterating when you experience an extended period without progress.[82] At that point, you either call it a final product, set it aside and come back, or completely move on from that particular idea. The important thing is to understand that you will know, deep in your gut, what the right call is when the time comes. It may not always be an easy call, but it'll be the right one.

Remember that most of your ideas will be thrown out. That's okay. If you generate a thousand ideas and only one ends up being successful—*that's all you need.*

---

[82] Or a point at which progress is no longer noticeable or impactful. More on this in the Law of the Finish Line.

17
Create for Yourself

The Law of Specificity

Make for yourself and you will appeal to many. Make for many and you will appeal to none.

Green Thumb, Green Pen

Emily Dickinson is one of the most iconic poets of the twenty-first century. She wrote nearly 1,800 poems during her lifetime, and there are countless exposés and biographies exploring the woman behind the work. How did she become an internationally acclaimed poet and, even more impressive, a household name?

In 1844, Dickinson was fourteen years old when tragedy struck. Her close cousin, Sophia Holland, died from typhoid. It marked the first of what would be a lifelong relationship with pain and death. Up until that point she was a happy, mild-mannered child, about as normal and well-adjusted as they come.

Her cousin's death traumatized her, changing her demeanor entirely. Life's veil had been pulled back prematurely, and what was revealed shook her to the core. No longer did Dickinson laugh and play like the other kids. Her parents had to visit her at boarding school to bring her back from darkness, which, thankfully, they were able to do.

Out from the gloom, Dickinson jumped into academics at Amherst Academy. She studied a host of subjects: arithmetic, geology, history, philosophy, botany, and, of course, literature. Back home, after finishing her seventh and final year, Dickinson's love for poetry reached a crescendo when she discovered the works of William Wordsworth and Ralph Waldo Emerson. The way they used words moved her deeply.

At some point in the mid-1850s, while taking care of her chronically ill mother and tending to the homestead, Dickinson began to write.

In her free time, if she wasn't gardening or managing chores, she was up in her bedroom, alone, penning line after line of poetry. Over time, Dickinson built up a small collection and began to share them with her friends and family. They enjoyed her writing so much that they urged her to send them off to get published. Eventually, she did.

Dickinson was first published in 1858 in the *Springfield Republican*, a few years later in the *Brooklyn Daily Union*, and finally alongside other poets in a book called *A Masque of Poets*. She continued to write, exploring topics of joy, pain, and death in everyday life. Her unique style and voice evolved with each passing verse, and by thirty-five years old she had written over 1,100 poems.

One hot summer day in 1886, Dickinson was baking in the kitchen when, without warning, she fainted. She remained on the floor all day before finally being found in the late evening. Sickness followed. Less than a year later, she died at fifty-five years old.

Aside from her friends and family and the few people who

read the handful of poems she published years before, no one knew her name or remembered her writing.

Fame Is a Bee

How did Emily Dickinson go from an unknown writer to a household name—*after* her death?

Dickinson's sister Livinia, who was tasked with getting Emily's things in order, discovered a locked chest in her room. She was surprised to find that it was filled with some forty booklets of poetry. The vast majority had never seen the light of day. Livinia became obsessed with getting them published, and, after a journey of her own in discovering who and how best to do it, she finally accomplished her goal.

Four years after her sister's death, *Poems of Emily Dickinson* was published. It was an immediate hit, with the second and third books released soon after. They changed the course of American literary history. Dickinson is credited as the reason why Americans read and buy poetry books at all.

Creators die every day, though, and they don't become posthumous icons—what made Emily Dickinson different? As it turns out, she asked herself the same thing: "What makes a few of us so different from others? It's a question I often ask myself." The key separator between her and the rest is that she didn't look for recognition while living. Her aforementioned published poems? They were either published anonymously or, sadly, without her permission.[83]

---

[83] Editors also reworked her poems to be more appropriate for the times, often removing dashes and capitalizations in favor of more traditional sentence structure and punctuation. Nasty stuff.

In fact, Dickinson was so uninterested in having her poems shared that she didn't even organize them. Very few were dated, and out of her near-1,800-piece collection, less than ten of them had titles. Decades later, scholars had to study her handwriting to organize them chronologically, and the only way we can refer to her poems is by their first lines.

Emily Dickinson wrote entirely for herself. And, because of that, she didn't have to live by anyone else's expectations on how things "are supposed to be done." Instead, she did what made her happy.

At the time, poets wrote epics—long-form poetry that told stories or spoke about the times—but Dickinson, instead, preferred short verse that looked inward rather than out. Her writing itself was quick, casual, almost conversational. Her punctuation was dramatically deviant. She generously employed dashes rather than periods, and she would capitalize regular words within sentences as she saw fit.

Perhaps she knew that, in the end, to be famous would be fleeting. She wrote a brief poem on the subject later in her life:

Fame is a bee.
It has a song—
It has a sting—
Ah, too, it has a wing.

The English major inside me would dissect it as: Fame is a double-edged sword / It is beautiful, for a moment / But it comes at a cost, always / And it is ultimately fleeting.[84]

---

84 My degree in design wasn't my first rodeo. Before that, I studied English literature and philosophy.

As if Dickinson knew what would come after her death, in another poem she says:

Luck is not chance—
It's Toil—
Fortune's expensive smile
Is earned.

At nearly two thousand poems, she certainly toiled. But because they were all for herself, she derived a special kind of joy—and formed a unique style—that was all her own.

A Tale of Two Gloves

It's easy, and almost logical, to get sucked into the belief that the broader your idea is—the more general—the more people will be able to relate. But if you try to make something that appeals to everyone, it very often appeals to no one.

Let's take gloves, for example. The following are two approaches, one attempts to target the greatest amount of people possible, the other, the least.

- **Broad:** Imagine the most generic looking, inoffensive gloves possible: dark gray, seams only where necessary, one type of material with no texture whatsoever. On paper they should appeal to damn-near the entire planet—everyone has hands, right? But if they're so generic, so plainly colored, and so straightforward, why buy them at all?

- **Narrow:** On the other hand,[85] imagine a pair of gloves

---

[85] Yes, pun intended. I'm perpetually practicing my dad jokes.

that are ultra-thin but still highly insulated, have zero padding, are waterproof, and the thumb and index fingers have special touchscreen-compatible fabric sewn into the tips. They'd be terrible for manual laborers, people who ski or snowboard or do other sports, or those who intend to spend long periods of time outdoors—which immediately excludes millions of people. But they're perfect for going from your house to your car and back. They solve for a very specific problem, and because of that, in that particular use case, they'll beat out the generic gloves every time.

Even though a broad approach appeals to the widest audience, the narrow approach categorically beats it bar none: There are gloves for working outdoors, gloves for golfing, gloves for handling hot metals, gloves for boxing, and so on.

How, then, do we master the narrow approach? You make things for yourself. You solve your own problems. You look to strum your own heartstrings before you worry about plucking those of others. James Joyce, the Irish writer responsible for the masterpiece that is *Ulysses*, once said, "In the particular is contained the universal."

The particular manifests itself differently for every person and for every profession.

- An **accountant** might ask themselves, "What makes the clearest financial model *for me?*"

- An **entrepreneur** might ask, "What problems *do I personally experience* that I can solve?"

- A **programmer** might ask, "What part of this code confuses *me*?"

- A **graphic designer** might ask, "How *do I feel* about what I'm looking at?"

- A **paramedic** might ask, "What would *make me feel* most comfortable in an emergency?"

- A **lawyer** might ask, "What would convince *me*?"

- A **juggler** might ask, "Aside from what's actually difficult, what looks the most difficult *to me*?"

These are all great examples of how creativity isn't relegated to the fine arts. Traditionally, when people hear the word "creativity," they think of painters and sculptors and the like. But, as you can see, whenever you address a problem from your own point of view, you're being creative.

Asking the right questions—ones that are particular to you—is the first half of the equation. How you approach answering them is the second. The Law of Expression leverages your unique perspective. The Law of Disruption dares you to challenge prescribed answers. The Law of the Unknown emboldens you to continue in the face of fear. And the Law of Rebellion (discussed in a later chapter) invites you to stand up for your ideas.

In the end, when you create for yourself and make gloves that fit you perfectly, you will realize there are a lot of other people out there with hands just like yours.

Summary

Creating is more than just making something—it's making something *personal*. Whether you are hired to make for others or are voluntarily doing it for yourself, find the part of the task you can relate to and explore it through your own lens.

On the surface, broad ideas may seem to appeal to more people. However, narrow ideas, despite a seemingly smaller audience, will win every time. Force yourself to get as specific as possible, for in the particular, you will discover the universal.

The best way to create for yourself is to constantly look inwards. Introspection—asking yourself questions—will sharpen the edges of the problem you're looking to solve. And answering them, without preconceived notions or limitations, will give you the best chances of striking gold.

18
Don't Discount the Obvious

The Law of Plain Sight

Many answers lie in the open. They do not need to be uncovered, but, rather, recognized. Fight the urge to discount ideas that are not derived from toil. Judge each idea on its merit alone.

The Million Dollar Napkin

Paula Scher, partner of the accomplished design firm Pentagram, was in a boardroom full of businesspeople in well-tailored suits. The New York City skyline was visible through floor-to-ceiling windows that spanned the room. Two companies, Travelers and Citicorp, were doing a merger, and they needed a new brand to go along with the new entity.

Pentagram was hired because they were the best, and Scher was chosen because she was the best of the best. Her portfolio included brands like Microsoft, Bloomberg, Perry Ellis, and Coca-Cola. Her clients were seated in a half crescent around her, chipping in on what the new brand should say and how it should feel.

When each person spoke, Scher gave them her attention,

listening not only to what they were saying but what they were *not* saying. She made sure everyone in the room had an opportunity to share their thoughts, barely speaking herself. Her hand rested on a glass of water, which she sipped intermittently as she watched the condensation roll down the glass and absorb into the napkin below.

At some point, Scher had heard enough for a picture to form in her mind. Her imagination flashed. Ideas from around the table morphed into an answer. Without any warning, she calmly removed her glass from the napkin, pulled out a pen, and made a quick sketch.

She slid the napkin across the table to the head of the group. "This is your answer," she said. The group looked from the napkin to Scher and back again, bewildered.

Citi paid a cool $1.5 million for Paula Scher's services. Today, the logo drawn on that napkin is the one used by Citi across the globe.

Inevitable Solutions

Milton Glaser, the renowned designer responsible for *I <3 NY*, described design as "The process of going from an existing condition to a preferred one." When the transition from existing to preferred is complicated or unclear, we call it a problem.

In Paula Scher's case, she was hired as a brand expert to address the problem of branding two merging entities as one: Citi. Her first move was to engage in conversation with those who knew more about the situation than she did. While both groups were participants in the same discussion, they were having entirely different experiences.

Scher's immediate goal was not to find a solution but to clearly define the problem. While greatly contributing to her process, the businesspeople in the room were operating from a solutions-based mindset. They made suggestions for logos, shared their ideas both visual and abstract, and pointed to other brands they wanted to imitate.

As discussed in the Law of Precision, defining a problem, which often requires research and repetition, enables one to discover a solution more quickly. Scher began her research by going to the source, the people who owned the problem and who knew the scenario best. She asked questions that were often fueled by the same underlying thoughts but phrased differently to understand the full scope of the challenge she was hired to tackle.

In the moment, it seemed to those around her that Scher had pulled off a magic trick. In the blink of an eye, she went from near-complete inaction—just sitting and listening—to sketching the answer. Those around her were dumbfounded, but the action she took was inevitable.

Let's look at a more straightforward design problem: a growling stomach. What's the existing condition? Hunger. What's the preferred condition? Satiated. What's the solution? Eat food. For us, the jump from problem to solution happens instantly because it's such a familiar issue, one we're regularly faced with.

Eating food when hungry may sound obvious, but it is, of course, the best solution to the problem. It's only obvious to us because we are all experts at the skill of operating the human body. We eat when we are hungry, we sleep when we are tired, and we shelter when we are exposed. Those problems have long been parsed.

In Scher's case, with her experience and skill, finding out how to merge two brands into one is, in many ways, like eating food to solve the problem of hunger. To Scher, designing logos is as familiar as eating is to the average person. This is, of course, overly simplified, but the point holds: experience weighs heavily on the speed at which a solution is found.

Answers are uncovered faster with more experience. They can occur so quickly that, sometimes, the results are questioned. It is incorrect to correlate difficulty and time with the solution's reliability, yet that is our tendency. Resist the urge to doubt the obvious, and you may find answers begin to come more easily.

When Paula Scher handed her napkin to the person in charge, she was met with disbelief.[86] They asked her why they paid so much money for five minutes of work.

"You didn't," she said. "You paid for forty-five years of experience."

Obviously Excellent

There is no intrinsic relationship between the amount of effort spent on a problem and the time it takes to find a solution. Most of the problems that plague our thoughts are big, mysterious ones. These stand out, and they incorrectly teach us that all problems require significant effort to solve. Every day, however, we instantly solve the majority of problems we encounter. But because they are so fleeting, they don't leave an impression.

Join a brainstorm session amongst designers and the phrase "That's too obvious" is bound to be uttered during the

---

86 Check out the napkin and the final logo at lawsofcreativity.com/citi-logo.

discussion. It's an immediate signal that, as it's so often put, "anyone could come up with that." And sure, that claim may be true, but that doesn't make it a poor solution. Be careful not to let ego cloud your judgment. Not every creative expression needs to be new and novel. Sometimes the simplest answer is the best.

Take Apple's logo, for example: It's an apple.

Is that too obvious? Did you ever question it? Did the little icon of an apple, at any point, seem inappropriate? You could call it an obvious solution to the problem of creating a logo for the Apple brand, and you wouldn't be wrong.[87]

Thanks to the Law of Plain Sight, we allow ourselves to entertain ideas as obvious as Apple's apple. But it doesn't end there. As we learned in the Law of Simplicity, strict parameters invite *even more* creativity. Using an apple as your anchor (Law of Grounding), you have a basis for infinite ideation, where everything you come up with always speaks to the core idea.

Rob Janoff, the designer of the Apple logo, still had countless options to explore even after deciding an apple was the answer. We know that he ended up using a rainbow-striped apple with a bite taken out, but he could have just as easily made the apple a zillion other ways.[88] Off the top of my head, how about: a red apple with a leaf in the shape of a computer chip; a cross-section of an apple that shows the seeds inside, shaped like tiny batteries; two apples side by side, forming a

---

[87] And no, it wasn't grandfathered in. The original Apple Computer Inc. logo was a black and white illustrated scene of Newton sitting under a tree. The apple in the image took up a fraction of the illustration.

[88] Yes, a "zillion." It's fair game if we make it so. You knew what I meant, right? That's language—it never stops evolving.

display; an apple with movement lines to call back to Newton's experience; an apple made out of the letter A to integrate into the word itself; or maybe a simple, clean cut apple slice with no meaning at all.[89]

The obvious answer is often correct. It's derived from an immediate connection to the problem and usually built upon knowledge that already exists.

Janoff said, "The most important thing a good design has to do is communicate." There is no clearer communication than seeing an apple and thinking: *Apple*.

Danger of Overconfidence

Combine the Law of Plain Sight, however, with excess confidence and we have a recipe for abuse. Sprinkle on top of that a healthy dose of the Dunning-Krueger effect, a cognitive bias in which people with low skill at a task overestimate their ability, and the situation gets even more uncertain.

People with high levels of confidence fall into two distinct groups: those that deserve it and those that do not. Those in the first group earn their confidence through application, trial and error, and experience. Those in the second one delude themselves into thinking they are part of the first.

Keep in mind that the people in the second group are entirely unaware of their self-deception. It is likely that, at some point in our lives, we have all fallen victim to overconfidence and mistakenly asserted our ideas in a situation where we had no right to claim authority. The question then becomes: How

---

89 With a little peanut butter on top. Mmm.

can we trust our first instinct—how can we trust *ourselves?* The answer is clear: due diligence.

Paula Scher may have discovered the solution in the first few moments of the Citi rebranding project, but she spent the next twelve weeks working with her team to confirm it.

Understand that the Law of Plain Sight does not ask us to immediately approve our gut reactions, but to be open to the possibility that those first insights can hold as much validity as those developed further in the process. It is up to us to spend the necessary time confirming whether or not they hold up.

Summary

Ideas that emerge suddenly and without toil are often viewed with doubt, when, in fact, they are like icebergs: a small sliver may be peeking above the water, suggesting a lack of structure or reasoning, but that sliver is often connected to a massive slab of solid logic floating just below the surface.

Disconnect the amount of work done with the value of the solution uncovered. They are entirely unrelated. Instead, recognize that, as Occam's Razor so eloquently puts it: the simplest explanation is often the right one. Not because it is the first to rise, but because it is a sliver of your vast experience peeking above the waves.

Above all, remember to validate your ideas, whether they took a moment or a month to emerge.

19
Go Where Others Are Not

The Law of Obscurity
Do what others do, and you will get results that others get. Instead, do what is not being done to get results that are fresh and novel.

Ancient Nemesis

Smallpox is believed to have originated around 10,000 BCE, right when human beings transitioned from hunter-gatherers to agriculturalists. It may have started in the Fertile Crescent, but by the time year zero rolled around, smallpox was the scourge of every populated land mass across the globe. Thanks to trade, exploration, and conquerors doing their conquering, whether populous trade hub or remote village, all were threatened and often devastated by it.

The disease was so harmful that, depending on the strain, mortality rates were anywhere between 30–50 percent. The *best-case* scenario was a one in three chance of dying. For those who survived, 65–80 percent were left with tissue scarring and disfigurement, most commonly located on and around the face.

In general, the disease killed 10 percent of the world's population *every year*, and up to 20 percent of those living in cities. For several millennia, smallpox was the greatest adversary of the human race.

On May 6, 1749, in Gloucestershire, England, the Reverend Stephen Jenner and his wife Sarah had a boy, whom they called Edward. Because of his father's standing, Edward was afforded a good education at Katherine Lady Berkeley's School in a nearby town. It was there that he was inoculated for smallpox through a process called variolation.

Getting smallpox was a life-altering diagnosis, and, at the time, variolation was the best means of preventing it. Essentially, it was the process of taking organic matter from someone else's ailment, in this case skin tissue or pustule fluid[90] from a person suffering from smallpox, and injecting it into the skin of a patient not yet affected. If all went well, the patient would develop light symptoms that would go away within days. Then their immune system would be better prepared to fight off the disease, increasing immunity. Unfortunately, that wasn't always the case. The variolation performed on Edward Jenner ended up having an adverse effect on his general health for the rest of his life.

In his teens, Jenner took an apprenticeship to study anatomy and surgery, which burgeoned into a full-on career. He was eventually elected to the Royal Society (short for The Royal Society of London for Improving Natural Knowledge). Throughout all of this, the effects of his smallpox inoculation and the impact it had on his life were not forgotten.

As the story goes, one day Jenner overheard a milkmaid brag

---

90 Pause for collective cringe.

to another, "I shall never have smallpox for I have had cowpox. I shall never have an ugly pockmarked face." The milkmaid's braggadocio, combined with his own lifelong experience, eventually led to Jenner's world-changing discovery.

The stars aligned when Sarah Nelmes, a local milkmaid, turned up at his practice.

Nelmes had contracted cowpox and was looking to be treated. Jenner took this opportunity to test his theory, that the relatively harmless cowpox could prevent contraction of smallpox. Using variolation, he scooped up some of her cowpox flakes and gave them to his gardener's eight-year-old son, James Phipps. After a brief illness, James fully recovered, healthy as ever. Jenner then exposed James to smallpox—numerous times—with no ill effect whatsoever.

In Latin, the word for cow is *vacca*, and cowpox is *vaccinia*. Jenner used these roots to give name to his revolutionary new procedure: *vaccination*.

Banished Beast

Edward Jenner, who is known today as the "father of immunology," is credited with single-handedly saving more lives than any other human in history. And he did it by going against the grain, by looking around the problem rather than directly at it.

Before Jenner's discovery, medical practitioners around the world only knew how to fight fire with fire. They tried to combat smallpox by inoculating people with more smallpox. As a child, he himself was subject to that line of thinking. After variolation was performed on him, Edward had to quarantine for days with other sick young boys. Some made it through, some didn't.

Smallpox had ravaged humanity throughout the ages. Everywhere humans went, it followed. When the conquistadors explored the new world, Smallpox was right behind them. It contributed to the fall of the Aztec and Incan empires just like it had done before with the Roman Empire, and with Chinese and Indian empires before that. Across all that distance and throughout all that time, no one figured out how to fight the disease except to slightly infect people and hope it didn't outright kill them. Even when they survived, a third went blind on top of being disfigured.

Despite all the people who tried and failed to fight smallpox through the centuries, how could it be that a milkmaid knew the answer? As we learned in the Law of Plain Sight, oftentimes the answer is obvious to those who are paying attention. It's just about recognizing it. In this particular case, one person had done the knowing and another had done the recognizing, but regardless, the process was the same. Never before had people thought to use one disease to fight another.

Even when Edward Jenner tested his thesis with little James Phipps and then afterwards proved its validity, the Royal Society rejected his paper that explained his hypothesis and observations. His idea went against everything they knew at the time. Jenner, refusing to give up (and enacting the Law of Rebellion), decided to publish the paper himself. He released a booklet titled *An Inquiry into the Causes and Effects of the Variolae Vaccinae, a Disease Discovered in Some of the Western Counties of England, Particularly Gloucestershire and Known by the Name of the Cow Pox*.[91] Suffice to say, it wasn't immediately met with open arms. It took several years before his peers began

---

91 Hell of a title. People back then weren't in a rush, that's for sure.

to come around to the revolutionary idea, but eventually it was accepted and spread far and wide.

On May 8, 1980—over 230 years after Edward Jenner performed the first vaccination—the World Health Assembly officially declared that smallpox had been eradicated from the world.

The Exocoetidae

To go where others are not is like swimming against the current. It's much easier to lie back and let the waters of society and assumption carry you along. Very little energy is needed. Instead of pumping away, head down in the murk fighting for every inch and breath, you can float, arms out, as the warm sun beats on your chest.

The problem with floating along is that you don't have any control of where you're headed. You get swept away and end up exactly where everyone else is: somewhere downriver in a place that's populated and explored. If you're looking for something new—say, a fresh idea—it won't be found there.

Swimming upstream is exhausting.[92] If you aren't prepared, you'll either have to give up or drown. If you are prepared, you know that you'll be facing oodles of external doubt. Everyone you pass will look at you strangely, for in a field of complacent flowers, you appear an unruly weed. In fact, there will be so much scrutiny and doubt that you'll begin to question yourself. But if you endure, if you continue putting one arm in front of the other, you'll begin

---

92 If you're waiting for a salmon metaphor about swimming upstream, you won't find it here. If *everyone* is going upstream, then the literal upstream becomes the metaphorical downstream.

to pick up speed. Those you pass will be but a blur, their opinions no longer a matter of concern. And at that moment, when you feel like the only fish in the river, you'll begin to fly.

No longer does the water beat on your shoulders as you pull yourself forward. No longer do deep stares and quizzical looks tug at your peripherals. You exist above the water, separate from the flow entirely. And from up here, you can see *everything*.

Going against the grain takes practice. Like anything worth doing, being comfortable with existing outside the pack requires effort. But if you're willing to do it, little by little, you'll become the fish that realizes he has wings.

Start small. Focus on a single experiment. Back in high school, I knew a kid, let's call him Andy, who, on the very first day of freshman year, went up to every single person he crossed paths with—students and staff alike—and shook their hands. He would say, with a colossal smile and eyes locked on theirs, "Hi, I'm Andy Smith! Nice to meet you." No one else was introducing themselves with anywhere near as much jubilation and warmth. I'll never forget it because three years later Andy was nominated and elected as the senior class president.

Perhaps we could shrug that off as unrelated or a fluke, and I'm sure Andy continued with his good spirits throughout high school. But I decided to run a test of my own. Throughout the first days of college, I walked up to everyone, held out my hand, and said, "Hi, I'm Joey!" with as much warmth and joy as I could muster.[93] To my utter amazement, I was nominated and elected as hall council president.

---

93 This is incredibly important: Don't do anything that isn't *genuine*. If you don't have it inside of you, that's fine. You have other things inside. But don't fake anything, people will see right through it.

Lucky me, I got to test my hypothesis a second time. I finished up my first round of college right in the heart of the financial crisis. There weren't many jobs for an English and philosophy major during normal times, but the job market I entered was even worse. Thankfully (and surprisingly) I was able to finagle my way back to school for an undergrad degree (again), this time for design.[94] At the start of the year, I shook everyone's hands, said my hellos—and was nominated and elected as hall council president *again*.

Doing what others are not will immediately separate you from the herd. How you manage it, and what you do with that separation, determines where it can take you—and just how high you can truly fly.

Eyes Everywhere

As we learned in the Law of Expression, the nail that sticks out invites the hammer. There are a few common pitfalls to avoid when you decide to leave the safety of the fold.

1. **Tread carefully.** This may seem obvious, but it is easily forgotten, especially when you're having fun and get pulled in. Don't forget: the sheep that strays from the flock is more likely to get attacked by a wolf. To deviate is to be vulnerable, so it must be done with care.

2. **Know where the pack is.** You must have a clear understanding of where the pack is to know where it *isn't*. You don't need to partake in their habits, rituals, or activities,

---

[94] Most people who decide to go back to school do a two-year master's program. I went back for a full four-year bachelor's degree.

but you must have an awareness of them to hone your ability to recognize different from same.

3. **Don't stray just for the sake of it.** Above all, do not be different just for the sake of being different. If you don't find a genuine reason for stepping outside the bounds, don't do it. It's a waste of energy and the results will be empty. You wear clothes and go to school and do a host of other things, like everyone else, because they work.

This is not a warning against paving your own path, but a reminder that those new paths require more tools to tread. Until your ideas are validated—which may take time—you will find that others often try to pull you down or minimize your efforts. Sure, sometimes that may be appropriate—if you were trying to sell couches made of live beehives, for example—but often it's merely a reaction by others to those unlike themselves.

Shania Twain, bestselling singer and songwriter, put it well: "I find that the very things that I get criticized for, which is usually being different and just doing my own thing and just being original, is the very thing that's making me successful."

Summary

Being different is about knowing when to responsibly wander from the beaten path. It requires either evidence or a hunch that what lies just beyond the brush is worth the time and effort it takes to get there.

However, you will never be 100 percent sure of what fruits you will discover (if any). Taking risks is an inherent part of going where others have not. When doing so, it's important to keep an open mind and regularly assess whether it's time to turn back or push forward. The only way to get better is with practice.

When you do decide to push forward: don't go anywhere you can't make it back from, be aware of where everyone else is so that you can better measure your progress, and don't just wander off because you feel like it—have a reason.

Every new breakthrough, in all of history, came from someone exploring a new frontier. So grab your bag of tools, pull up your socks, and head out into the lush wilds of discovery and innovation.

20
Talk Out Your Ideas

The Law of Collaboration

Join forces with others to maximize knowledge, speed up ideation, and minimize wheel-spinning. Share what you know and you will, in turn, have others share with you. Multiple heads truly are better than one.

Frames and In-Betweens

Fifteen-year-old Walt Disney walked out of the cinema, deep in thought. The year was 1916, and he had just seen the original live-action *Snow White*. He thought the movie was entertaining, but there was something missing that he couldn't quite put a finger on. That thought stuck in the back of his mind for close to two decades.

In 1934, Disney finally got the chance to answer the question he asked as a teenager, to explore what it was that had left him so unsatisfied. He stood in front of a room of storytellers and animators and described his idea for the first ever Hollywood full-length animated feature film, *Snow White and the Seven Dwarves*.

He explained how he envisioned the story but couldn't fill in all the gaps. He told them how he imagined the characters would realistically move and sound, but he didn't know how they'd achieve it. And he guessed at how much it would cost to make the movie, but he wasn't certain that would be the case.

For every idea he presented, the room asked ten questions back, most of which he couldn't answer.

Disney knew he didn't have all the answers; hell, he didn't even have half. But he *did* have an undeniable vision, one he believed in—and that was enough to get people on board. In his mind, the destination was crystal clear, despite not knowing exactly how to get there. Using his signature Walt Disney panache, he recruited over twelve hundred people to help Walt Disney Studios bring his vision to life.

Disney met regularly with a dedicated group of people responsible for shaping the story and putting ideas into action. Together they reconstructed the narrative again and again. The queen, for example, was originally a frumpy, maniacal character, but ended up transforming into the staid, regal one we all know. And they made over *fifty* versions of the dwarves, all with their own unique names and personalities. The more interesting ones include Burpy, Gabby, Nifty, Baldy, Tubby, and—the oddest one of all—Hickey.

As development progressed, more people joined. At one point, *Snow White* had thirty-two key animators, over one hundred inbetweeners,[95] and nearly three hundred production staff

---

95 In hand-drawn animation, animators draw what are called "key frames," spaced-out pieces of a character's scene. Then the inbetweeners come in and do all the illustrations in between, essentially like connecting the dots, but with full drawings.

responsible for inking, layouts, background, sound, and more. Disney was so committed to realism that he hired live actors as animation references.

Walt Disney looped himself into a never-ending cycle: debating character intention with the story crew, reviewing ideas and experiments with the animators, innovating camera layering and other technologies with the production crew—all while exploring the question he had first posed at fifteen: *How can* Snow White *be truly special?*

In an effort to find the answer, Disney pushed far beyond his initial budget. He estimated the movie would cost $250,000, but they were rounding the corner on a million dollars.[96] The press was starting to refer to his project as "Disney's Folly."

No one thought the movie was going to see the light of day. Even teams within Walt Disney Studios were concerned at one point, and it was later discovered that he had mortgaged his own home to finish it. But Disney—a premier connector of human beings and master of motivating beyond limits—pulled everyone through.

In December 1937, *Snow White and the Seven Dwarves* premiered in Hollywood to a standing ovation. The following February, it released publicly to critical acclaim. It pulled in over $8 million in ticket sales upon initial release, and the film has since been rereleased numerous times. All combined and adjusted for inflation, *Snow White* has pulled in over $1.5 billion in revenue, making it the highest grossing full-length animated feature film, ever.

Sixty years later, in 2008, the American Film Institute named

---

96 They ultimately spent $1.4 million.

Snow White the number one animated film of all time—while the original live-action movie has been all but forgotten.

Dreaming and Doing

How did Walt Disney answer the question that had been nagging at him all those years? How did he manage to answer the scores of questions from that room full of people?

He didn't.

Disney understood that while the big question was his—*How can* Snow White *be truly special?*—it would take a lot of smaller questions to figure it out. And their answers didn't need to come from him. In fact, very few of them could.

Like all great connectors, he went out and found people who knew far more than he did on a myriad of subjects and stuck them in rooms together. They were puzzle pieces, each contributing a part of the answer that would together form a beautiful whole—as long as Disney could let himself see it.

Thankfully, he could. Walt Disney was able to set aside his ego to let others shine, but at the same time employ his ego to confidently decide on how to continue moving the project forward. Collaborating is a delicate give and take—one that requires careful consideration of others' ideas—but also demands sheer will to make decisions and prevent stagnation.

Disney managed to keep production going and spirits up long enough, despite numerous setbacks and poor public opinion, to get the team to create 1.5 million individually hand-drawn frames. To put that into perspective, *Snow White's* animators produced roughly fifty thousand frames per month for nearly three years.

Having hundreds of animators collaborate on tens of thousands of frames and have something sensible come out at the end, let alone award-winning, is a collaborative feat worthy of being called a great wonder of human achievement. Never before had that many artists worked together to create a full-length animated feature film.

It wasn't luck. Disney knew exactly what he was doing.

The creative process was so clear to Disney that he figured out how to formalize its structure and maximize its output. He literally divided an area of Walt Disney Studios into three separate rooms for the three general types of thinking required to create.

In the first room, only **Dreaming** was allowed. There were no limitations, no filters. Any and all ideas were given the space to be heard, no matter how ridiculous or impractical. By creating an "anything goes" atmosphere, Disney invited collaborators to speak freely, to have fun, and to dream big.

The second room was for **Building**. It had a do-your-best, let's-give-it-a-shot atmosphere. It was where they attempted to take the first room's favorite ideas and turn them from thought into reality. Oftentimes they'd hack things together—it was about experimenting, not finalizing—but sometimes they'd cobble together a plan of action when action itself was out of reach.

Ideas then entered the third room for **Critiquing**. While first two were for imagining and playing, the third was where reality was applied. Ideas were scrutinized (never the people who thought of them), plans were analyzed (never the people who made them), and, depending on where the cracks in the sidewalk formed, they'd be sent back to either of the previous rooms to be re-Dreamt or re-Built.

Ideas ping-ponged back and forth between the rooms until finally they emerged pristine, undeniable, and ready for production. The three-room strategy was so effective that to this day, nearly a century later, Walt Disney Studios still uses it.

Three Rooms in One

Think about those IKEA instructions that have an illustrated character lifting alone with a red slash through them. The caption says, "Get help." Sure, you could probably lift the box yourself, but there's a good chance you're going to have trouble with it, and there's a possibility for real pain. Why do something alone when you could do it more easily with others?

Stanford did a study that found people who were primed to act collaboratively stuck to tasks 64 percent longer. They also reported higher success and lower fatigue. Forrester discovered that, at work, collaboration can increase productivity by 10 percent and save employees 5–10 percent of their time—that's a two- to four-hour refund per week.

It makes sense: If a problem requires, say, eighty Think Units (TUs) and a person with one hundred TUs is working on it, they're close to their capacity. That's a surefire way to get tired and burn out. But if that same eighty-TU problem is spread across two one-hundred-TU workers, now each only needs to give forty TUs and has sixty left for other work. Spread it across three people and each is left with close to three-quarters of a tank.

Naturally, not everyone brings the same type of Think Units to the table. Some people bring visual ones, others bring mathematical or logic-driven ones. There are as many varieties as there are people in the world. And when you put the right people on the right tasks, you start to get discounts. A problem involving geometry may cost eighty TUs for you but only twenty TUs for your math-minded collaborator.

The benefits of collaboration have been proven time and again. It doesn't take a rocket scientist (or a creativity scientist) to understand there are clear reasons for making sure person-to-person ideation and work is a part of your process. A few of the biggest reasons include:

- **Skill swapping:** The most obvious advantage to getting a well-rounded group together is skillset cross-pollination. Each person brings something to the table, the more diverse the better, and together there's always someone (ideally) who's familiar with an aspect of the challenge at hand.

- **Learning:** A byproduct of skill swapping: if you're paying attention to those performing what you don't know, you will soon learn. Depending on the group and time restraints, even better if there's an open dialog for teaching. Ask questions, get answers, learn.

- **Quicker resolutions:** Rather than having to self-educate or chase answers for questions you aren't personally prepared for, the group could provide answers instead. Excising the chase and flounder from the process saves a load of time.[97]

- **Efficient work:** Generally speaking, when you attack a problem with thirty-five steps to completion, the more people you divide the work across, the less work per

---

[97] Keep in mind, however, it can also lead to silos of information if the parties don't share or educate each other.

person. For example, one person does all thirty-five, but five people do an average of seven each.[98]

We can agree that the benefits are evident. Now that we know *why* collaboration is helpful, it's time to discuss *how* to collaborate—and do it well.

Unlike Walt Disney, we don't all have access to (or time for) three separate rooms. Most collaboration is done in small- to medium-sized groups together in a single location, often a classroom or conference room. Lucky for us, we can get the benefits of Disney's process without the physical demands of changing up our workspace.

There are an infinite number of ways to ideate. If you throw a bunch of open-minded people in a room and make sure they're honest with each other, that's really all it takes. For those of you who'd like a little more guidance, fear not, here it comes.

HOW TO COLLABORATE ON IDEAS
Step One: Ideate
Like Disney's dream room, anything goes. Don't limit yourselves and don't worry about quality; aim for pure quantity.

1. Pass out a bunch of sticky notes, index cards, or small pieces of paper. Each person in the group should have several—more than they need.

2. Set a timer for five to ten minutes. It should be long enough to get multiple ideas out, but short enough that people can't dwell on them.

---

[98] Division of labor doesn't usually divide perfectly even. Distribution depends on the skills of the people involved.

3. Require everyone to fill out as many sticky notes as possible, each one containing the basics of an idea (just a few words). Focus on quantity over quality.[99]

4. Once the timer goes off, collect everyone's ideas and put them on a wall or bulletin board.

Step Two: Review
Now we must float down from the clouds and measure our ideas against the realities of time and space.

1. Read all the ideas aloud, one by one. Then go back to the beginning and start taking votes on each, either yay or nay.

2. Collect the top ideas—the ones with the most yay votes—and ask for feedback. Anything goes. The goal here is to quickly separate the wheat from the chaff. Eliminate any ideas that no longer make sense.

3. With the remaining ideas, discuss the viability in depth: the pros, the cons, the challenges, and benefits.

4. Now choose a direction.[100] It's rare that a solution jumps out above the rest; instead, we're often left debating two to three solid approaches. This is when a leader needs to step up and make a call. Under a mindset of experimentation, it's time to move forward.

Step Three: Plan
Here we transform ideas to action. This is the part that's usually

---

99 Take a look at the Law of Iteration for additional insights.
100 If nothing floats to the top, that's ok. Start over.

undervalued by the "idea people" or prematurely jumped to by the "suits."

1. Start at the end—what is the final task that needs to get done? Write it down, then make a list of everything that precedes it, step by step.

2. When you think your list is ready, start attaching people to the tasks. Make sure to discuss who is best suited for each, and don't assign any more people per task than necessary.

3. Finally, apply time to the list of tasks. Depending on how long the list is, don't get too precise. Tying tasks to dates too soon will set everyone up for failure. The process will evolve as you go, and if the plan is too precise, then it will resist meeting needs as they arise. For example, list tasks by day for the first four weeks, and by week for the next four. Everything that has to be done three or more months in the future should be listed by month, not by week or day.

4. Get to work.

A Thousand Cuts

Collaborating with others is a wonderful, fulfilling practice that should absolutely be performed at every level of an organization, big or small. If you're an individual working on a one-person project, such as a book,[101] it's worth

---

101 We've gone meta.

gathering a few trusted individuals to replicate a collaborative environment.

Working with others is not without its dangers, however. Keep in mind the following and you'll be square dancing in no time.

- **Share selectively.** In the early stages, share with those that are extremely familiar with the subject or field you're working with. If you try to engage those who don't understand the context of what you're doing while your idea is still forming or you're still defining the problem, you may get shot down before the project has had time to build its wings. As your idea takes shape, broaden the spectrum of who you talk with; by the end, you can share it with anyone.

- **Make sure the group has variety.** There's very little value in getting together with a bunch of people who are good at the exact same things. You add productivity horsepower, sure, but if there's no skill diversity, then you're missing out on all the other benefits like skill swapping and learning.[102] Avoid redundancy at all costs—you're better off alone than in a group that's composed of copies of yourself.

- **Avoid ideation by committee.** The idea with the most votes isn't necessarily the best. It just means it's the most liked. Oftentimes, a good idea has to be pushed through by a vocal minority, which is why a capable leader is needed. The skills a leader must bring to the table include

---

102 If I only had a dollar for every time I met a startup founding duo made of two developers, two designers, or two businesspeople.

the ability to recognize a diamond in the rough, to have the vision to see beyond what the rest of the group sees—and to make the call.

- **Recognize better vs. different.** It's easy for an idea to get stuck in Ideation Land, forever tumbling around like it's in the Dryer of Continuous Rebirth. Practice recognizing when the group is making an idea better versus only making it different. It's a fine line, but one you'll get better at treading with awareness and practice.

In the end, the best way to determine if an idea is ready to share or if a collaborator is effective is to go ahead and try. You will quickly learn if the time or person is right. Trust your gut.

Summary

Most great achievements in the history of mankind were attained not by one person, but by many working together. Joining forces to achieve your goals is the secret to unlocking a myriad of benefits. You can swap skills to cover more knowledge bases, learn while doing it, reach your goals faster, and have it all feel easier.

The act of collaborating is as simple as getting together and being honest. Ensure that the goals are clear from the start. Remember to regularly redirect back towards them if ideas stray. And take your time going through the steps of dreaming, reviewing, and planning.

Make sure to assemble a group with a variety of skillsets to avoid redundancy. Do not give credence to an idea simply because it's popular; instead have someone in the group who's skilled at vetting ideas. Learn to recognize when an idea is on the edge (or inside) of the endless cycle of making it different rather than better.

Collaborating isn't just great because it's effective—it's also more fun.

21
Come Back to It

The Law of Stepping Away

Over-familiarity is poisonous to creativity—it produces boredom and blindness. The cure is space and time. When progress stagnates, take a break.

Six in the Drawer

Stephen King is one of the most prolific authors of the twenty-first century. His first story was published in 1965 and he's been going strong ever since. So far, King has written over seventy-five books and two hundred short stories. He has sold over 350 million copies of his work.

In his book *On Writing*, which is half memoir and half how-to, King shares all sorts of insights into how he's managed to be such a fruitful creator. For our purposes, we're going to talk here about one in particular: when he steps away from his work and for how long.

He likens working on a project to spending "day after day scanning and identifying the trees." You become intimate with the details but lose sight of the bigger picture. He tells us that at some point we must "step back and look at the forest." For King, that perfect moment comes after he's written a first draft. He puts the manuscript in a drawer for six weeks, moving on to other projects or taking a break altogether.[103]

Going back is as challenging as stepping away. What was once difficult to see becomes clear as day, and in many cases the results may not be pretty. King writes, "You are forbidden to feel depressed about them or to beat up on yourself. Screw-ups happen to the best of us."

Cells of Theseus

It is said that our body replaces its cells every seven years. Which would mean that the person you are at birth is physically not the person you are when you enter first grade, who is also entirely distinct from the human being you are as a freshman in high school. It's a fun thought, and a popular one that often gets cited. Unfortunately, it's just a myth.

Like most folk tales, however, there's truth behind it. Many of our cells do, in fact, die off as new ones replace them. For example, the cells in our skin are replaced every two to three weeks, and the ones in our stomach last just a few days. But others—such as our brain cells in the cerebral cortex, the rod and cone cells in our eyes, and the cardiac muscle cells in our heart—are all we get. Once they're gone, that's it. Still, the idea that we're born anew, so to speak, every seven years is an inspiring one.

---

103 I successfully employed King's technique to help me edit this book.

Stefan Sagmeister, the Austrian graphic designer, took this myth and built on top of it. Despite not being physically accurate, Sagmeister realized that, psychologically, the idea was more right than wrong. In every sense but the literal, we really are a different person every seven years. Think about who you were when you were born vs. first grade vs. high school vs. graduating college vs. your late twenties—the difference is staggering.

Running with the idea, Sagmeister outlined the average life: about twenty-five years of learning, forty years of working, and fifteen years of retirement. He decided to cut off five years from retirement and distribute them through his working ones by taking a full year off after every seven. Essentially, he steps away from *everything*—including his design studio—for a full twelve-month sabbatical, every seven years.

For his very first sabbatical in 2008, Sagmeister went to Bali. After a brief transition (it's difficult to turn off the ingrained "time for work" mentality) he began to feel the weight of the world lift from his shoulders. He started meditating. Experiments came more readily and were more enjoyable. The life that had been right in front of him all those years had suddenly become clearer. And, most importantly, his creativity began to bloom.

The Space Between

Even though Stephen King and Stefan Sagmeister step away using drastically different parameters, they're fundamentally operating under a similar premise. Whether six weeks or one year, the goal is the same: to minimize the familiar and maximize the unknown.

For King, who almost always works on just one project at a time, he's learned through trial and error that it takes six weeks for a manuscript to melt from memory. At that point, when he finally reads the pages after being away from them for forty-two days, it's almost like he's reading something that was written by someone else. He's separated himself long enough from the words on the page that he can go back with fresh eyes—and significantly more objectivity—to edit and get on with the next draft.

If you do the math, King has written an average of 1.3 books and 3.6 short stories *per year* for fifty-five years. After five decades of writing, he still makes sure to take the time to step away. There is no clearer indication that the fundamentals work—and apply to *everyone*—than this.

The seventh-year sabbaticals that Sagmeister takes have the same intention. In an interview, he explained that it's normal to get bored by the things we do, even if we love doing them. Once he came to that realization, he knew the only way to replenish his curiosity was to distance himself from the monotony of his work. So off he went.

Yes, Sagmeister's clients were there when he got back. And yes, he still remembered how to design. In fact, all the personal projects that followed in the next seven years came from the single year that he took off.

As we have learned over and over throughout *The Laws of Creativity*, existing within the unknown is a critical aspect of being creative. It's a place of possibility, of mystery and wonder, of endless curiosity. It's the ultimate state of creation. Conversely, familiarity is the death knell of ideation, a blanket that covers the sky and prevents all light from reaching our minds. Familiarity is the mother of boredom, and boredom is kryptonite to creativity.[104]

Thankfully, there's a straightforward remedy to familiarity: distance.

When you step away, you put space and time between you and your creation. You let the back of your mind settle its debts while the front of your mind takes a vacation. And, when you put the right amount of space in the right place at the right time, you come back supercharged.

Time to Go Tubing

Trying to force creativity is like waiting for water to boil: it takes agonizingly long, time is wasted rather than used, and the result is overhyped and underwhelming. Instead of staring at the pot, you could take out the trash or fold clothes; the water will be roiling before you know it *and* you'll get other things done. It's a win-win.

Similarly, there are benefits when you step away from your creative work. Aside from being able to destress and take care of other responsibilities, you also enter Float, Flow's sister state.[105]

In Float State, the mind directs you instead of the opposite. Float occurs when the prefrontal cortex (PFC), which oversees both focus and memory retrieval, is allowed to stop concentrating. When you step away, you deactivate focus and hand your PFC the reins. You let it excavate the mind to see if it can make

---

[104] To be clear here, boredom is not the same as stillness. Stillness is a wonderful creative tool for finding the present moment. Boredom is an apathetic lack of interest and motivation.

[105] More on Flow in the Law of the Now.

connections that were previously out of view. When you wake up in the morning with a solution to a problem or a great idea pops into your head while showering, that's Float.

THE ORDER OF FIVE

Now that we know what Float is and why it occurs, we can begin to actively leverage it. I came up with and use a basic system called the Order of Five to do just that. In a nutshell, it's a system for stepping away that increases magnitude in response to your needs. Use whichever level of step-away that makes sense for the task at hand.

- **Five Minutes:** Use this when you need a micro-breather. Like stepping outside for a breath of fresh air, it pauses your focus just long enough that when you come back you have to give it a jumpstart, which will bring in new thoughts.

- **Five Hours:** Use this pause when you feel like you've reached a dead end even though you know there's more road to go. Set your work aside, do something else (or nothing at all), and come back with a clear mind.

- **Five Days:** Use this pause when the problem seems almost impossible to work around, and always after you've dedicated a good chunk of time in an attempt to solve it. This is a mid-level palette cleanser. When you return, it should take effort to ease back into the thought process necessary to continue, which helps you more readily bring new ideas to the situation.

- **Five Weeks:** Use this pause when things still aren't coming together. Set the project aside, forget about it, and try again later. At this stage (and the following ones), it's best to start from scratch when you make your next attempt to pick up the task.

- **Five Months:** Use this pause when you aren't sure the problem is currently solvable. It could be because of your environment, the parameters, or a host of other variables that prevent success. This pause is long enough that even deeply rooted elements can change by the time you restart.

- **Five Years:** Use this pause when nothing is working, most likely because of multiple circumstances in your life that prevent your idea from being realized. You'll either come back to it years down the road or not at all. Both of which are acceptable.

The trick, if you want to call it that, is to actively manage Flow and Float. When ideas are effortlessly pouring forth, when time falls to the wayside, you're in Flow. It's not a constant state, but one that can be increasingly activated with select strategies that we discuss later on in the Law of the Now. When you're feeling blocked, when the resistance to progress becomes so great that it's counterproductive to continue—that's when you step away and activate Float state.

It's up to you whether you step away for six weeks like King, every seventh year like Sagmeister, or in line with the Order of Five. It takes practice to know when to sail down the river of ideas or drop the mast and let the current carry you. As long as you stay on the boat, you *will* make progress.

Summary

Intimacy with an idea is a good thing. It makes your efforts personal; it fuels your actions with passion—but there's a limit. Eventually intimacy trades for familiarity, which breeds boredom. And boredom is the antithesis of creativity.

Give your idea time and space to reveal strong and weak points. This strategy works when you are having trouble progressing, but it also works when you think you reached a solution. The amount of time to separate with your idea depends on a variety of factors, including severity of friction, size and complexity of the problem, and degree of familiarity. Use trial and error to hone your ability to make the right choice.

Alternate between Flow and Float—deep, timeless focus and interims of separation—to maximize your creativity and minimize wasted energy.

22
Wear Your Heart

The Law of Vulnerability

To be vulnerable is to be true. Exploring truths, especially those that are below the surface, reveal a piece of what it means to be human. You become relatable—and your message speaks to the heart of what matters most.

Above All This, I Wish You

In 1973, twenty-seven-year-old Dolly Parton came to a sad realization. It was time to part ways with Porter Wagoner, her longtime business partner and the person who contributed most to her success.

Wagoner gave Parton her big break when he chose her to be his co-host on *The Porter Wagoner Show* in 1967. Before that, Parton was a known quantity in her own right as a country music singer, but when she and Wagoner joined forces, they catapulted to the stars.

The show was a medley of country music, comedy, and short skits where the two shared center stage. The duo regularly sang duets with bright smiles tucked under Porter's blonde pompadour and Dolly's even-more-blonde bouffant. Their chemistry was clear to anyone watching. It didn't take long for *The Porter Wagoner Show* to become the number one syndicated program in America.

Dolly Parton wasn't in the mix from the start, however. Wagoner had a previous stage partner, Norma Jean, who left the show, opening up the spot that twenty-one-year-old Parton—originally writing songs for Jean to sing—ended up filling. Wagoner and Parton hit it off professionally, and Wagoner's choice was far more successful than he could have hoped for. But—as all things must—eventually their partnership had to come to an end.

After nearly seven years together, Parton reluctantly decided she had to move on to continue growing and challenging herself as a performer. Wagoner, for mostly selfish reasons, disagreed, and the two of them began to butt heads. Not only did she have a close working relationship with Wagoner, but she was keenly aware that it was he who gave her the opportunity that changed her life. Still, there was no getting around the fact that it was time for her to go solo. Parton went about it in the best way she knew how: by writing a song.

Dolly Parton went home, sat down, and poured her heart out into powerful verse. She laid bare her inner conflict: On one hand, she wanted to explore what else the world offered, but on the other she didn't want to leave Wagoner.

Those verses became the song *I Will Always Love You*. She wrote it in an evening, and the next day she sat Porter Wagoner down and sang it to him. By the end, he was in tears. He said if she felt that strongly, then he wouldn't hold her back.

The very next year, now on her own, Parton released *Jolene*, the hit record that included *I Will Always Love You*, which itself became a number one song—multiple times—and the rest is history.[106]

Better Than to Never

Dolly Parton had everything she could ask for: a job that allowed her to do what she loved, fame and riches, a fair and equitable business relationship, and more. For years, that was enough. But at some point, her need for growth and change became too strong to ignore.

To even admit that need requires an impressive connection with the inner self. Every day, people live lives of discontent, imagining what could be but not taking the steps to chase possibility.

In Alcoholics Anonymous (or any similar program), the first stride towards change is admitting there's a problem. Every time someone shares during a meeting, they introduce themselves, followed by "...and I'm an alcoholic." For most, getting to that point—being able to admit something so deep and fraught with baggage—takes *years*.[107]

For Parton to admit she wanted more from her career was to risk giving up everything she had. To come to terms with one's

---

[106] In 2007, Dolly Parton sang the song one last time to Porter Wagoner, on the day he died.

[107] For those of you out there who are fighting alcohol or substance abuse, please know that I fully support you on your journey and so very much wish you the best. I do not make light of AA, but mention it with the entirety of respect that it deserves.

own truth is no easy feat, but there is no way to become vulnerable or create from the depths without first coming face to face with innermost truths.

That was Parton's first step, to go on an inner journey up the harrowing paths and slopes of Mount Interior and find her way to the peak. The second, once she finally understood how she felt, was to plant a flag inscribed with her intentions firmly at the top of the mountain in the face of thin air and blustering winds—to share her truths and be vulnerable in the process.

Most of us take our realizations and communicate them in conversation, plain and simple. Using only fifty-eight unique words, Dolly Parton took it to the next level, putting all her feelings—sadness, doubt, love—into a song and singing it to Porter Wagoner herself. She communicated a truth so deep and relatable—the idea of loving someone but still hurting them in order to look out for oneself—that when the song reached the radio waves it hit a nerve with listeners everywhere, topping the charts.

I Will Always Love You came from a place of truth. It was shared at the risk of everything. And, to this day, it resonates with everyone who hears it—because we have all loved and lost.

Off the Deep End

Dolly Parton wore her heart on her sleeve when she wrote that song for Porter Wagoner, but being vulnerable, at its core, isn't strictly about showing your sensitive side and sharing your feelings. It can be, but that's more of an effect rather than a cause. The central aim behind the principle of vulnerability is to share ideas that may be uncomfortable or have opposition (or both).

Ever notice that when something hits a nerve, it usually comes from someone being vulnerable? Bradley Cooper's performance in *A Star Is Born* is a great example. Not only did he learn to sing for the role of Jackson Maine, a country music star, he performed the movie's songs live rather than recording them separately.[108] If that were it, that'd be enough—it takes a massive amount of vulnerability to surrender oneself to a new challenge. But, on top of that, he had to do it next to megastar and phenom singer Stefani Germanotta, aka Lady Gaga.[109] Actors are used to uncomfortable situations, but here it's taken to the extreme.

In addition, Cooper's previous roles included a grizzled sniper, the voice of a murderous (and hilarious) raccoon, and several comedic guys-in-trouble. Fans of his funny and action-oriented characters had to adjust to an entirely new archetype—a down-on-himself, past-his-prime country singer. When the role was first announced, as expected, there was opposition. But someone did something right because the move was an instant hit, and "Shallow," the track Cooper and Germanotta performed together, took home an Oscar for best original song.

Of course, it isn't just stars and superstars and megastars that need to be vulnerable for their craft. Everyday folks like you and me put our egos on the line all the time.[110] Whenever

---

[108] Cooper reflects on it: "I had no idea how to breathe. I knew nothing about singing—nothing. It's such a difficult art form to sing in front of people, because you lose your breath right away when you're nervous."

[109] Talk about being self-conscious.

[110] Or we should, at least. Some do it more readily than others. Either way, that's okay, one step at a time. Measure against yourself.

you're in a meeting and voice an opinion against that of the room's, you're being vulnerable. When you experiment with an approach that may not work, you're vulnerable. Building on an idea that comes from personal experience, that's vulnerability. You are putting yourself into the work, and if it fails, it could be taken personally, as if a part of yourself is rejected.[111] But if you don't go there, if you don't take that risk, you're losing far more than you're gaining by shielding yourself from it. In the end, if someone doesn't like your idea, no big deal. You can't hit the ball every time you're at bat.[112]

So how do you become more vulnerable? How do you find the places deep within that are worth mining?

Ask yourself more questions.

As we learned in the Law of Curiosity, asking questions is like digging a hole. Every self-inquiry is another shovelpluck of dirt. The more you ask, the deeper you go. And, with dedication to the hole-digging lifestyle, you occasionally uncover a treasure chest.

Dolly Parton wouldn't have realized she needed to move on if she didn't first ask herself why she was unhappy and, to a degree, bored. Even Porter Wagoner wouldn't have understood how Parton truly felt—they had discussed and disagreed on the subject for quite some time—until he was inspired by her song to ask himself why she went to such great lengths to express her feelings. Bradley Cooper wouldn't have been able to create the

---

111 More on this idea in the Law of the Unknown.

112 In 2018, the MLB batting average was .248. That means that three times out of four, players don't get successful hits. If pro athletes—who are at the top of their game and getting paid millions—are okay with that, then we can give ourselves a break.

character Jackson Maine if he didn't first ask himself if he could learn to sing, learn to play the guitar, *and* learn to play the piano. Stefani Germanotta wouldn't have played his counterpart if she didn't ask herself if she could act alongside the incredible actor that is Cooper.

Over time, you'll become familiar with the questions that help you in your line of work (or whatever it is that you're doing). As a designer, I often ask myself: *How does this make me feel? Would I get excited by this? Would I buy this? Can I do better? Can I do it differently? Has someone already done it this way? If I published it now, would I be happy with the result?* Each question helps me look at what I'm working on with a different perspective, and they add up to help me put together a result I'm proud of and happy with.

Professions and tasks have all sorts of questions that are specific to them, so you'll need to begin experimenting with what works for you. As you discover those questions, put them in your imaginary toolbox—then pull them out whenever necessary and get to digging.

Summary

Vulnerability is the key to relatability. Pulling from deep within yourself allows you to reach deep within others.

Truth is the most important tool in creating from the depths. You must be true to yourself—to admit what's inside and put that into your work. If you don't, or if you try to spin it in a way that imitates depth but removes the vulnerable parts, it won't work. People will see right through it. Or, perhaps worse, they won't see anything at all; it will be ignored completely.

Going deep takes practice. The best way to get there is through self-inquiry, to ask yourself questions that uncover your inner thoughts and feelings, layer by layer. Once you get to the heart of the matter, you've struck gold. Take that gold, melt it, and fashion it into whatever you like.

23
Champion Your Work

The Law of Rebellion

Progress, innovation, and the unknown are nearly always met with opposition. Stand up for your ideas or they will never take flight. What's resisted is often what matters most.

Hello, World

Every time you tap your phone to life or safely pass through a stoplight or interact with a computer in any way, big or small, you're benefiting from the work of a woman whose innovation—and fight for her idea—made it all possible.

Grace Hopper, an educator with three degrees in mathematics and one in physics, joined the United States Navy in 1943. She was assigned to a top-secret project at Harvard, but it wasn't until the day she entered the building that Hopper discovered what her assignment would be: working on the Mark I computer, a five-ton piece of cutting-edge machinery that was the first of its kind in the US.

As a girl, she had taken apart every clock in her house to see how they worked; between that and her affinity for numbers, the task was right up her alley. Hopper was given a week to learn how to program for the Mark I. Not only did she learn what was required of her, she tasked herself with understanding how the machine itself operated, and immediately began to explore ways of making it more efficient and user-friendly.

The first computers, including the Mark I, operated by processing machine language fed to them through a series of punch cards or long rolls of paper with holes.[113] The holes represent binary code, which is a series of zeroes and ones (bits) strung together in sets of eight (bytes) that tell the computer how to manage the flow of electricity. Using circuits, the computer either cuts off power for a zero or allows it for a one, which is how chips still function today.

When Grace Hopper first began working with computers, to have the Mark I output the word "hello" she'd have to punch forty holes to string together machine language that looks like this:

01101000
01100101
01101100
01101100
01101111

Would you be able to read that if you weren't first told what it

---

[113] Every now and then the machine would suddenly stop, caused by its inability to read input. Most of the time it was human error, a misaligned or misplaced hole was all it took. But occasionally it was due to insects that would creep in and get in the way. Hopper found a moth in the Mark I and taped it inside her notebook with the caption, "First case of bug being found." Hence, a computer bug.

says? Of course not, and Grace Hopper quickly realized that there were inherent issues with how programs were created, mainly how specialized someone needed to be to write them and how incomprehensible they were read.

Hopper proposed to her superiors that they work on a way to teach computers to speak human language rather than continuing to have humans speak machine language. They immediately told her it wouldn't work, that programming was for people like her with PhDs in mathematics, that no one else would be able to work with such complex machinery and logic.

Hopper disagreed, and in her free time she continued to develop ways of integrating human and machine language. She figured out how to better organize the capabilities and information stored inside the computer, which was as big as a room and stored data like a library stores books. Instead of only entering machine language, she was able to index various physical locations, give them normal human-word names, and use those names to recall data.

Despite her success, those in charge still didn't find the endeavor worth pursuing. Hopper pushed forward, regardless of support.

In 1952, Hopper came up with the first version of her crowning achievement—the compiler—a program whose sole job is translating human language to machine language. It was named A-0, and it allowed the Mark I to understand and put to use a short list of human commands. For the first time, a person could write human language (just like the words on this page), hand it off to the compiler, and the compiler would output machine language that the computer could then process.

A few years later, at the American machines manufacturer

Remington Rand, Grace Hopper was finally given the opportunity to go all in on compiler technology. She developed FLOW-MATIC, the first fully human programming language, for the UNIVAC I, a general-purpose commercial computer and the forefather of the personal computer. Here's an example of FLOW-MATIC code in action:

> (0) INPUT HELLO FILE-A .
> (1) WRITE FILE-A .
> (2) STOP . (END)

Thanks to Grace Hopper's invention of the compiler, even if you don't understand the nuances of what's happening, you get the gist that the code is saying hello in some way. In this case, "hello" is stored in *FILE-A* and being output, or written, via the *WRITE* command. Compare that to the binary code a few paragraphs back and the importance of Hopper's innovation is apparent.

In 1959, Hopper's FLOW-MATIC became the foundation for COBOL, the first widespread commercial human programming language. It contains over six hundred human word commands, and today, some eight decades later, COBOL is still used to process over 80 percent of all business transactions.

Honor in Battle

If Grace Hopper didn't fight to invent the compiler, we wouldn't be living in the world we do today. It's easy to look back on the impact she had and ask how anyone could deny her the opportunity to innovate, but that's exactly what happened.

How did Hopper know that her idea was worth fighting for?

Why did she stick her neck out several times when life would've been less stressful if she had let it go?

To judge whether the fight was worth it, Hopper had to analyze the problem, not the idea itself. In her case, the problem was clear:

1. Computers would be more important over time.
2. Programmers would be increasingly needed.
3. Programming required too much specialty knowledge.

Ahead of everyone around her, she realized that as time went on, the demand for programmers would far outweigh the supply. As technology continued to progress, finding enough highly math-oriented individuals and training them to speak machine language would be a losing battle.

At first, she simply presented the solution to her superiors, but because they couldn't see the causes themselves, they shot her down. Then she tested her idea on a small scale by indexing the innards of the Mark I, proving that basic human language in programming was beneficial. While her work was appreciated, her insights weren't clear to those in charge, and so they deemed it progress enough. It took *years* of persistence before Hopper found someone who could both understand the problem and provide her the opportunity to solve it.

New ideas almost always face opposition. It's why creativity—the practice of ideas—is viewed with so much apprehension and fear. Its very nature requires that the unknown be explored, that new paths be scouted. Because of this, there will often be friction when presenting an idea to a general audience, regardless of the quality of the idea itself.

Though Grace Hopper had opposition at the leadership level, she had the support of her close peers. Those who worked with her had a similar experience. They didn't have to extend themselves to understand the problem she was attempting to prevent because they could see it coming firsthand.

IDEA VALIDATION

As we learned in the Law of the Muse, ideas are cheap. Creativity necessitates iteration (Law of Iteration), not only with the thing being made but with the ideas involved. It's normal to go through hundreds of ideas before finding one that works. But if that's the case, how do we know when an idea is the right one?

There's no magic bullet here. In the end, publishing your work *will* require a leap of faith. The strategy, however, is to minimize how much faith you need. Faith has a spectrum that goes from "No idea" to "Absolutely certain." You will never be at the extreme ends of either side, but rather somewhere in the middle. Which means that there's always an inherent doubt to any decision to move forward (or stop going). The goal is to be as close to certainty as possible, and the closer you get, the more likely you'll prosper once you put your idea into the world.

THE CERTAINTY SPECTRUM

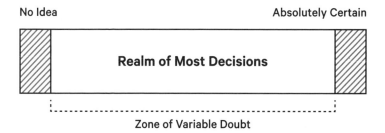

There's a spectrum of certainty—confidence in a judment—that goes from having no idea whatsoever to being absolutely certain. In real-world application, nearly all of the judgments we are tasked with making exist between the two extremes. We rarely have no idea what to think; equally as unlikely, we rarely have complete certainty about a decsion.

Here are a few ways to minimize your faith requirement and maximize your probability for success:

1. **Review your premise.** Starting from the fundamental concepts that your idea is built upon, review each element that contributes to your creation. Take a counter position to your own and attempt to argue *against* your idea. Break down those arguments and evaluate them one by one. If they are valid, revisit your idea and patch up the holes. If they are weak or nonexistent, that's a good sign.

2. **Find others with insight.** When trying to validate your ideas, search for people who have similar experiences and knowledge to those that brought you to your conclusion. You may find several people who can help, sometimes there might be just one, or it may be the case

that there's no one at all. If you do find people who can help, ask for their perspective. Don't feel like what they say is the ultimate truth—very often others miss what's right in front of them—but use their input to responsibly weigh your insights.

3. **Run a test.** If you can, test your idea on a small scale: hand out prototypes, start using your creation, post it to a message board or text some friends and assess their reactions, etc. You will quickly discover what works and what doesn't. Depending on the idea, this isn't always possible, but when it is, take advantage.

Regardless of support, if you do decide your idea is worth the trouble, you're going to have to make the decision, when the time is right, to take a leap of faith and put it out there. It's likely that you will eventually be called to stand up for your idea, perhaps even several times like Hopper. If you do, always remember to be respectful and do no harm.

Thankfully, Grace Hopper fought for her idea and succeeded. Today the global computer developer population includes over twenty-five million people, all of which code in various human programming languages that use her invention, the compiler, to speak to machines.

Power and Purple

History is littered with great ideas whose thinkers had to fight tooth and nail to get heard.

Nikola Tesla battled Thomas Edison and his direct current for years before people accepted that Tesla's alternating current was a more efficient way to light homes and power machines. Their feud was so severe that Tesla had to pull a nuclear move to win: he sold his patent rights to Westinghouse to provide alternating current with the backing it needed to take hold, surrendering years of royalties for the sake of a better world.[114]

In Tesla's case, the fight was about the results of creativity, as it often is. But occasionally, the fight itself includes creativity. Take the musician Prince's battle with his record label, for example.

With the exception of 1983, Prince released an album annually from 1978 to 1992. After fourteen albums, Warner Brothers decided they wanted him to slow down and publish less, worried that he was saturating his audience with too much music. Prince vehemently disagreed. He wanted to publish music as fast as he made it, but ultimately the label controlled what was released. They had even gone so far as to trademark his name.

"Prince is the name that my mother gave me at birth," he recalls. "Warner Brothers took the name, trademarked it, and used it as the main marketing tool to promote all of the music I wrote. I became merely a pawn used to produce more money for Warner Brothers."

---

114 Tesla won against Edison, and today alternating current powers nearly everything we interact with. Unfortunately, he achieved success at great cost to his own personal wealth and died broke living in a New York hotel.

So what did Prince do? He changed his name to an unpronounceable symbol: a combination of a cross and an arrow—those for female and male—which together created a shape that somewhat resembles an Egyptian ankh. There was no way to write or verbalize it, which is why people gave it the description of "The Love Symbol," and eventually started referring to him as "The Artist Formerly Known as Prince."

While he couldn't break the contract, there was nothing in there that said he couldn't give the label a hard time. It's difficult to sell records when no one knows what to call you. And once his contract expired, he went right back to calling himself Prince, thus concluding his incredible and creative act of daring rebellion.

I learned all of this during *my own* act of creative rebellion. In 2013, I was invited to participate in a design competition, all expenses paid.[115] Normally I wouldn't have gone, but I'd never been to Minneapolis before and figured it would be a fun trip.

The competition was similar to a reality cooking show like *Iron Chef*, but with the audience voting rather than judges. There were three rounds, one per day for three days straight. Each day was a different design challenge, which myself and my fellow contestants had just twenty-four hours to complete. Seven designers started, only one came out.

A few weeks before my flight, the organizers sent over the first design brief: rebrand Prince.

---

115 I am not a fan of industry competitions like these. They're ego fests that don't correlate to ability. Aside from sports athletes, think about a role model you have and ask yourself if they ever needed to prove themself by competing in or winning a contest. Measure against yourself, not others.

I spent day and night learning about him, listening to his music, and trying to figure out, as best I could, who Prince was beneath the celebrity. He had done so many rebellious things in his career and defied so many social expectations, that by the time I was done researching, trying to brand him felt like a betrayal. Prince was a person who strived to define himself, not have others do it. Yet that is exactly what I was tasked to do. This thought led me to the only question that mattered: *How would Prince rebrand himself?*

The day finally came. My design was projected on a forty-foot screen along with the six other contestants' work. Every one of them designed complex glyphs full of sharp lines and intricate details. Mine, on the other hand, was just the name "prince" in purple and typed using Comic Sans, the font that designers despise the most.

I walked up to the mic in front of two-thousand people, all designers. There were boos scattered throughout the crowd. Instead of taking it to heart, I smiled, laughed, and defended my idea: "A guy who can make high heels, purple boots, and turquoise leather jackets sexy—could probably make Comic Sans sexy."

As it turned out, my approach resonated.

The audience voted for me, and I survived the first day. And the second. And, on the third day, I won the entire competition. I approached design as a non-designer—in rebellion of the expectations that the industry places on us (like any other industry)—and fought for what I believed in: that designers shouldn't design for other designers, but for everyone.[116]

---

[116] The event organizer wasn't happy that I won, and I was never invited back to speak like other winners were.

The third design that helped me seal the deal and win? A software concept designed to help people drive safer—which, if created, would only be possible thanks to Grace Hopper and her compiler.

Summary

Do not confuse rebellion for anarchy. Rebels have a cause—an idea—that drives them. It just so happens that many of history's greatest achievers were called troublemakers: George Washington and the founding fathers, Nelson Mandela, Martin Luther King Jr., Abraham Lincoln, and so on down a near-infinite list of people who shaped the world we live in.

Twyla Tharp, the innovative American choreographer, said, "Creativity is an act of defiance." Picking a fight is not something that should be done out of aggression or malice, but out of a belief that the world will be a better place—even if only slightly—because of your idea.

It's paramount that the idea you go to bat for is validated in some way. There's a difference between it being misunderstood versus being a poor idea. Learn to recognize the difference. You can test your idea in small doses, or you can pass it by those who have the right knowledge and experience, but in the end you're going to have to take a leap of faith.

24
Publish Imperfection

The Law of Good Enough

Aim for perfection and you will find yourself smothered by perpetual searching and disappointment. Instead, publish the simplest, clearest version of your creation, and go from there.

Chalkboard on a Screen

Sal Khan sat in a small office chair with his feet propped up on the windowsill, his back against the opposite wall. A notebook rested on his lap, filled with notes for a math lesson. Aside from a modest desk, he was surrounded by books from floor to ceiling. It was 2009, and Khan had just quit a comfortable job to work full time ... in a closet.

Khan was on a journey that started a few years earlier when he had been working as a hedge fund analyst. In school he studied mathematics, electrical engineering, and computer science—fields which his hedge fund job barely scratched the surface of.[117] Through the family grapevine, he found out that his cousin, Nadia, needed tutoring for her seventh-grade algebra class. Khan jumped on the opportunity to use his knowledge and volunteered.

There was just one problem. He was in Boston and Nadia lived halfway across the country, in New Orleans. There weren't many remote communication options available in 2004, but Khan managed to come up with a simple enough solution: YouTube. Rather than align his schedule with Nadia's to teach live or find a service to privately host his videos, he instead posted them to his newly created channel. It was easy, free, and fast.

Khan's videos were rudimentary: A black screen, similar to a chalkboard, his own handwriting in various colors just like a teacher using colorful chalk to differentiate ideas, and a voice-over of—you guessed it—Sal Khan himself. The videos weren't edited. They didn't have music. There were no intro or outro screens. And he didn't even make an appearance in them. As Khan described his method, it's like he's "sitting next to the person and we're looking at the paper together."

In fact, he didn't even run through the problems beforehand. When asked about his preparation routine, he said: "I'm 95 percent of the time working through that problem in real time.[118] Or I'm thinking it through myself if I'm explaining something, and to see that it is actually sometimes a messy process, that it isn't always this clean process where you just know the answer. I think that that's what people like. The kind of humanity there."

---

117 A sobering truth: Only 27 percent of college graduates work in a field related to their major.

118 His willingness to "fail" in front of others is a great example of the Law of Continuity. Failing isn't true failure of you learn from it.

All of Khan's videos were publicly posted to YouTube. He figured there was no need to keep them unlisted, as there was nothing private about them. He didn't expect others to start watching. At first it was just a few dozen, but in a short time, his videos began to collect hundreds of views. Then thousands. Then tens of thousands.

It was undeniable—he was on to something.

In 2007, he named his YouTube channel Khan Academy with the mission to create "A free world-class education for anyone, anywhere." By 2009, his videos had been viewed by millions around the world. It was then that his wife suggested he quit his job and run the academy full time.

Agreeing that he was onto something, Khan took his wife's suggestion and quit his comfortable hedge fund job. He leapt headfirst into the world of entrepreneurship and nonprofits. Every month, another five- to ten-thousand dollars disappeared from his savings as he worked to bring Khan Academy to life.

"I was probably at my lowest point," Khan recalls. "I was waking up with cold sweats, not able to sleep. I would go for a run in the middle of the night to calm my nerves." He was aware that, compared to other education platforms at the time, his videos were crude, and the delivery method was unsophisticated. "At the time," he later explained, "no one took YouTube seriously."

Committed, Khan continued pushing forward. In order to grow Khan Academy, he needed to attract investors and hire a bigger team. Pitch after pitch failed to convince others to join him on his mission, however. "I was getting no traction. I had gotten rejected at that point by twenty or thirty foundations," Khan said of his early days building the business.

Throughout all this struggle, he still made videos every day.

Even though he wasn't getting traction in board rooms, people everywhere were taking his lessons in greater and greater numbers.

Then a tipping point occurred.

In an interview, Bill Gates revealed that he used Khan Academy to teach his own children. From that point forward, everyone was on board with Khan's revolutionary idea. On *60 Minutes*, Sanjay Gupta called Sal Khan the "Most watched teacher in the world." And TIME magazine named him one of the 100 Most Influential People in the World.

Today, Khan Academy has over sixty million registered students. His videos have nearly two billion views. And they are still made with a black screen, handwritten text, and a voiceover.

Now Presenting

Salvador Dali famously said, "Have no fear of perfection—you'll never reach it." He understood what most do not, that striving for perfection inherently dooms a project to be steeped in feelings of disappointment. If you aim to create something perfect, there are only two possible outcomes:

1. **Perfection is endlessly pursued.** Since perfection is unattainable, by reaching for it the creator condemns themselves to a taxing chase with no end.

2. **An imperfect creation is reluctantly published.** By aiming for perfection and "falling short," the creator is effectively pigeonholing themselves into perpetual dissatisfaction.

How did Sal Khan avoid these two scenarios? How did he handle perfection?

Khan was not immune to the internal second guessing that comes with perfectionism.[119] Once he decided to make Khan Academy his full-time job, mixed emotions began flooding in. In an interview, Khan admitted that he often questioned whether he had made the right choice, thinking to himself, "Who do you think you are, Sal? You're just some guy. You're not a formal educator. You're a guy operating out of a walk-in closet. You have no business model. You have zero experience in the non-profit realm." And while "It was hard to go through a day without several moments of self-doubt," Khan continued to publish videos, believing in his idea and his mission.

Khan knew that the process of putting something into the world requires two elements: First, the creation itself. Second, the presentation of the creation.

As we've discussed, creativity is the practice of ideas, and a creation is the expression of said ideas. The creation generally solves some kind of problem or expresses a concept.[120] Once it's made, there's the challenge of presenting—or publishing—which is the second layer of creation. For example, chocolate makers spend years cooking up the perfect recipe, but then they still need to figure out what shape to mold the bars and how to package and sell it. Even if you're making something as straightforward as a spreadsheet, you still need to set up the information (the creation) in a way that other people can parse it (the presentation).

In Khan's case, he chose to focus almost exclusively on the

---

119 We're all human. Doubt is natural and common. It's what we do with doubt that determines our success.

120 Take a look at the Law of Grounding for Problem vs. Concept Anchors.

creation itself: communicating a single math concept per lesson. He let the creation fully dictate the presentation. While everyone else was making highly refined "professional" education videos, Khan just got to the point. He didn't worry about flashy introductions, being in the spotlight, or stumbling over a word or two. And it resonated. Not just with his cousin, Nadia, who immediately started improving at school, but with strangers all around the world.

Plato's Playdough

Everyone publishes imperfection. This isn't a guess or an estimation. It's not hyperbole—it's a fact. How do I know this? Because perfection doesn't exist, yet everywhere we look, all sorts of things *do* exist.

For every object in your kitchen or bedroom or wherever you are right now, someone (probably a team of people) had to stop the gears of creation and say, "This will do."

And that's okay.

While there are probably a few items in your kitchen that you find unsatisfactory, you use most of them without a second thought. Your spoons don't need exact edges or flawless finishes to scoop soup from a bowl to your mouth. It's very likely that you bought your silverware after looking at dozens online or in a store, all with similar but slightly different engravings, and ultimately chose one of several sensible options and said, "This will do."

While perfection itself is certainly not worth striving for—and unnecessary, as is evident in the fact that the world continues to spin—exploring the *idea* of perfection in your mind is still a valuable exercise.

The Greek philosopher Plato came up with what is now simply called the Theory of Forms. Essentially, it's the philosophical understanding of abstract ideas as they relate to their real-word counterparts.

Take the form (or idea) of a circle, for example. It's a round, flat shape where all points are *perfectly* equidistant from the center point. In concept, it's simple. In your mind, it's perfect. But in the real world, creating a perfect circle is impossible. That doesn't stop us from trying, however. Circles surround us. You can find them on clocks, bottles, plates, windows, headphones, and so on. None of them are perfect in the sense of true mathematical perfection, but they all accomplish their creator's goals.

In your own creative endeavors, you must do the same. Use the *idea* of your creation—the Platonic Form—to guide you in your process. It is there not as a goal to achieve, but as a model to imitate.

If we aren't heading towards the perfect, then where *are* we heading? Without a goal, it's easy to slip back into a perfection mindset or work endlessly towards an impossible end. Thankfully, we have a clear target: the **Prime Construct**.

The Prime Construct is the simplest version of your idea that can be shaped into an effective creation. Measuring whether you're at the simplest version is a matter of pulling away components. If a creation no longer functions with even a single current component removed, you're at the prime level. If it *does* function, then keep that component removed and take away yet another until you've reached prime.

Depending on the nature of your project, the Prime Construct may or may not be the version you publish. If you're making YouTube videos like Sal Khan, you can publish the

Prime Construct because of how easy it is to update if needed. If you're writing a book, such as this one, the Prime Construct (commonly referred to as the first draft) requires several passes before publishing because of the permanence of a physical book.

If we can never reach perfection, at some point in the process we must come to terms with the truth—that the actual creation in front of us will never be exactly like the idea in our mind—and make the active decision to say, "This will do."

Summary

Perfection is a double-edged sword. If wielded correctly, it can serve you well. If wielded incorrectly, it can harm you rather than help. Accept that perfection is unattainable in the physical world. Understand that to strive for it would be like trying to find the legendary (but nonexistent) lost city of Atlantis.

Appreciate the Platonic Form—the perfect version of your idea—for what it is: an immaterial, impossible goal. But recognize that it can still be an inspiring blueprint. Grounded in reality, let the form guide you in creating your Prime Construct, the simplest version of your idea.

As Plato said, "The greatest wealth is to live content with little." Start small and be proud of what you've made—who knows where it will take you.

25
Let It Go

The Law of the Finish Line

The end is a fallacy. You don't reach it, you choose it. And when you do, when your creation leaves your hands and enters the world—it is no longer yours.

Hero's Journey

The Alchemist, written by Paulo Coelho, is one of the bestselling books of all time. It's right up there with other legendary tales like *The Catcher in the Rye* and the Harry Potter series. The book didn't start that way, though. Originally it was a flop when Coelho released it in 1988. What happened later, however, once it was out of his hands, changed the novel's trajectory entirely.

The story of *The Alchemist* is one of an archetypal hero's journey. In this case, a young shepherd boy named Santiago goes off on a journey to Egypt in search of treasure. Coelho wrote the book in just two weeks. He claimed that it was "already in his soul." The ease at which words came out was also partly because the story was so familiar to him—Santiago's journey is a metaphor for Coelho's own life.

Coelho was born in Rio de Janeiro in 1947. From childhood, he had a fascination with writing as well as a tendency to cause trouble. At the age of seventeen, his parents committed him to a psychiatric facility, forbidding him from being a writer. He resisted, and as a result, ended up spending the remainder of his youth in and out of institutions. At one point, he was even put in prison and tortured for writing a supposedly subversive comic strip. Briefly, he attended law school but dropped out soon after. No matter what anyone did, the rebel within him could not be quelled.

Coelho's passion for writing survived years of oppression. At long last, he was a free adult. Much like Santiago, he began the search for his own personal treasure. He experimented with psychedelics, played music, and generally lived a life one would expect from a young adult in the 1960s and 70s, all the while continuing to write.

In 1988, Coelho published *The Alchemist*. It was his second novel, and the publisher agreed to print nine hundred copies. Unfortunately, sales were poor and they decided against printing a second run. He remembers, "There was one month in my life where I could really quit my dream. If I was not perseverant enough, *The Alchemist* would not be the worldwide success that it is today." Through sheer force of will and an unwavering passion for storytelling, Coelho continued his journey as an author.

In 1990, Coelho published his third novel, *Brida*. With it came international literary success, which caused interest in his earlier books and prompted them to be reprinted. While the two books weren't instant hits, they continued to sell steadily.

Then something curious happened.

The Alchemist re-released, along with its e-book version, right around the time the internet and peer-to-peer file sharing was booming. Coelho soon discovered that his book, like many other authors', was being pirated on websites and in chatrooms with users from all around the world. At the time, publishers played whack-a-mole, searching for illegal e-books and removing them (as best they could), only to have ten more pop up overnight.

Coelho realized publishers were fighting a losing battle. He decided to do something no other author had ever done—certainly not something he remotely imagined doing himself. He went online, found the best pirated versions of his books, and launched his own site, Pirate Coelho. It contained all of his works linked and downloadable entirely for *free*.

In the years that followed, Paulo Coelho's sales rocketed. As of today, *The Alchemist* has graced the *New York Times* best-seller list 315 weeks, has been translated into more than eight languages, and has sold over sixty-five million copies.

Pirates and Payments

Even if you haven't read it, *The Alchemist* is a title that very few haven't heard of. Nowadays, many high schools require it as part of standard curriculum, as the lessons it teaches are both lifelong and timeless. The question begs to be asked:

Would Paulo Coelho's book be so ubiquitous if he hadn't given it away for free?

First, let's make a distinction: if the book wasn't phenomenal, it never would have risen to its current status, regardless of how many smart moves or marketing tricks were used. *The Alchemist*, at its core, is a rare combination of fantastic storytelling and beautiful line-to-line writing. If you haven't already read it, you should.

Coelho spent just two weeks writing the first draft, but he spent months wrapping up the final manuscript. During that process, there's no way he could've predicted what would happen next. But once a work is out of the author's hands—whether it's a book or a product or a spreadsheet—it's not theirs anymore. Sure, they may own the rights to it, but you don't ask the makers of your toaster if it's okay to put hash browns in there. You just do it.

Hearts sank across dozens of industries when digital piracy first emerged. For books, authors spent months, oftentimes years of their lives on a single project, only to see their work downloaded illegally for free. Nowadays it's common, but back then it was shocking.[121] Coelho's decision was steeped in the idea that "If you can't beat 'em, join 'em."

At first, it may seem like Coelho betrayed the Law of Obscurity (going where others are not). He more or less decided to do what the masses were doing: sharing books and other digital media, for free, peer to peer. But, if we peel back one more layer, we reveal that he embodied the law: he went where *his* peers were not. By giving his books away for free, he did the opposite of what every other author and publisher was doing at the time, and that made him stand out. As Coelho put it, "The ultimate goal of a writer is to be read. Money comes later."

---

121 To those of you who paid for this book: Thank you for the support.

Let It Go

Radiohead, the rock band out of the UK, followed Coelho's example in 2007 when they released their new album, *In Rainbows*, under a pay-what-you-want format. I remember my college roommate at the time excitedly telling me all about it. Once I was caught up, I purchased the album myself just to see if the offer was real or not.[122] It was, and the strategy was so successful that the band ended up selling three times as many copies as their previous album.

Don't worry, this isn't a marketing book and I'm not here to tell you that giving away your work for free is a good idea. In fact, I don't think it is, mostly because everyone is doing it now. Coelho and Radiohead did it when it was unheard of, and they were already known quantities to begin with. For the average person, for whatever it is you're making, assign a fair value and stick to it.[123]

After publishing *The Alchemist*, it was out of Paulo Coelho's hands, subject to the ebbs and flows of cultures and peoples. Like others did in the 1990s, he could've easily succumbed to the seemingly dismal reality of piracy. Instead, Coelho paid attention to what others were doing with his book, which was now in their hands, and, almost like a collaboration, responded in kind.

To this day, the acclaimed author looks back positively on Pirate Coelho. And—best of all—the website is still live.[124]

---

[122] I don't remember too well, but I think I tried giving $5 to see if the website was truly going to spit out an album afterwards. And it did. They earned a fan that day because I've purchased every Radiohead album since.

[123] If you want to give a portion away for free—a taste of the full product or service—go for it. It doesn't always make sense, but when it does, why not.

[124] At least at the time of publication.

Half and Half and Half and Soup

Anything that we decide to make we must also decide to stop making. The end—the finish line—will never come of its own volition. As Leonardo da Vinci, legendary polymath and grandmaster of creativity, once said, "Art is never finished, only abandoned."[125]

To help us understand, let's take a look at the Greek philosopher Zeno's dichotomy paradox. Imagine two points—let's call them the beginning and the end—and a straight path that connects them. Euclidean geometry (the stuff most of us studied as kids) states that between those two points there are an infinite number of connecting points. Zeno extrapolated this concept, claiming that if we start at the beginning and proceed in halfway chunks—50 percent of the distance to the end each time—then we will never reach the end point. For example, if the two points are one hundred meters apart, the first step would be fifty meters, the second twenty-five (half of the remaining fifty), the third 12.5, and on and on into infinity, but never to completion.

Think of creating in much the same way.

---

125 Art, schmart—don't let the word distract you. Anyone who does something with heart and passion is an artist. Anything they make with that mindset is art.

ZENO'S PARADOX VS. PROGRESS

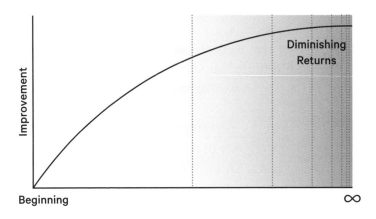

DOTS: Zeno's Paradox depicted. Over time, equal amounts of effort translates to smaller returns. Eventually, you reach a point in which effort becomes inconsequential or invisible to the average viwer. This is a natural ending; effort should cease.

GRAPH: Zeno's Paradox applied to quality of improvement. In the early stages of a creative project, improvements are easily achieved. Later on, improvements are minor and eventually not worth the effort. The point at which improvement decelerates is when an ending should be considered.

In the first step, you start with zero—nothing. And then go to one—something. The difference between the two is vast. Then you continue working until you shape your creation to be in a more preferable state than when you first began, and, while the difference isn't as dramatic, there is noticeable progress. Keep doing this and eventually you get to the point in which your changes, though they still add progress, are so minuscule or insignificant that they aren't worth the time and effort anymore.

If I were designing, say, an album cover, the first few steps—adding the title and an image—would transform a blank sheet of paper into a functional (albeit plain) piece of communication. In the next step, I'd choose a better typeface to match the genre and tweak the photo to fit the mood. Now the viewer would know what to expect just from glancing at it. (For example, a gothic illustration with sharp red text would immediately convey heavy metal.) Then I'd spend time improving the finer elements of the design, like tweaking the layout, adjusting the space between letters, and making sure there's a hierarchy to everything. That can take the cover from good to great, but if I'm not careful, I could begin to obsess over tiny things that the average viewer won't notice. If I go too far, I cease to make it better and just start making it different.

It's critical that when the steps I take become inconsequential, I voluntarily decide to stop.

Understanding how creative progress works is essential because deciding to stop is the first part of letting go. The best way to know when to call it quits is to recognize, deep within, that it must be a proactive choice. Like the spoken word whose speaker may have one intention but a listener could perceive something else entirely, once you let go, what happens next is out of your hands.

In 1962, Andy Warhol, the American pop artist, presented his new work in a modest Los Angeles gallery. It was a collection of thirty-two canvases that is known today as *Campbell's Soup*

Cans.[126] Each canvas features a different can of soup with the signature red Campbell's label. The collection became iconic—it took the mundane and elevated it. Warhol's work ushered in a new era of fine art, with Campbell's at the center.

The second part of letting go is acceptance. In most cases, there is very little that can be done to control the life of a thing once you release it into the wild. You've made something, but you can't control how people will respond to or use it. Sure, you can have an idea of how you'd like things to play out, but ultimately you must let go, like a parent whose child has grown into adulthood.

Can you imagine being the CEO of Campbell's Soup? Or the designer responsible for the labels? At no point did they plan on—nor give Warhol permission for—their image being reused, yet their product suddenly became a part of American pop art, subject to the whims of its citizens and culture. It's easy to imagine a scenario where they presented Warhol with a cease and desist, or publicly disparaged the works, or even outright took him to court. After all, it could be quite damaging to a company to have their brand appropriated. So what did Campbell's do?

They enjoyed it.

So much, in fact, that they reappropriated Warhol's appropriation. In 1968, Campbell's introduced "The Souper Dress," a paper dress with a soup can pattern printed from top to bottom. To get one, all you had to do was send $1 and two soup labels to the company. A few short weeks later, you'd receive your dress in the mail, folded neatly in an envelope.

---

126 If you've seen a Campbell's soup can printed on a shirt or blanket or anything that isn't a grocery store brochure, you can thank Warhol for it.

Summary

There is no such thing as a true finish line. Even a sprinter who passes the checkered flag is already thinking about the next competition. In reality, the true end comes only when you decide it's time.

Creative work, after a point, has exponentially diminishing returns. In the beginning, the act of starting is alone a tremendous step forward. But as progress continues, each step becomes less effective until, eventually, the work being done is inconsequential. To continue would be a waste of energy. This point must be recognized, and a decision must be made to call it quits.

Once you wrap up and give your creation to the world—whether it's a song or a blanket or a presentation—it's no longer yours. Then comes a process of acceptance. What once was held in secret—built with pieces of your very self and toiled over—must now be let go. Like a parent letting a child grow into adulthood, you must accept that whatever happens next is out of your control.

If you proactively choose to end and accept what comes next, you have truly let go. It's at that point that the ensuing results can be harnessed and channeled into something even better.

PART 3
EXCELLENCE

How to Rise Above the Rest

The Laws of Greatness

"Be a yardstick of quality. Some people aren't used to an environment where excellence is expected." —Steve Jobs

---

Take a close look at top performers and you'll notice common traits: They all have unique methods of expression, they employ copious amounts of self-discipline, and—perhaps most importantly—they know how to set their stage for success and capitalize on opportunities when they appear.

To be better than the majority—the average—you must do more than the majority does. You will have to go farther, longer, and deeper in all aspects of your practice.

We will discuss excellence as it relates to the practice of creativity, but know that the next set of laws, like so many in this book, apply not only to creative acts, but also to the greater experience of life.

The following section contains a short list of laws that, when combined, propel the average performer into the realm of greatness. As with the two previous sections, it's recommended that you take your time with each law. Let them sink in before moving on to the next, perhaps have a conversation about them with friends, family, or at work. Keep an eye out for trends you see in your life because if you look closely, you'll see them everywhere.

Remember, creativity is a skill. Here's how to master it.

26
Do the Work

The Law of Showing Up

Do the work and you will reap the rewards. Attempt to skip to the end or cheat the process and you yourself will be skipped over or cheated out. Instead, convert passion into energy, believe in yourself, and begin.

Reference Letters

The year was 1884. A little boy named Albert Einstein was five years old and lying in bed, sick. Unable to read and bored with his toys, there was nothing for him to do but suffer and wait to get better. To lift his spirits, his father Hermann surprised young Albert with a brass pocket compass. It worked. Before long, his son was not only distracted from his illness, he was set on a path of—and lifelong obsession with—learning more about how the universe works.

By twelve years old, Einstein had taught himself algebra and geometry.[127] By fourteen, he had mastered advanced calculus.

---

[127] Key words here: "taught himself." He wasn't born with advanced mathematics knowledge; he worked for it.

He was certain that the mysteries of nature could be uncovered and expressed through mathematics, and he was determined to prove it.

At sixteen years old—two years younger than the norm—he applied to the Swiss Federal Polytechnic School in Zürich. He failed the entrance exam. Undeterred, he tried again at seventeen and was accepted. In 1900, Einstein graduated with a teacher's degree in math and physics. His ultimate goal was to become an academic, to teach his favorite subjects to young minds and, in between, do research to develop new hypotheses.

To no one's surprise but his own, Einstein's aspirations were met with resistance. He was unable to find a job because of the reputation he had unknowingly developed. As exampled in his early application to school, Einstein rarely waited for the permission of others to make progress. Because of this, he was often ahead of the class—and even his professors. He would correct professors when they were wrong or if there was a simpler way to solve a problem. Eventually he stopped showing up to class entirely, preferring to spend more time in the lab.

When it came time for recommendations, no professor would vouch for him. And without peer support, it was nearly impossible to secure an academic position. After trying and failing for two years, Einstein finally accepted his fate. He famously took a job in the Swiss patent office. As it turned out, it would be one of the best decisions of his life.

Einstein divided his day into three equal parts: Eight hours working at the patent office, eight hours working on his personal mathematics endeavors, and eight hours sleeping. And so he worked in obscurity, stamping papers in the daytime (spending downtime on study and research) and exploring ideas in the evenings.

In 1905, he shocked the scientific community—not once, but four times in a single year.

In the span of seven months, Einstein published four papers—each on a different subject—that radically changed our understanding of the universe. First, in March, he put forth the idea that light was a particle rather than a wave. In May, he proved the existence of atoms. In June, he theorized that the speed of light is a constant, culminating in his theory of special relativity. And finally, in September, Einstein solved the relationship between energy and mass, presenting the now-iconic formula $E = mc^2$.

It wasn't long before he had the attention of every academic in the world. Mathematicians and physicists pored over his work, astounded by the simplicity and elegance of his ideas. He finally got the letters of recommendation he was looking for, including one from Marie Curie herself, who called him "one of the most original thinkers I have ever met."[128]

A decade later, he introduced his masterpiece, the theory of general relativity, which presents gravity as the result of the curvature of space and time. When it was validated by another scientist four years later, Albert Einstein was launched into mainstream consciousness, where he still exists today.

---

[128] Translation: Einstein was one of the most creative scientists of his generation. She complimented his ability to think originally, not the horsepower of his intellect.

Zeitgeist Inflection

Albert Einstein is traditionally held up as the picture-perfect definition of a genius: original, groundbreaking, and creative (our favorite). There's no argument there, he is all those things. But what about the twenty-something years he spent working in obscurity?

Imagine a timeline that goes from left to right, past to present. In the very center there's a vertical line that splits the timeline in half. That vertical line represents the Zeitgeist Inflection, the point when the person becomes a known quantity. As far as mainstream media is concerned (and therefore mainstream knowledge), that center point is treated as the starting point.

THE ILLUSION OF SUCCESS

Zeitgeist Inflection = False Beginning

Creators work on their creations much longer than the creations are known. At some point, after significant effort, an inflection point occurs that brings the creator's work into the consciousness of others. That inflection point is often treated as a starting point, disregarding all the effort that led to its cause, and perpetuating the myth that success is created in a single moment.

Einstein presented his four extraordinary ideas in 1905, which is now referred to as his "miracle year." It's when people began paying attention to him. In their minds, one moment Einstein didn't exist, the next he did, *along with all that he had accomplished.* It's easy to be intimidated by success when we don't account for everything that came before the inflection point. Because of this, it's even easier to think that we are incapable of doing great things because they don't fall into our laps the way Einstein's ideas seemingly fell into his.

For the remainder of his life, Einstein fought against the belief that genius led to his success. In a way, it was an insult. Attributing his success to some kind of mythical mental prowess negated all the very real, very hard work he had put in to build his theories. Einstein is even on record trying to push back against this sentiment, saying, "It's not that I'm so smart, it's just that I stay with problems longer," and, "If you thought about this as much as me, you'd figure it out too."

Einstein stayed with problems longer because he was fueled by passion. His mind lit up the moment his father gave him that compass, and from that day forward it never stopped exploding with curiosities. For every answer he found, he also discovered a host of new questions. Einstein chased those strands of thought until he inevitably reached answers that no one had previously formulated.

It's easier to think that personal greatness is impossible, that the potential for it is something very few are born with. Because the opposite would mean accepting that it simply takes a lot of work and time, more than you're willing to give. Which means that you're then *choosing* not to be great.

Are you willing to show up and do the work?

Let You Be

It's been claimed that Einstein said, "Everybody is a genius. But if you judge a fish by its ability to climb a tree, it will live its whole life believing that it is stupid." No one has been able to prove these words are his, but regardless of whether he said it or not, the reason the quote has endured is because there's truth behind the thought, and it falls in line with his beliefs on intelligence and hard work.

I started designing when I was eight or so. As soon as we got our first family computer, I was off making flyers and greeting cards for friends, family, and neighbors. I continued right through high school and into college when I got a job doing marketing. Since there was no designer on the team, I filled that role as well. And so it went for several years. I worked when I had a problem to solve, but never for the sake of just learning and improving. I made progress, and at that pace I would've been a capable designer, if average.

At the time, I was still a fish trying to climb a tree. Despite designing for years, I went to university for literature and philosophy. I was (and still am) a voracious reader. Since I learned to read, I've been consuming several dozen books a year, so when the prospect of college came up, I figured literature was my passion. And sure, I enjoyed it. But for the most part, I was more interested in consuming books than creating them.

Unfortunately, I had little passion for the activities of class. Rather than read and discuss, I just wanted to read, read, read. I became bored with my classes and, for many of them, stopped going entirely. Over the course of four years, I ended up failing fifteen classes—forty-five credits' worth!—and finally left without ever getting a degree.

In a series of unexpected events, I found myself at design school.[129] Finally, I let my passion lead *me* rather than the reverse. That's when everything changed. I was compelled to create, to push myself further than I'd ever pushed in anything else I'd done.

All my time was spent either in class, at my computer designing, or sleeping. I rarely hung out with friends. It wasn't that I didn't want to be with them, but I wanted to design *more*. Without planning it, I noticed I was taking greater and greater leaps forward. When we put our work on the walls in class, my projects began to rise to the top. I went bigger, deeper, and further than everyone else, over and over.

I wholly enjoyed designing and wanted to do it as much as possible. My obsession facilitated the accelerated development of my design skills. Over time, I started to get noticed. I would recoil when people called me "talented," as if I was born with it. On the contrary, I had to work hard. But all that work was invisible to others. It happened before my localized Zeitgeist Inflection and behind doors after it.

To close friends and family, I joked that I was "One of the greatest designers that no one knows about." I could design books, posters, packaging, all sorts of print applications, websites, apps, other digital formats, physical goods with a host of materials including paper, plastic, metal, fabric, and more. Every day, I found myself designing in 2D, 3D, and 4D (with time, i.e. moving images). I didn't learn all these mediums because I wanted to be better. It was either out of pure curiosity or necessity. Sometimes I just wanted to experiment. Other times I

---

129 A story for another time.

had an idea that pushed the boundaries of my capability, so I extended those capabilities.

Throughout all of this, nothing about my progress was remarkable. *What* I did and continue to do can be done by anyone. If there's one thing, however, that I do find special about the way things played out, it's *how* they happened. If I didn't allow myself to be directed by my true passion—to design (to create)—then I would have absolutely continued down a path of mediocrity.

Every one of us is the person we are. Most elements of our self can't be changed. If you love movies and scorn books, you're never going to be a trailblazing author. It may seem obvious in this example, but our lives are, of course, more complex than that. Society (and family) pressures us to fit expectations, even when doing so is averse to who we are within. You can meet those expectations and live a fine life. Comfortable, even. But without passion, it's impractical to expect to achieve greatness. Not because you can't theoretically achieve it, but because you're going to be competing against those who *are* passionate. They will work longer and harder because it feels less like work and more like play.

If you want to be great, you must recognize and follow your passion. Few people achieve greatness who are not passionate, on some level, about what they're doing. Understandably, it's easier said than done. Even so, this is the truth of the matter. You must *be you.*

Do you want to be a fish trying to climb a tree, or do you want to be a fish exploring the vastness of the oceans?

Summary

When it's sunny, it's difficult to imagine the rain. When it's raining, it's almost impossible to imagine the sun. We must remember that what is in front of us is not all that has existed. There is more to each story than meets the eye.

Every role model, icon, and legend had to put in the work—often for years—before they began to bear fruit. If we neglect to acknowledge their hard work, which is a common mistake, then we lose touch with the reality of how they accomplished their achievements. Without a realistic perspective, those achievements begin to take on a mythical quality, one which easily convinces us that greatness is a gift one is born with. This is an extremely detrimental mindset. You *can* reach incredible heights, but first you must put in the time.

So keep your perspective grounded in reality. Understand that every single enduring achiever has worked for it. Know that no one can do the work for you.

The first step is to simply show up—whether rain or shine.

27
Develop Self-Discipline

The Law of Order

Greatness requires great effort. No one can actualize your potential but you. Develop the discipline to go longer and further than you originally thought possible.

Good Red X

Red light bounced off the low ceilings of a nameless New York City comedy club. It was late, sometime between 11 p.m. and 2 a.m. Jerry Seinfeld was leaning on a table, a barely visible smile rested on his lips, eyes out of focus. He listened through a thin wall as the comic on the other side told joke after joke. Seinfeld was the headliner, but he arrived ahead of time to show support and enjoy the evening.

An up-and-coming young comic had been standing across the room building up the nerve to approach him. Finally, he walked up, white knuckled, and said, "Excuse me? Mr. Seinfeld?"

Seinfeld told him to call him Jerry. He asked for a name, shook hands, and made a joke about how they must be serving the right food out there because the audience was eating it up. The young comic agreed and asked if he could ask Seinfeld a question.

"I don't know, can you?" Seinfeld responded in that if-anyone-else-said-it-they'd-be-a-jerk-but-not-Jerry way.

The young comic stammered, laughed, and stammered again. It took a few tries, but the burning question eventually emerged. "What's the secret to your success?"

Seinfeld took a sip of his drink, letting the youngster absorb the moment.

Then Seinfeld told him that the secret was ... that there's no secret at all. He simply explained that if you want to be better than everyone else, you have to do better than everyone else.

Seinfeld shifted his weight from one foot to the other as he began to recall the early days of his career. As an aspiring comic, he wrote new material every single day. Even if he wasn't feeling inspired. In fact, *especially* when he wasn't feeling inspired.

When he was up-and-coming, Seinfeld put a calendar on his wall with the entire year in view. He told the young comic he had committed to writing at least one joke every day. Once he wrote his joke, he'd put a big red X on that day. He said, "After a few days you'll have a chain. Just keep at it and the chain will grow longer every day. You'll like seeing that chain, especially when you get a few weeks under your belt. Your only job next is to not break the chain."

The young comic was visibly dissatisfied. Instead of a secret, some kind of approach that could give a leg up on the rest, the only thing that was shared was seemingly obvious: be disciplined. That surely couldn't be the secret to Seinfeld's success.

As the youngster walked away, Seinfeld called back. With that signature smirk, he winked and said, "Don't break the chain."

The Do Board

Jerry Seinfeld went from selling light bulbs for pennies to becoming one of the most well-known comics to grace the stage and screen. He did it not only by showing up and doing the work, but by putting in more consistent effort than his peers. He formed a simple habit—one joke a day—that, over time, launched his career into the stratosphere.

Habits are part of our identity. We have good ones and bad ones, and for the most part, we accept them as they are. If you bite your fingernails or sometimes forget to take your shoes off at the door, that's generally just how it goes for you. On the flip side, if you have good habits like reading every night or doing the laundry first thing on Sunday mornings, they're also part and parcel of the package that is you. Rarely do we work to significantly alter the landscape of our habits but doing so is exactly the type of discipline it takes to excel.

When we talk of discipline, most people imagine working out or saying no to chocolate (and those aren't wrong), but it's more than doing things we should or shouldn't do because others say so. True discipline is *one's own decision* to regulate one's actions. It is the proactive, rather than reactive, effort towards forming good habits and eliminating bad ones. As James Clear, author of *Atomic Habits*, puts it, "Every time you successfully perform a habit, you're putting in another vote for the person you want to become."

In Seinfeld's case, he built a system for himself. He understood that writing seven jokes over seven days was more valuable than writing all seven in one day. The former requires consistency. It breeds a habit of writing. It keeps writing on the mind at all times. And it allows those seven jokes to come out easier than if he consolidated his work to a single writing session.

When I was in design school, I read about Seinfeld's calendar in a magazine I was flipping through while waiting to see a doctor. It was a novel idea at the time—nowadays it's commonly called "habit tracking"—and it stuck with me. When I got home, I pulled an unused mini whiteboard from under my bed and listed the skills I wanted to improve: Design, Write, and Draw.

I called it my "Do Board."

THE DO BOARD

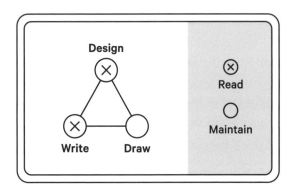

Illustration of the "Do Board" I created to keep myself disciplined. The three habits on the left—Design, Write, and Draw—all contributed towards my primary goal of being a capable, ever-improving designer. The two habits on the right—Read and Maintain—helped me to continue learning and keep my life in order.

Every day I committed to learning one new thing about designing, writing, and drawing. Not by reading about the subjects, but by doing them.¹³⁰ Once I learned something, I filled in the respective circle on my board and, at the end of the day, recorded the total number on a wall calendar. Having a three was a perfect day.

Soon after, I added two additional habits—Read and Maintain—to make sure I was learning from others and taking care of my life (taking out the trash, buying groceries, etc.).

Within a few weeks, I dramatically improved in all areas. I was *literally* designing in my dreams. I wrote more essays and poetry than ever before. My drawing ability significantly developed. I was also devouring books and managing the responsibilities in my life became effortless. Despite what Seinfeld said, it was as if I *had* stumbled on a secret.

Today, over a decade later, I still track my habits every single day.¹³¹ They've changed over time, but the core idea is still the same. Each habit builds upon a skill that contributes to where I'd like to take my life.

If this sounds tedious and obsessive, you aren't wrong. Tracking habits is somewhat challenging, but it's also tremendously rewarding. Granted, if I tried to force myself every day to do gymnastics or bake pastries, then I most likely would've given up long ago. Instead, I chose to commit to the things I already wanted to do, and that has made all the difference.

As Seinfeld described it, "Find the torture you're comfortable with."

---

130 Hence the name.

131 Every year I take approximately 1,700 steps forward in my habit journey.

The Truth of Discipline

It's rare that discipline is taught. When it comes to those with true discipline, most develop it as the result of an internal choice rather than one of external pressures. They all reach a point, myself included, when they realize life isn't serving them well because they aren't serving themselves well.

It's a sobering experience to realize there's no reason your goals deserve to come true when you don't go out of your way to achieve them. We all dream of success—financial freedom, professional acclaim, personal happiness, whatever it may be—but few do more than those around them.

How can you excel beyond the rest when you don't perform beyond the rest?

The first and most important element of discipline is the decision to commit to your goals, to make sacrifices today that will pay off tomorrow. It isn't easy—if it were, everyone would do it—but it does work. If there's a secret to success, it's not in what people do—the actual act isn't a secret—but *that they do it at all.*

Achieving excellence is straightforward. The difference between those who reach incredible heights and those who don't is their difference in work ethic.

What you're about to read *will* work. Even still, most readers won't try because it's hard. But if you do, you will find it to be one of the most rewarding commitments of your life. To date, very few have made the decision to achieve self-discipline and followed through.

Will you?

THE THREE PRINCIPLES OF DISCIPLINE

Discipline is self-governance. For the first eighteen years of our lives, we are presided over and regulated by our parents or guardians. We go from them telling us what to do at home to teachers at school to bosses at work. It is no wonder so many of us never learn how to become our own directors.

There are three key principles of discipline:

1. **Point your trajectory.** First, choose your goals for yourself. If you want to be a doctor but your parents are pushing you to be a lawyer, no amount of self-coercion is going to make you love law. Once you know where you want to end up, pinpoint the skills or actions that will take you there. To be a doctor, for example, you could Study Anatomy (e.g. five pages or a single element of the body) and Read Medical Journals (e.g. one article) every day.

2. **Act on your commitments.** This is the meaty part, the step that separates the greats from the crowd: follow-through. Now that you know what you must do, it's time to stop dreaming and start acting. Show up every day without fail. Track your efforts. It's easy for progress to *seem* like it's happening, but the work that's being done must be of true quality, not mere wheel spinning.[132] Do not mistake the illusion of progress for actual progress. No one is forcing you—you must hold yourself accountable.

---

[132] Have you ever heard someone talk about the book they've been writing (for years) or about how often they go to the gym (and nothing changes)? That's wheel-spinning at its finest.

3. **Review your progress.** Regularly review how you're doing. One must routinely assess whether the desired trajectory and the actual trajectory are aligned. If they aren't, an adjustment is necessary. How often you review depends on your goals. Someone studying to be a doctor may only need to check in every three to six months, but an entrepreneur starting a business may need to review weekly, and a person creating a spreadsheet may need to reassess hourly.

As you develop discipline you will find that everything in life becomes easier. No longer do you first see the ways in which something will be challenging, but the ways in which it can be achieved. Consistency breeds confidence, which in turn delivers results.

As you continue, your tiny snowball of perseverance becomes an unstoppable ice boulder until, finally, it catapults itself into orbit as a brand new, tide-changing moon in the sky.

Summary

To reach beyond the rest, one must go beyond the rest. If you push less than those around you, don't expect to excel. Conversely, if you push more, then the probability of excellence is in your favor. In order to do this reliably, you must employ discipline.

Discipline is the measured combination of planning, acting, and reviewing. It's staying accountable to your goals and true to reality as it is, not as you wish it to be. Your wish can still come true, however, if you accept the truth of your reality at a given moment in time. Because then you can change it.

While there is no secret to easy success, the true secret is that most people will not go to the lengths required to reach their goals. Compare your goals to your daily actions, and ask yourself—am I truly doing what I need to do to achieve my dreams?

28
Adapt to Circumstance

The Law of Chaos

Learn to be adaptable rather than presupposing an outcome. You will not only mine the most from the immediate circumstance—you will also enjoy yourself more.

Talent Show Dare

A seventeen-year-old girl stood on stage wearing a frayed dress and dirty work boots. The year was 1934. The stage was The Apollo, Harlem's preeminent venue for all things new and hip. In front of the girl sat hundreds of people waiting for her to jump to life, but jump she did not. Instead, she stood frozen, paralyzed by the moment and the eyes and her thoughts.

The day before, the girl's friends had dared her to apply to dance at The Apollo's talent show. Thinking nothing of it, she threw her name in, not believing she'd ever get selected. After all, who would let a homeless girl from the street up on such a fancy stage? Someone did because before she knew what was happening, the girl was backstage alongside fellow performers getting ready to do their bits.

One by one, each act was invited on stage to put their hearts on display. As they performed, the others stood behind the side curtains stealing glances in between conversation and laughter. The girl, however, had no one to speak to. Her ragged clothes and haggard hair kept everyone at bay. Instead of chatting away the stage jitters, hers simmered below the surface as she stood in silence watching act after act.

There wasn't a set list, so no one knew when they'd be called. The MC had full command of the stage. He was building the show as he went, calling up acts based on who had just gone and how well they were received.

Two sisters had just finished an incredible dance piece. The audience was clapping furiously in response. Suddenly, the girl heard her name boom throughout the music hall and across the audience.

It was her turn.

The girl's face dropped. She was a good dancer, but she only danced for fun. There was no way she could follow those sisters. They were legitimate professionals. The girl thought about leaving, but there was nowhere to go. Before she knew what was happening, a fellow performer ushered her onto the stage. In a flash, she had gone from the safe sidelines, standing quietly behind a curtain, to the very-wide-open center stage where fifteen hundred pairs of eyes clung to her every move.

As the audience stared at her, all she could do was stare back. Time crawled. Each second felt like an hour. In slow motion, the audience members' smiles began to turn to scowls as they registered the obviously homeless girl in front of them.

They began to boo.

The girl felt the urge to walk out, but everyone backstage

had stopped chattering and clogged the exits. She could either jump into the crowd and run—or perform.

"Just do something," the MC whispered.

With no way out and complete certainty that she couldn't do a dance worth watching, she turned to the only other skill she had: singing. The girl opened her mouth and began to channel her fear and doubt and sadness into song. It wasn't long before the audience had closed their mouths, now sitting in awe at the incredible voice that was floating out of such an unexpected source.

By the time the girl finished singing, the audience's mouths were open again, this time alternating between shocked awe and cheering for more.

She ended up winning the talent show. The girl's name was Ella Fitzgerald. In just a few months' time she was headlining events with Chick Webb, the legendary jazz drummer and band leader. Fitzgerald went on to become a celebrated jazz singer in her own right. She traveled the world, made the move to film and television, and even sang for presidents.

Last-Minute Maneuvers

Today, Ella Fitzgerald's name is synonymous with not just jazz, but music as a whole. It's difficult to believe that someone who has reached such a prestigious level didn't meticulously plan and angle for it, but that's exactly what happened. Be careful, however, not to minimize the role she played in getting there.

Very often, if not most of the time, life happens to us in ways we don't plan for. In Fitzgerald's case, it happened twice in one evening. She didn't expect to get accepted into the talent show, and she certainly didn't expect for the act before hers to be a phenomenal dance performance. Both times, her expectations were subverted, and both times she chose *against* the path of least resistance.

Imagine being up on a bright stage. The center spotlight is illuminating you and nothing else. You're standing in front of hundreds of well-dressed, expectant audience members. That's already tough for most, but then add to it the fact that you're poorly dressed, and everyone can tell you haven't had a shower in days. If that sounds terrifying, or at least uncomfortable, know that you could decide at any moment to simply not do it. There wouldn't be any repercussions. Despite being in that same situation, Fitzgerald went ahead anyway.

Once she was up on stage, she yet again faced a situation she didn't *have to* proceed with. When the two sisters performed their dance set that left the crowd clapping and whistling, she could've easily turned around and left. Sure, she'd have to push a few people aside, but no one was forcing her to go out on stage. She remembered initially thinking, "There's no way I'm going out there to dance." Yet she persevered. In the moment, Fitzgerald made the call to switch things up and sing rather than dance. Up until a few minutes earlier, the thought hadn't crossed her mind. But when she knew dancing was a no-go, she made a last-minute call that changed her life.

In both circumstances, Fitzgerald exhibited one of the most important qualities in achieving greatness: adaptability. Her expected outcomes didn't match reality. Instead of turning back and abandoning things altogether, she reacted to the new realities that were presented to her. As we've learned, it made all the difference.

When Chick Webb invited her to sing, she was hesitant. Fitzgerald didn't believe her singing was as good as people claimed. Later—after she had attained lasting success—she candidly confessed in an interview that she thought her singing "was pretty much hollering." Singing for a living was never part of Ella Fitzgerald's plan, but life delivered unexpected circumstances and she chose to make the best of them.

There's a time for planning and, as we've just learned, a time for throwing plans to the wind. To maximize the likelihood of positive results, you must know the difference between the two and when to employ each.

Be the Tree

Bruce Lee once said, "The oak tree is mighty, yet it will be destroyed by a mighty wind because it resists the elements. The bamboo bends with the wind, and by bending, survives." When they bend, bamboo trees are metaphorically indulging their impulses. Let me explain.

Discipline takes the form of several self-regulated practices, including planning. Impulse is the opposite; it involves reacting to the situation at hand. The fundamental natures of planning and adaptability are at odds: planning focuses on the future, adapting focuses on the present. When you plan, you sacrifice the current moment to account for—and hopefully improve the return of—future moments. When you adapt, you potentially sacrifice future returns for present efficiency.

Can you precisely predict the future? Of course not. Which means planning has a limit to how effective it can be. If one only focuses on planning, they may get great results, but they may also incur great disasters. Sticking too tightly to an imagined path can blind you to the actual path you're on. It's a recipe for wasted effort and missed opportunity.

Conversely, if one only focuses on adapting to the moment, they may have a wonderful time in the present, but without accounting for the future, the joy that's received over time is sure to diminish. Allowing yourself a plan—one that adapts in reaction to circumstance—enables you to create with the knowledge that your efforts are building on one another.

Ideally, planning and adapting occur in cycles. The future should be regularly assessed, and the present should be constantly explored. Like trees in the wind, there's a time to stand tall and bask in the sunlight, but there's also a time to give in to the moment and bend.

What will you choose to be—oak or bamboo?

How to Be More Adaptable

Have you ever wondered why we say "play an instrument" rather than "use" one? It's because music is inherently tied to the present. The moment you stop playing, it ceases to exist. Like musicians and children, people of all ages must remember to take time to play, which inherently makes us more adaptable.

The biggest difference between children and adults is how often they allow themselves to explore the present without concern for the future.

THE FIVE RULES OF PLAY

Playing is an innate practice. It's a dance with the present moment—exercising adaptability in real time. No one teaches us how to do it. It's a natural part of being not only homo sapiens, but mammals.[133] As humans, we tend to forget how to play as we get older. There are five key rules.

1. **Be curious.** Curiosity is magnetism to the present moment. Allow yourself to be fascinated by what's going on around you. Give your attention to something that catches your eye. Focus on having fun and enjoying yourself.

2. **Do things that don't matter.** When you let the moment take you, don't worry about whether it's efficient or necessary. When you try to figure out if it's worth the time, you've unknowingly detached yourself from the present to assess the future.

3. **Ignore what others think.** Everyone who has ever made something—from legends and superstars to you and your neighbors—has, at some point, had to fend off criticism to bring their creations to life. If you stop when others look at you funny or make jokes at your expense, you'll never get anywhere.

4. **Let yourself fall.** If you worry about falling, you're concerning yourself with the future. Accept that falling is guaranteed, but so is standing back up. When kids fall at the playground they don't ask to go home—they brush themselves off and keep playing.

---

133 Ironically, what sets us apart is our ability to plan, but without temperance—without balancing planning with play—it also destroys a big part of what makes us happy, creative creatures.

5. **Expect nothing.** To expect results is to bring the future into consideration. You must avoid this at all costs. You will find time and again that those who are most successful also love what they do. They don't necessarily need results because the act itself is enjoyable. This is a form of play, of letting go of all expectations.

You will find that some of these are easier than others, and that they're all fundamentally tied together through various levels of presence. As you practice playing, it will become easier. The better you become at perceiving and adapting to the situation at hand, the more likely you are to overcome challenges and reach new heights.

Remember: You're a natural.

Summary

Thomas Edison was signing the guest book at a party when he came across a column titled "Interested in." The other guests listed their professions or hobbies. Edison, a person of many skills and interests, couldn't choose. So he wrote "Everything." It is no wonder that Edison was so successful. He indulged his curiosities—his impulses—whenever he got the chance.

Historically, the word "impulsive" has had a negative connotation. Yet we are repeatedly reminded—through stories like Ella Fitzgerald's and experiences in our own lives—that positive results come from impulsivity all the time. It's so common there's even a term for it: happy accidents.

It's important to value discipline and planning, but it is equally important to balance them with impulse and adaptability. Remember to weave in and out of future and present thinking. Let your curiosities guide you. Don't be concerned with where they'll take you or how they'll be judged.

Above all, remember what's fair game: *everything*.

29
Tailor Your Surroundings

The Law of Habitat
Tend to your mind and your surroundings before you tend to your work. To do so is to leverage probabilities in your favor. Otherwise you force yourself to put in more effort than necessary.

Encyclopedia Reformation

Michael King was the respected pastor of Ebenezer Baptist Church in Atlanta, Georgia. In 1934, he took a trip to Germany for an international conference. While there, he learned about the work of Martin Luther, the leader of the Protestant Reformation. So inspired by his story, King changed his name—and the name of his five-year-old son—to Martin Luther King. Little did he know, his son would grow up to inspire a reformation of his own.

Martin Luther King Jr. was a child in a time and place in the United States that's historically referred to as the segregated

South. While the legal doctrine that was set in the late 1800s claimed that African Americans were "separate but equal," in reality they were anything but. Funding was dramatically uneven, opportunities were limited and low paying, and nearly all the facilities that were supposed to equally cater to Black communities were less robust in every way.

For Black Americans, the entire country was—to grossly understate—a poor habitat for success.

Growing up in this environment and determined not to be held back by it, King used whatever was at his disposal to learn and excel. As unlikely as it sounds, King's rise to prominence can be traced back to a single book. By chance, he discovered a family encyclopedia as a child and began to study it religiously. Over time, his vocabulary grew, and with it, his confidence. From the pages to his mind, a world of ideas blossomed. He used those words and ideas to develop into an increasingly masterful speaker.

In 1944, at the age of fifteen, King's speaking abilities earned him an invitation to a speech contest in Dublin, Georgia. It was there that he first openly expressed his discontent with society, powerfully stating that, "The finest negro is at the mercy of the meanest white man." When he was done, it was clear to the audience and the judges that he not only had an incredible ability to speak, but he also had a lot to say. King won the contest despite it being his first public speaking event.

On the bus heading back to Atlanta, King and his teacher were asked to give up their seats for white passengers. He initially refused, but his teacher urged him to comply. It was illegal to resist, and his teacher was focused on getting King home in one piece. King later recalled, "That night will never leave my memory. It was the angriest I have ever been in my life." The irony of the (award-winning) speech he'd just given juxtaposed with being forced out of his seat by a white man was a turning point in his life—one that foreshadowed future events.

A decade later, the state of things wasn't much better.

Claudette Colvin, also fifteen, refused to give up her seat on a bus in Montgomery, Alabama where King now lived. She recalled, "History kept me stuck to my seat. I felt the hand of Harriet Tubman pushing down on one shoulder and Sojourner Truth pushing down on the other." Colvin was arrested. Nine months later, Rosa Parks also famously refused to give up her seat and was arrested.

The same evening Parks made her stand, King was chosen by the community to lead the Montgomery bus boycotts. Initially unsure of himself, he used his personal experience to fuel his message. Three hundred and eighty-five long days later—and after several violent attacks and unjust arrests—King and the Black community of Montgomery won. The US District Court ruled in their favor, prohibiting segregation on Montgomery buses.

Going forward, Martin Luther King Jr. became *the* national figure for the civil rights movement. Event after event, he used his incredible speaking ability to spread his message far and wide.

In 1965, King was awarded the Nobel Peace Prize for his nonviolent resistance. Posthumously, he was awarded the Presidential Medal of Freedom and the Congressional Gold Medal. He is one of only three Americans—including George Washington and Abraham Lincoln—to have his birthday celebrated as a national holiday. Martin Luther King Jr.'s message remains as important as ever as the fight against inequality continues today.

A Truth, Self-Evident

Whether your environment is as localized as the setup of your desk or, as in Martin Luther King Jr.'s case, as vast as an entire society—your surroundings have a profound impact on how you operate in the world. If that environment isn't conducive to positive outcomes—if it prevents happiness, productivity, success, or freedom—then it must be changed.

On August 28, 1963, King gave his famous "I Have a Dream" speech. It is a perfect example of changing one's environment on a large scale. As we know, while the law deemed all peoples "equal but separate," that was far from how everyday life played out. Segregation, by its nature, creates division. It invites an us-versus-them mentality. And when a group of people who are already marginalized is pitted against a group who is not, it's impossible for a mutually positive outcome to occur. King understood this deeply.

On the steps of the Lincoln Memorial, King spoke the powerful claim made by the founding fathers in the Declaration of Independence: "We hold these truths to be self-evident, that all men are created equal." By uttering those words, it was clear to him and the two hundred thousand people who came to listen that society was not embodying such a belief. He went on to say, "I have a dream that one day out in the red hills of Georgia the sons of former slaves and the sons of former slaveowners will be able to sit down together at the table of brotherhood. ... I have a dream that my four little children will one day live in a nation where they will not be judged by the color of their skin but by their character."

Charged by his own experiences, by Claudette Colvin and Rosa Parks, by the people and stories he was exposed to daily,

King knew that for the Black community to prosper, their environment had to fundamentally change. He used his ability to move the minds and souls of those who listened to him to affect that change. It didn't happen overnight—it's a struggle that's going on to this day—and it didn't happen without sacrifices.

Change, however, did come. The year after his speech, the Civil Rights Act of 1964 was passed, which banned segregation and prohibited discrimination on the basis of race, gender, and religion. It was a major turning point, not just for Martin Luther King Jr., but for Black Americans everywhere.

Habitat de la Influence

Before you can do good work, you must create an environment for it. Think about what you need to succeed, as well as what you don't, and do the work to get closer to your ideal habitat.

There are two habitats each of us must tend to: the external and the internal. Oftentimes, a person is great at managing one and not the other. For example, one may have a fantastic job, no debts, and want for nothing, yet still feel unhappy or unsatisfied with life. This is more common than the opposite, which is to have peace of mind but live an otherwise unfulfilling life that does not contribute to the happiness of others or the productivity of society as a whole.

INTERNAL HABITAT

Your internal habitat is the constant, inescapable environment of the mind: your thoughts. Know that your thoughts become your actions, and your actions become (or halt) your progress, which then generates more thoughts as the cycle continues. To change your actions, you must literally change your thinking. This is often as simple as reminding yourself of who you are and who you'd like to become. In effect, you must be your own cheerleader.

When first starting Baronfig, I had a traumatic experience on a trip to Japan that ended with me in the hospital. It took five days to recover, but eventually I was able to get on a plane and head back home to New York City. Unbeknownst to me, something was deeply lodged in my mind. On my next international trip, I found myself having a panic attack, all alone and thousands of miles from home. With no one to lean on and nowhere to go, I came up with a mantra that summed up how I wanted to view my perseverance and inner strength:

"I am a champion."

I endured the sixteen-hour flight home by quietly repeating that phrase to myself over nineteen thousand times.[134] By saying it over and over in my head, I was not only convincing myself of a preferred narrative, I was blocking anxious thoughts from having space to create a narrative of their own.

Methods for Internal Tending:

- **Talk about your thoughts and feelings.** Whether it's with a close friend or a mental health professional, conversation allows you to dig deeper. It helps you peel back the layers of your mind to find the true source of anxieties, fears, traumas, and so on.

- **Keep a journal.** Writing in a journal just three times

---

[134] Roughly once every two seconds for about two-thirds the flight, sleeping the other third.

a week for fifteen minutes has been proven to reduce stress, boost your mood, improve your memory, and even strengthen your immune system.

- **Develop a personal mantra.** If you've identified a recurring negative thought, create a positive mantra that counteracts it. Repeat your mantra whenever those thoughts or feelings begin to emerge.

On a regular basis, think about what you're good at, what you've succeeded in, what you're proud of. Remind yourself of these things frequently, such as every morning while getting dressed or every night while brushing your teeth.

Reprogram your thoughts, and your actions will follow.

EXTERNAL HABITAT

Your external habitat is just that: your surroundings. Unlike the habitat of the mind, the habitat of the body can change. One day you may work at home, the next at the office or in class or at a friend's place. Every location has its own unique impact on how you think and act. That's why we go to "a quiet place" such as a conference room or the library when we want to get real work done.

When the author Henry David Thoreau had trouble writing in the city, he dramatically changed his environment by moving to a small cabin next to a pond in the woods. The new location changed his thinking so significantly that he ended up staying there for over two years. It inspired him to write *Walden*, the book that would become his crowning achievement.

Thoreau later went on to write the essay "Civil Disobedience," a treatise on how to peacefully protest. It eventually found its way to Martin Luther King Jr., who said, "I was so deeply moved that I reread the work several times. I became convinced that noncooperation with evil is as much a moral obligation as is cooperation with good. ... As a result of his writings and personal witness, we are the heirs of a legacy of creative protest."

Methods for External Tending:

- **Optimize your primary space.** Rarely do we stop doing something to assess *how* we're doing it. Often, however, it's our workspace that may prevent us from doing our best. Take time to assess how you do what you do before you jump in and do it.

- **Change locations.** The more locations you try, the better equipped you are to evaluate any single habitat. Fill your data banks with multiple experiences and compare benefits and drawbacks. When possible, combine the best parts and eliminate the worst.

- **Ask others.** You can't be everywhere and try everything, so the next best thing is to talk about habitats with others. Ask them what works and what doesn't. Use your collective knowledge to mutually benefit.

Your external habitat can be viewed in two dimensions, localized and expansive. Like Thoreau going from the city to the woods, you can alter or replace your immediate surroundings—your localized external habitat—to have a positive impact on your personal thoughts and actions. Or, as Martin Luther King Jr. did through nonviolent protest and extensive speaking, you can move to change your universal surroundings—the expansive external habitat—to influence the thoughts and actions of many.

Summary

Leverage the habitats of your mind and your surroundings. By altering or replacing poor environments with favorable ones, you increase the likelihood of positive outcomes. You also invite better results with less effort, which not only allows you to move more efficiently, but to retain the stamina to go further than the average.

The habitat of your mind—your thoughts—affects everything you do. Tina Turner, the rock-and-roll queen, said, "Sometimes you've got to let everything go—purge yourself. If you are unhappy with anything, whatever is bringing you down, get rid of it. Because you'll find that when you're free, your true creativity, your true self, comes out."

The habitat of your body—your localized and expansive surroundings—defines your capabilities, which in turn contribute to your actions. On a localized scale, you can make small and large changes that affect you personally. On an expansive scale, the changes you move towards can affect people around you.

Next time you have a poor thought or find your environment working against you, take the time to adjust them directly before you continue. It will make a world of difference.

30
Engage in Quality Practice

The Law of Intention
Practice at the edge of your capabilities and steadily broaden their borders. Focus, and spend little energy to great effect; slack, and you will go to great lengths just to find yourself exactly where you started.

Hot Dog Hot Dog Hot Dog Hot...

Every year since 1972, thousands gather on Coney Island in New York City to watch a spectacle that is simultaneously impressive and unsettling: Nathan's Hot Dog Eating Contest. Held on Independence Day, it brings together the best eaters for an annual showdown to see who can stomach the most hot dogs in twelve minutes.

In terms of eating competitions, Nathan's event has been described as the "Super Bowl, Masters, and World Series rolled into one." Over time, it became clear: the bigger the human, the bigger the stomach, the better the eater. To give you an idea, past champions include 317-pound, fifty-year-old Steve Keiner and 330-pound, thirty-four-year-old Ed Krachie. As the contest gained in popularity, it attracted more viewers and even more powerful eaters. In 2001, it reached entirely new heights.

The sun was out and people from everywhere flocked to watch what had become an iconic event. Contestants from all around the world were registered and shaking hands. Reporters interviewed the well-known participants, asking how many hot dogs they would eat this year. The previous winner had eaten twenty-five hot dogs—a new world record—and eaters were predicting numbers just above that in their visions of glory.

Standing between towering champions with names like "The Crusher," "Cookie," and "The Doginator" was the 130-pound, twenty-three-year-old Takeru Kobayashi. He was a skinny, mild-mannered kid from Nagano Prefecture, Japan. As others were answering questions and enjoying the limelight, the majority of attention on Kobayashi came in the form of side glances and snickering. Very few people expected what would happen next.

The eaters lined up, side by side, on a wide stage. A long table divided the audience from the participants. On it sat all the hot dogs one could desire (and more). Glasses of water were lined up in front of each person. For twelve minutes, both food and liquid were in infinite supply. The bell rang and the contestants started eating.

Immediately, the crowd began cheering on their favorite eaters. Some contestants raised their fists in the air while chewing to elicit more whoops and hollers. Whenever a contestant finished a hot dog, a sign was raised behind them to keep count. Excitement in the crowd grew to a fervor as the minutes passed. People began to take notice of a particular count. The time limit was only halfway through, but one contestant had already surpassed the previous year's record.

It was Kobayashi.

He was consuming hot dogs faster than anyone *ever*. When he hit thirty, the person next to him was only finishing their eighth hot dog. When they realized how far behind they were, they actually took off their shirt and waved it like a white flag in surrender.[135]

At the end of twelve minutes, Kobayashi had consumed a whopping fifty hot dogs, *double* that of the previous year's winner. The crowd was stunned. The contestants were in shock. One eater later commented, "Kobayashi was like a conveyor belt. He was just putting them in two at a time." Another could only shake his head, repeating, "The kid is incredible."

In reflection, Kobayashi said, "People think that if you have a huge appetite, then you'll be better at it. But actually, it's how you confront the food that is brought to you. You have to be mentally and psychologically prepared."

Takeru Kobayashi went on to win Nathan's contest six years in a row. He holds over a dozen eating world records, including 227 buffalo wings in thirty minutes, 159 tacos in ten minutes, and twenty-one *pounds* of soba noodles in twelve minutes. Kobayashi has been described on more than one occasion as the godfather of competitive eating.

---

[135] A great (and hilarious) example of knowing when it's time to call it quits.

Jaw and Throat and Belly

Starting with his incredible performance in 2001, Takeru Kobayashi is widely credited with elevating competitive eating from entertainment to sport. He was able to blow away expectations thanks to his practice regimen, which has been compared to Olympic-level preparation.

In order to eat so much food, Kobayashi first prepares his jaw, esophagus, and stomach. He uses specific practice methods for each to maximize their total potential.

The faster he's able to crush food, the easier he can stuff more food in. To train his mouth, he chews upwards of five sticks of gum at a time. When it starts to get dense and tasteless—right about when the rest of us would throw it away—that's when his practice begins. A seasoned competitive eater, such as Kobayashi, can easily have a jaw capable of 250 pounds of force. That's stronger than a German Shepherd's bite.[136]

The more Kobayashi can shoot down his esophagus, the quicker he can swallow. He practices by swallowing entire gulps of water at once, which stretch the esophagus and allow food to go down easier. When swallowing a mouthful is effortless, he moves on to soft foods, then more dense foods, until finally he's practicing with the same foods he'll be competing with.

Finally, the more food his stomach can fit, the more he can eat. Eating fifty hot dogs, for example, requires that the stomach have over three times its normal capacity. "I have to put something inside the stomach to make it expand, but it doesn't

---

[136] German Shepherds have a bite that's 238 pounds of force per square inch. The dog with the strongest bite, at 743psi, is the Kangal Shepherd. Historically, they were relied on to fight and defend humans from lions, bears, wolves, and more.

necessarily have to be food," Kobayashi explains. By using water rather than food, he gets all the practice benefits without any of the health risks. He slowly increases how much he can drink each session. This process takes about three months, but by the end he can easily take down three gallons. He then switches to food in the days leading up to the event.

In addition to his physical training, Kobayashi has a host of techniques he uses during competitions to expand his potential even further. Through experimentation and disciplined practice, he has developed a set of tools that propel him to victory: He's mastered a body wiggle, often called the "Kobayashi Shake," that forces food through his esophagus even faster. He coined the "Solomon Method" of removing hot dogs from their buns, breaking them in half, and eating the two halves simultaneously. He also innovated by dunking the buns in water to make them easier to eat.

Everything Takeru Kobayashi did to prepare for his 2001 win has since become standard practice amongst competitive eaters. Through sheer will and discipline, he showed that practice and dedication give phenomenal results.

Practice, Practice, Praxis

There's no such thing as "talent." What people mean when they call someone talented is that they're skilled. By using the word *talent*, they're actually making an excuse as to why they themselves aren't as skilled in something. They convince themselves that skilled people are born with an innate ability. This isn't true at all. Every skilled person acquired their skills using the same method: practice.

If you're guilty of using the word "talent" in the past, don't be hard on yourself. It's easy to come to the false conclusion that someone has an innate ability because, in nearly all cases, their practice is invisible. Most of the time we just don't see it.[137] Plenty of greats went to extreme lengths to acquire skills, but rarely did others see them do or discuss those lengths:

- **Demosthenes**, ancient Greek orator, spoke with stones in his mouth to learn how to better articulate his words.

- **Julia Child**, expert chef and author, spent ten years refining her recipes before publishing her first book, *Mastering the Art of French Cooking*.

- **Philly Joe Jones**, renowned jazz drummer, spent his entire life mastering drum patterns from a single book, which he then mixed together in near-endless ways.

- **Joe DiMaggio**, one of baseball's greatest hitters, practiced swinging in a dark basement where he did thousands of repetitions for each type of pitch.

- **Beyonce Knowles**, legendary singer and performer, had four private and six group vocal lessons *per week* starting when she was eight years old.

- **Kobe Bryant**, all-star basketball player, hit the court at 4 a.m. to warm up, then did cardio, lifted weights, went back to sink five hundred jumpers, and *then* started practice with his team.

---

[137] See the Law of Showing Up to learn more about the invisibility of effort and the danger of misunderstood inflection points.

- **Joyce Carol Oates**, prolific author, writes eight hours a day and uses various typewriters for different projects; to date she's published fifty-eight novels, averaging exactly one per year for her entire writing career.

- **Pablo Picasso**, iconic fine artist, made over fifty thousand works in his life in pursuit of excellence (that's 1.5 per day for ninety-one years).

- **Ben Franklin**, accomplished polymath, converted book passages into rhyme and then, later, back into prose to practice having access to the right words when he needed them.

Greatness and practice clearly go hand in hand. What may seem extreme at first, such as speaking with rocks in your mouth, makes more sense when we combine it with the Law of Order, which states that to be better than the rest we must go further than the rest. Before we achieve greatness, we must first learn how to practice correctly.

THREE ELEMENTS OF PRACTICE

Practice is the act of focused effort with the goal of increasing a skill. There are three core elements to effective practice:

1. **Trajectory:** You must have a purpose before you can fulfill one. Know what your goal is—where you'd like your efforts to carry you—and use that as your guiding light.

2. **Intention:** Similar to trajectory but focused on the practice session at hand. Know what you're looking to

accomplish *today* and work towards achieving it. If done correctly, you will push into your discomfort zone.

3. **Repetition:** Continuously stretch your comfort zone by habitually working towards your trajectory with intentional sessions. Target the fringes of your ability and patiently move them forward.

When your practice is uncomfortable—perhaps even painful—you know you're on the right path. As discussed in the Law of the Unknown, our fears point us in directions of potential growth. The more discomfort you allow in your practice sessions, the more you are growing.

If it all sounds obvious, that's because it is. Most things are simple, it's the human mind that complicates them. Focus on the quality of your practice, not the quantity, and you will prosper.

This method has proven true countless times in my own life. You don't need to spend hours a day practicing to learn a new skill. I tested this by challenging myself to learn to play the trumpet, which I specifically chose because up until that point I had been terrible at all things music. I committed to practicing just ten minutes a day. Each session, my goal was to strengthen my ability to play the previous two pages in my music book and push forward another quarter page. Within a few months, I could play entire songs. At the end of my first year, I could sight read new music.

That's not an isolated experience. Over the past two decades, I've learned multiple unrelated skills by visualizing where I want to be, practicing with intent, and regularly facing discomfort. In addition to learning to play the trumpet, other skills include writing nonfiction, coding for the web, presenting in front of others, exercising and workout building, and all sorts of design disciplines (print, web, industrial, textile, etc.).

Even Luigi, my dog, has benefitted from the principles of practice via five-minute daily training sessions. At one year old, he already knew more than thirty commands.

Consistency is key. Focus and be honest with yourself in how much discomfort you're allowing. If you do it right, you can take great leaps in short time.

Summary

There's a couplet in rapper Macklemore's song "Ten Thousand Hours" that effectively says: The greatest painters weren't great because they could paint from birth. / They were great because they painted a lot.[138] These lines represent the epitome of skills versus talent. Skill is the result of vision, focus, and discipline. Talent is a farce, an illusion derived from the fact that most practice is done behind closed doors.

Practice is the act of focused effort with the goal of increasing a skill. When you practice, integrate the three principles: trajectory, intention, and repetition. Before you know it, you will find yourself propelled forward on the spectrum of skill in whatever it is you're learning.

Above all, make sure you are practicing that which makes you uncomfortable. Discomfort means you're doing something new. New means you're learning. And learning means you're growing.

---

[138] Listen to the full song—inspired by Malcom Gladwell's 10,000-hour rule, which states one has to put in that many hours to be an expert at a given skill—at lawsofcreativity.com/ten-thousand-hours.

31
Push Mental Endurance

The Law of the Will

Often the deciding factor between success and failure is not skill, timing, or luck—but the willingness to endure. Success has its own timeline, one you cannot control. Patience, then, is the most powerful tool against failure.

Five-Year Cuffs

Harry Houdini was known as The King of Cards. He was a magician who had built his act around sleight of hand, misdirection, and clever mechanisms. In his early twenties, Houdini began inviting his audience to bring handcuffs up to the stage for him to escape. Combined with his showmanship, which was second to none, his act—and his name—began to spread like wildfire. It was the illustrious evening of March 17, 1904, however, that almost single-handedly earned him a new title.

Houdini had publicly claimed, "No prison can hold me. No hand or leg irons or steel locks can shackle me. No ropes or chains can keep me from my freedom." And now he was to be tested.

On that fateful evening at the Hippodrome Theatre in London, Houdini accepted his greatest challenge to date. He was tasked with escaping a set of steel cuffs whose creator, a blacksmith from Birmingham, had spent *five years* designing. The blacksmith claimed that "no mortal man" could escape from them. In front of a crowd of four thousand, Houdini allowed himself to be shackled. The lock was tested. He then went behind a red velvet curtain to begin his escape.

Houdini always performed his escapes behind a curtain, in a box, or covered by some other object blocking onlookers' view. He wasn't necessarily doing anything deceitful, however. It was far more compelling, Houdini knew, to allow the audience to fill in the blanks themselves. "The secret of showmanship consists not of what you really do, but what the mystery-loving public thinks you do," he once explained. The mystery drives the attraction.

Twenty-two minutes later, Houdini briefly peeked out. The crowd's quiet murmur dropped sharply as he held his still-shackled arms in the light to get a better look. As quickly as he appeared, he was gone. Those in the crowd who missed him didn't believe he had even shown.

At thirty-five minutes, he fully emerged. Again, conversation dialed down as the moment transitioned from social to spectacle. Houdini was still cuffed. His collar was unbuttoned, sweat poured down his face. He asked for a cushion to kneel on and disappeared behind the curtain.

The audience erupted with chatter. "Can he do it?", "He didn't look so good," "It's not going well," they said.

Exactly one hour from when he was cuffed, Houdini again came into view. He asked the challenger, a reporter from the

Daily Mirror, if he'd unlock the cuffs so that he could take off his jacket. Fearing trickery, the reporter refused. Not to be deterred, Houdini flipped a pocketknife into his mouth, tossed his coat up over his head, and proceeded to shred it to pieces. The audience ate it up. Houdini again stepped behind the bright red curtain.

As the minutes passed, the crowd began to finally grow restless. Houdini had been at it for over an hour with no results. Just five days earlier, he had escaped in minutes from one set of cuffs after the other. The sentiment amongst the audience turned from one of anticipation to concern. It was only a matter of time, they thought, until Houdini would admit defeat.

Just when the audience seemed to be at their limit, Houdini reappeared. Eyes went wide as mouths closed shut. Everyone was standing and staring. The moment hung in the air, frozen in time—then the auditorium erupted in celebration.

Houdini stood at the edge of the stage. His arms were held high. This time the cuffs were in his hands rather than on his wrists. The applause was so loud, the cheering so forceful, that one couldn't hear the person next to them. Houdini was scooped off the stage, hoisted up by outstretched hands, and carried around the auditorium as the band played their hearts out.

It was at that moment that Houdini broke down in tears of joy. His legend was solidified. That night he earned himself a new title: The Handcuff King. To this day, Harry Houdini is still the most famous magician in history. A century later, people all over the world still call it "pulling a Houdini" when someone performs an unexplainable escape.

Controlled Breathing

Little did Houdini know, that night at the Hippodrome would be a turning point in his life. He had uncovered an entirely new aspect to his performance. Without any trickery at all, and only employing pure determination and will, he put on his greatest performance to date.

After escaping the inescapable shackles, Houdini immediately recognized the allure—and the power—of going further than the norm. He knew he wouldn't have gotten the same reaction from the crowd if he took the cuffs off after five or ten minutes. Pushing the limits of the human body, of defying expectations, became his new focus. Houdini's realization inevitably escalated to maximum stakes: his life.

Over a ten-year period, Houdini went from escaping handcuffs to straightjackets to being buried alive. His first attempt at the latter occurred in 1915. In a rudimentary performance, he had his assistants bury him under six feet of dirt without a casket or box of any kind. As the dirt began to pile up, it dawned on Houdini that he was in real danger.

With no other option but to fight for his life, he clawed his way back to sunlight. His hand breached the surface just as he fainted. His assistants pulled him out, saving his life. Houdini called it, "The narrowest squeak in my life," describing it in his notes as, "Very dangerous. The weight of the earth is killing."

Several years later, despite his near-death experience, he was back at it again. Houdini caught wind that a rival magician claimed to have supernatural powers and could survive being sealed in an airtight casket for one hour. Not to be outdone, Houdini announced that he could do it longer—*and* make it harder. In front of a crowd,[139] he was sealed in a casket and, to prove that it was airtight, lowered into a pool where he remained for an hour and a half. When asked how he did it, he said there were no tricks or supernatural abilities, just controlled breathing. He willed himself to stay calm and use less oxygen.

Finally, in 1926, Houdini proved why he is to this day the greatest escape artist of all time. At the top of his game, and still ever challenged to take things further, he combined everything he had done before into a single grandiose performance. It was titled "Buried Alive" and pitched as a "quadruple smothering imprisonment." Beneath the simple name was a complex act. Houdini was to be strapped in a straitjacket, sealed in a glass casket, locked in a giant glass vault, and buried under one ton of sand. Houdini diagrammed the feat in one of his notebooks, ending with a short notation that read, "I like it very much."

Harry Houdini exampled incredible willpower in each of his escapes. For most people, being confined to a small space, even briefly, induces panic. Add to that the responsibility to keep calm and free oneself, and the expectations for the average person decrease substantially. It was in this space—between expectation and possibility—that Houdini discovered the power of the will.

In addition to the will required to perform each escape, the compounding dangers from one feat to the next required further application of the will. It allowed him to up the ante time after time.

Ultimately, there are two aspects of the will in play when we face repeating or escalating challenges:

---

139 As always.

- **Micro Will:** The willpower to endure an individual challenge from start to finish.
- **Macro Will:** The willpower to endure a sequence of challenges over time.

Actively challenging your Micro and Macro Wills allows you to strengthen them as if they were a muscle in your body. Over time, you can accomplish more than you or anyone else ever thought possible, simply by pushing beyond your perceived limits.

Houdini understood this well, noting: "My chief task has been to conquer fear. The public sees only the thrill of the accomplished trick; they have no conception of the tortuous preliminary self-training that was necessary to conquer fear." He pushed far beyond the limits of acceptable comfort.

Just a Little Bit

David Blaine, inspired by Harry Houdini, is a contemporary magician-turned-escape artist. Determined to push his own limits, and admittedly "obsessed with Houdini," he transformed himself into what can only be described as an endurance artist, which is what he is most famous for.

Dropping almost the entirety of the performance aspect that Houdini had mastered, Blaine put the majority of his focus on endurance alone. It was where Houdini, the father of endurance art, left off that Blaine began.

Blaine was buried alive, where he stayed for seven days. Among other feats, he was also entombed in ice for over sixty hours, stood on a hundred-foot-high pillar for thirty-five hours, was suspended over the River Thames in London for forty-four days, and, perhaps most impressively, held his breath underwater for *seventeen minutes.*

Houdini and Blaine repeatedly challenged themselves to go one step further—a lesson we can bring into our everyday lives. These magicians make it easy (and entertaining) to witness someone pushing not just their own limits, but humanity's. But don't fall into the trap of thinking that mental fortitude is something that must be a larger-than-life spectacle. The truth is far from it.

In Blaine's own words, "We are all capable of infinitely more than we believe. We are stronger and more resourceful than we know. And we can endure much more than we think we can."

Every time a designer decides to do one more version or a student takes one more stab at a difficult math problem or an office worker makes the choice to add yet another complexity to their spreadsheet, they're expanding their personal tolerance. And, as a result, they're expanding their personal *possibilities.*

Whenever you actively make the decision to do "just a little bit more," you're broadening your potential. Putting in three more minutes of effort may not seem like much in a given moment, but when you do it day after day, it adds up.

I have a personal manifesto—a short document that lives on my phone—that I read every morning. It's filled with various reminders of things I've learned in my life. Each one is a commitment I've made to myself. One of them reads:

"Be diligent, don't cut corners, give my full self to what I'm doing. Always go the extra mile that makes the difference between them and me."

Ask yourself: *How often do I go the extra mile?*

All Day, Every Day

There's more to pushing yourself than the aforementioned examples of the designer, student, and office worker. Sure, those moments are great for inching your craft, knowledge, or career forward, but they are few and far between in days filled with all sorts of activities. How, then, do you prepare for them?

Simple: you practice the act of pushing. Like many of the truths in this book, the how-to isn't that entertaining. In fact, it's mundane. But as we've learned, coming to terms with the mundane—accepting repetition—is one of the keys to excellence.

So how do you practice pushing? You push *everything*.

PUSH YOURSELF DURING CREATIVE ACTS

- Learning music scales? Practice them over and over, despite how repetitive it may feel at first, until you can dance between the notes.

- Developing your figure drawing? Draw the same pose until you can do it without source material.

- Improving spreadsheet dynamics? Create a sheet on a different subject, every day, pushing yourself to integrate new features until they become second nature.

PUSH YOURSELF OUTSIDE OF CREATIVE ACTS

- Done eating dinner? Don't put the dish in the sink; clean it off right then and there.

- Trash filled? Don't wait until the next piece of rubbish doesn't fit; take it out the moment you notice it's full.

- Running low on socks? Do the wash now instead of waiting until you're down to the last pair.

Every day there are dozens, if not hundreds, of opportunities for you to do better. The more you apply this approach to the small things, the easier it is to bring it to the big ones.[140] Forego the "fun stuff" in favor of continuously refining your fundamentals. Before you know it, your standard mode of operation will be far more efficient, and effective, than that of the people around you. It's then that you'll begin to naturally rise to the top.

Summary

Great creators have great moments. Michael Jordan repeatedly sank game-winning shots, Stephen King releases chart-topping bestsellers year after year, and Michelangelo painted the final dab on the Sistine Chapel to create one of the largest frescoes ever made.

As incredible as those moments are, they are red herrings to what truly made these three people legends. Greatness is not achieved in one fell swoop but earned in all the small moments leading up to those striking finales. Every day, Michael Jordan was the first on the court and the last to leave. Each morning, Stephen King sits at his desk and doesn't let himself leave until he writes two thousand words. For four years, Michelangelo showed up, day after day, to stand on scaffolding and paint.

You can do the same.

---

140 After all, small things tell big stories.

Harness the power of your Micro and Macro Wills by consciously going one step further at every opportunity. Before long, your baseline will be beyond what others consider normal. As you keep pushing, your standard will be others' excellent. And, if you keep going, little by little you will find yourself in the realm of greatness.

32

Expose Yourself to New Things

The Law of Adventure

Routinely venture into the unknown so that your pool of inspiration never grows stagnant. New ideas come from new experiences. Allow yourself to engage in opportunities you might initially reject.

Brush and Code

It is said that hindsight is 20/20, and looking at Zaha Hadid's career is a prime example of why this expression is so true. Hadid, now, is considered one of the greatest architects of all time, but when she first began her career, greatness was far from predictable—at least to the outsider.

Hadid grew up in Beirut studying mathematics. In 1972, when she was twenty-two, she moved to London to study architecture. It was during her studies that her professor, Rem Koolhaus, first recognized something special, describing her as "a planet in her own orbit." Her designs were unique and pioneering, even at a young age. Koolhaus called Hadid one of the best students he'd ever had. He was so impressed that he hired her.

At the time, architecture was typically comprised of straight lines and ninety-degree angles. Hadid noticed that her ideas were constantly butting up against the tools architects would use to express those ideas, such as grids and rulers. These tools were helpful, but there were so many more expressions to be had if she broke away and didn't lean on them. Finding herself at the limit of what current techniques could attain, she adopted an entirely new one: painting.

Going against the grain, Hadid tossed aside the straight lines and right angles of traditional architecture in favor of stretching, melting, flying curves. By adopting painting as part of her design process, she was able to go beyond what others were doing at the time. In her own words, she painted "to unveil new fields of building." She wasn't taken seriously for years. That is, until her approach began to produce forms that had never been done before.

Technology became more integrated into architecture as time went on. Hadid, now with her own firm, respected the advances in her field but still insisted on painting and making handmade models to break beyond the limits of what computers were able to do. Again, others in her industry criticized her approach as old-fashioned, certainly not something to carry into the age of computers. However, while she fought the limits of technology, she embraced the benefits.

It became apparent to Hadid that there were things computers could do which human beings would never be able to. Specifically, complex mathematical computation. A person's mind can only grasp so many variables at a given time, but a computer's processor was nearly limitless. Using technology, she pioneered computer-led architecture using forms derived from algorithms. This technique would eventually be called parametricism.

Hadid went on to use painting and parametricism to create iconic architecture around the world. Her designs included the flowing concrete Vitra Fire Station in Germany, the shining steel Bergisel Ski Jump in Austria, the part-bridge part-expo center (and aptly named) Bridge Pavilion in Spain, the jutting glass-triangle-covered Guangzhou Opera House in China, and many more.[141]

Her pioneering work was widely recognized: *Forbes* named her one of The World's Most Powerful Women. *TIME* named her one of The Most Influential People in the World. After her death in 2016, London's *Guardian* newspaper called Zaha Hadid "The Queen of The Curve," saying she "liberated architectural geometry, giving it a whole new expressive identity."

Reservations Unknown

Imagine having the best job in the world. In an interview reflecting on his career, Anthony Bourdain claimed to have exactly that. Getting there, however, wasn't a straight and easy path.

Bourdain went on a trip to France as a kid, where—on a fisherman's boat—he tried oysters for the first time. The taste, the freshness, and the wild unfamiliarity struck a chord. He

---

141 See these buildings and more at lawsofcreativity.com/zaha-hadid.

couldn't shake the experience. In fact, it rooted itself so deeply that it changed the direction of his life entirely.

Years later, Bourdain decided to drop out of traditional university and go to culinary school instead. Twenty years and several restaurants later, he was promoted to head chef of Brasserie Les Halles, a French restaurant in New York City. It was the pinnacle of chefdom—or so he thought.

Armed with insights from years of working in kitchens and fueled by his flair for going against the grain, Bourdain wrote *Kitchen Confidential*. It was a behind-the-scenes look at what goes on in the back of restaurants. In the book, he revealed industry secrets alongside warnings for his readers. These warnings include avoiding eggs Benedict at Sunday brunch because it's probably made from melted butter left over from the week, and that one should first check a restaurant bathroom's cleanliness before ordering, as it usually reflects how clean the kitchen is. Needless to say, the book was a raving success.

Not only was he an accomplished head chef, but he also became a bestselling author.

Everyone wanted a piece of Bourdain, and he was happy to give it to them. In 2002, the Food Network premiered his new show, *A Cook's Tour*, which featured Bourdain traveling all over the world exploring various cultures and their cuisines. It was a hit, and in 2005 he signed a deal with the Travel Channel for a new show, *Anthony Bourdain: No Reservations*. Similar to his first, this one found him traveling the world tasting food and sharing his thoughts along the way. He finally went on to explore even more remote culinary experiences in *Anthony Bourdain: Parts Unknown*.

Bourdain pushed the limits of safety and sensibility to try

new dishes. In Libya, his team had to hire the local military to keep them safe. In Vietnam, he ate a still-beating cobra heart, describing it as a "very athletic, aggressive oyster." In the deserts of Morocco, he ate roasted sheep's testicles. In Namibia, he ate warthog, specifically the anus. In Cairo, he ate a delicately cooked feral pigeon, calling it "utterly delicious." The list goes on.

Later in his career—after nearly two decades of traveling the world—he was asked his thoughts about *Kitchen Confidential,* the book that launched his career. Without hesitation, Bourdain responded, "I was so wrong about so many things. I regret saying that you should check out the bathroom and leave if the bathroom's filthy. So many of the best meals of my life over the past seven years have been in absolutely septic environments with chickens and pigs running around."

Today, Anthony Bourdain is regarded as one of the pioneers of culinary commentary, both in written format and on screen. *Kitchen Confidential* went on to become a *New York Times* bestseller. His shows collectively aired over 290 episodes across twenty-five seasons—and won a total of eight Emmys for outstanding work.

Here, There, Everywhere

On the surface, it would seem that Zaha Hadid and Anthony Bourdain took different paths to greatness, but upon deeper inspection we find that is not the case at all. There was one specific tendency that allowed Hadid to break ground in the field of architecture and Bourdain to cook up new ideas in the field of culinary arts: exploration.

They both had strong inclinations towards the unknown.

Simply stated, they enjoyed doing things and going ways that were unfamiliar. While the underlying motivations were analogous, their explorations were expressed in different ways. Hadid explored the adjacent; Bourdain explored the remote.

The two fundamental methods of exploration:

- **Adjacent Exploration:** Exploring that which is near—within daily grasp—to expose oneself to ideas, methods, people, and places that are not being leveraged.

- **Remote Exploration:** Exploring that which is distant—outside of your normal life bubble—to expose oneself to entirely new ideas, methods, people, and places.

At first, Hadid's contemporaries thought she had an obsession with old ways. Everyone around her seemed to be using modern methods while she favored classic ones. As technology became more useful, however, she quickly assimilated it into her toolbox against the expectations of others.

To Hadid, painting was as functional as programming. The two were just for different uses. In the end, she employed the freedoms afforded by brush and canvas as much as those of code and terminal. Painting granted her the ability to imagine shapes and curves that standard tools didn't allow, and programming gave her the power to compute complex architecture that otherwise was unthinkable. Ultimately, Hadid was propelled by a simple idea: "Not to have any ninety-degree angles." Her Adjacent Exploration allowed her to do the things she was already doing, but in new ways.

In Bourdain's case, it seemed like he had life all figured out. He went to culinary school, earned rank by toiling in kitchens, achieved head chef status, and wrote a book. That's a trajectory right out of a modern-day fairy tale. He traveled upward until he reached the pinnacle of his career, there was nowhere left to go but outward. So away he went, using the medium of cooking and the vehicle of television to explore the world.

Perhaps he knew that travel would be the path of growth but probably not in the way he expected. Exploring abroad gave him a greater appreciation for all kinds of people, cultures, and, of course, food. In one episode, after years of traveling, Bourdain looked right into the camera and said, "This is what you want. This is what you need." He briefly glanced down at a bowl of noodles and then scanned his surroundings. "This is the path to true happiness and wisdom." His Remote Exploration helped him see the world in ways that he couldn't possibly imagine beforehand.

You must take the time—and accept the inherent discomfort—to explore both your adjacent and remote worlds. Without consistently dipping new ideas into your well of existing thoughts, you will eventually use up your stores and your ideas will run dry.

Familiar, Yet Unknown

How much do you really know about a loaf of bread? If you were asked to make one right now, could you? Up until I was thirty-three, I couldn't. Ariana, my wife, showed me how. And Ariana didn't know either until she decided to figure it out while we were stuck inside during the COVID pandemic.

For those who don't know how to bake bread, here's the recipe we use:

Ingredients:

- 1.5 cups warm water
- 1 tablespoon yeast
- 3.5–4.5 cups flour
- 1 tablespoon honey
- 1.5 teaspoons salt

Directions:

1. Preheat oven to 400 degrees.
2. Combine warm water, honey, yeast, and salt. Let sit for 10 minutes.
3. Add flour, one cup at a time. Knead until no longer sticky.[142]
4. Form into loaf on pan and cover with towel. Let sit for 20 minutes, then cut slits across top.[143]
5. Bake for 16–20 minutes. Enjoy!

Why did I go through the trouble of sharing an entire recipe? Because it's an easy place to start your Adjacent Exploration. If you haven't made bread before (which is most people), it will allow you to have a new experience in under an hour and for less than ten dollars.

You can start by having adventures right at home. In doing so, you will get more comfortable with the uncomfortable. Then you can take that approach and begin applying it beyond the safety of your front door.

---

[142] Tip: Don't knead the dough too much; it will get dense, and the bread won't bake well.

[143] Bonus: Throw cheese on top and/or garlic inside for an extra tasty outcome.

Here are a few more ideas to shake things up:

ADJACENT EXPLORATION IDEAS
- If you usually drink coffee, try tea (or vice versa).
- Take an ice-cold shower.
- Sleep in a different room.
- Eat a meal you've never had.
- Visit a local shop or restaurant you've never been to.

REMOTE EXPLORATION IDEAS
- Visit a friend who lives somewhere you've never been.
- Take a different form of transportation on your next trip.
- Visit a biome that is opposite or unlike the one you live in.
- Learn the basics of a language and visit that country.
- Let someone else create the entire itinerary for a trip.

Remember that chasing the New can be a dangerous affair. Too much focus on freshness can make us forget to appreciate the beauty of the everyday mundane. As a creator, however, it's necessary to find newness and regularly add to your pool of possibilities. We learned in the Law of Connection that creating is a misnomer—you're really just combining. In order to facilitate a healthy stream of ideas, one must have a steady flow of experiences to supply the fundamental components that combine into those new ideas.

A Note on Reading

Reading is indispensable. Still, there's only so much you can get from a book. As wonderful as they are—and as much as I love them—they are no substitute for lived experience.

When considering the difference between real life and reading, I often think about what Robin Williams' character said to Will Hunting on that park bench:

"If I asked you about art, you'd probably give me the skinny on every art book ever written. Michelangelo, you know a lot about him. Life's work, political aspirations, him and the pope, sexual orientations, the whole works, right? But I'll bet you can't tell me what it smells like in the Sistine Chapel. You've never actually stood there and looked up at that beautiful ceiling. ... I can't learn anything from you that I can't read in some *[expletive]* book."

You have to experience things to truly learn from them. You can't be exploring 100 percent of the time, however. Books are an essential way to supplement your Adjacent and Remote Exploration.[144]

Summary

To create is to bring into the world a thought that has not been expressed in exactly the way you're expressing it. It may manifest physically, digitally, through audio, or by written word, but it is always the result of your personal experiences. To continue to create quality thoughts necessitates that you continually add to your experiences.

The world can be dipped into in two ways: Adjacent and Remote Exploration. Adjacent experiences exist within your

---

[144] You should always have a book in progress, and make sure you're reading regularly.

daily bubble. Remote experiences exist outside of it. The former is more accessible, the latter is more radical. Having a balance of both will keep your thoughts fresh and your ideas flowing.

Alan Watts, Zen Buddhist and bestselling author, said, "Real travel requires a maximum of unscheduled wandering, for there is no other way of discovering surprises and marvels." Whether adjacent or remote, you must include *unscripted* experiences—only then can they be called adventures.

33
Never Stop Learning

The Law of Growth

Learning has no limits. Don't be content to master one skill and neglect others. Without diversification, your strengths can turn into weaknesses. Commit to being a student for life.

Street Fighter

To say the name Bruce Lee brings immediate visions of martial arts movies. Close your eyes and there he is, face drawn in a serious expression, still as stone until—bam!—he strikes his foe down before movement even registers. Few realize, however, that his legend goes far deeper than film.

Bruce Lee grew up in Hong Kong where, as a kid, he got picked on for being small and relatively frail. Beyond bullying him with words, the kids in his neighborhood would beat on him whenever they got the chance. His parents, fearing that one day he could get truly hurt, sent him to learn martial arts at age thirteen.

Lee, determined to be able to stand up for himself, worked harder than any of his fellow students. In a short time, he became the best of the bunch. Not long after, he turned the tables, beating up the very same kids who had plagued his early childhood. His parents couldn't breathe a sigh of relief, however. They no longer worried about him getting hurt, but about *him hurting others*. Lee had transformed from a helpless kid to a dominant street fighter.

In fact, the situation escalated so severely that the local police sent a warning to his parents. If he got in one more fight, they said, he'd be at risk of going to prison. Fearing the worst, his parents put him on a one-way flight to the United States. He was only eighteen and had just a hundred dollars in his pocket.

Lee landed in San Francisco and traveled up to Seattle, Washington, where he stayed with family friends, working at their restaurant to pay his way. Shortly after, in 1961, Lee applied to the University of Washington as a philosophy major.[145]

Due to Lee's bravado, word quickly spread about his martial arts abilities. Within weeks of starting school, fellow students were begging him to teach them Wing Chun-style Gung Fu.[146] And teach them he did.

Anyone who wanted to learn, and was physically able to do so, was a fine student in Lee's eyes. Before long, he had more students than he could handle in an informal setting. Lee opened his first school, the Jun Fan Gung Fu Institute, in 1963.

At this point, Lee began to get into trouble all over again.

Local martial arts masters frowned on Lee's willingness to teach martial arts to everyone. In their eyes, it was a sacred part of Chinese culture and should be kept as such. Lee, however,

---

145 Didn't see that coming, did you?

146 Gung Fu is commonly referred to as Kung Fu, though Lee preferred the former spelling.

believed the opposite, writing, "Under the sky … there is but one family." Teacher after teacher spoke out against Lee, mocking his abilities and dragging his name through the mud. One teacher, Wong Jack Man, was so angry with Lee that he formally challenged him to a fight.

Reluctantly, Lee accepted even though he didn't care about proving his skills. The two met in private to settle the score, bringing only a handful of supporters. Wong was a master in the martial arts of Tai Ji Quan, Xing Yi Quan, and Northern Shaolin, and believed that his abilities were far superior to Lee's. There's no official documentation of the fight, but from eyewitness accounts, the widely accepted story tells quite the opposite tale.

According to those who were there, the fight lasted only three minutes. Wong's style of attack, as elegant and captivating as it was, was no match for Lee's direct and flourish-free movements. It is said that Lee was so fearsome that Wong turned and ran. Lee—borne from the unforgiving nature of the streets—gave chase and pounced. He beat Wong to the ground and forced him to verbally admit defeat.

With no one else willing to contest him, Lee had stood his ground. His school was going to teach martial arts to anyone willing to learn, and no one was going to stop him. He was at the top of his game in all regards—students, mastery, renown—and then he did something unexpected.

Out of seemingly nowhere, Lee began to publicly condemn the traditional practice of mastering any single martial art, *including Gung Fu*. Despite being considered a master, Lee denied such labels in favor of being a perpetual student. He voraciously studied every martial art he could, including taekwondo, judo, karate, tai chi, aikido, savate, boxing, and even fencing.

Bruce Lee's passion for martial arts solidified into what he called Jeet Kune Do, which translates to "The Way of the Intercepting Fist." It wasn't a style, but a philosophy. And it was this philosophy—the style of no style—that resulted in Lee being named the father of mixed martial arts, which endures to this day.

Final Dragon

Bruce Lee was a philosopher. He had over two thousand books in his private library. Beyond being an athlete of the body, he was a thinker of the mind. After he beat Wong Jack Man, a thought planted itself, one that Lee couldn't shake:

If Wong was a grandmaster of his art, why was it so easy to defeat him?

Lee used Wing Chun style Gung Fu to handily defeat Wong. With nothing left to prove, the other teachers backed down, leaving Lee to operate how he saw fit. But if he won, why did he criticize traditional martial arts? After all, it had worked.

Unable to stop thinking about the fight, the question consumed him until, finally, he came to a conclusion that was both troubling and yet strangely peaceful. Lee realized that Wong's greatest strength, his mastery, was also his greatest weakness.

Wong's fighting style just happened to be a poor match against Lee's. Like paper always being weak against scissors in the game Rock, Paper, Scissors, it wasn't that Lee was more masterful than Wong; he was simply the beneficiary of an asymmetrical matchup. Lee wasn't necessarily better; he was just different *in the right way*. Lee was struck with an unsettling awareness: As a master of Wing Chun Gung Fu, he could just as easily be on the wrong side.

In what seemed like a sudden change from the outside, Lee could find no other solution to the problem than to fiercely criticize traditional martial arts. As a master himself, he had unknowingly opened himself up to the same vulnerability as Wong.

Traditionally, a martial artist focused on one or two styles and worked from novice up to master. They would follow, without deviation, the methods and movements prescribed by that particular style. This created admirable practitioners. People spent their whole lives perfecting their chosen martial art. But, as Lee came to realize, it also opened the door for immense weakness.

Instead, Lee became a proponent of formlessness. "Have no rigid system in you, and you'll be flexible to change with the ever changing." He decided that the only way to truly be prepared was to study all styles of combat and then use whatever made sense for a given situation: Jeet Kune Do.

Speaking in an interview, Lee explained his philosophy with a metaphor: "Be formless. Shapeless. Like water. You put water into a cup, it becomes the cup. You put water into a bottle, it becomes the bottle. You put water in a teapot, it becomes the teapot. Water can flow or it can crash. Be water."

Rather than concern himself with mastering each new style, he would pick and choose what made sense for his interests and preferences. "Absorb what is useful, discard what is useless, and add what is specifically your own," he would say to his students. When the time came to fight, one was to react to the demands of the moment—like water.

We, too, can do the same in our own lives. Learning various practices allows us to see connections where single-minded practitioners see nothing at all. For example, a master pianist is useless in a room full of guitars, while a musician with no mastery but intermediate ability with several instruments can still pick up a guitar and play. Perfecting the art of Microsoft Word is useless when all you need is an Excel document. Lifting weights on its own makes for a strong physique but a weak runner. And so on.

Now, this is not to say that one must avoid mastery. Like all things, there's a balance. The ideal approach involves striving for mastery in one or two areas—like Lee and Wing Chun—but still actively studying and learning from everything else.

As it turned out, Lee's ability to learn and integrate went beyond martial arts.

After moving his family back to Hong Kong in his late twenties, he played the leading role in his first martial arts movie. Three more movies followed. By 1972, he was a star. Then Lee hit it even bigger, starring in *Enter the Dragon*, his first Hollywood film. Unfortunately, it would also be his last. Lee unexpectedly passed away, at age thirty-two, just a month before the movie premiered.

Lee starred in just five major films—and only one in Hollywood—in the last three years of his life. So the next time someone refers to Bruce Lee as a movie star, you can remind them that he was much, much more. While his star didn't burn long, it certainly burned bright.

Eat Responsibly

In today's world, the word "consumer" often has a negative connotation. And that's fair when mention of the word brings to mind scenes of people sitting in front of the TV all day, swiping on social media, or endlessly browsing the internet. What is usually missed, however, is the importance of consuming if you expect to create.

Being a creator does not mean you need to abstain from being a consumer. In fact, it's detrimental if you do. Would you expect a chef not to explore foods and taste other chefs' dishes, but to only silo themselves in their specialty cuisine? Of course not. Similarly, we must do the same.

When you're creating, the things you consume become your building blocks.[147] The Law of Connection teaches us that "base concepts can neither be created nor destroyed; they simply merge to form new combinations." The more you're able to ingest the world around you—even things seemingly unrelated to your craft—the more resources you're able to pull from.

Be mindful to not follow trends, however. Make sure what you consume speaks to your interests, to who you are within. As we learned at the very start of this book, you must allow yourself to be weird. Chase the things that excite you and let them influence what you create, regardless of if they are a little unusual.[148]

The trick, if we can call it that, is to consume responsibly[149] by balancing two primary factors:

1. **What:** As with food, you are what you eat. If you consume low-quality content, then, in turn, you will produce low

---

[147] If an artist tells you to abstain from "like, society, man," then they probably aren't creating anything worth seeing.

[148] Weird is different, different is unique, unique is original. And everyone wants to be original.

[149] Everything in moderation.

quality creations. Of course, enjoy your entertainment, but also balance it with content that enriches your thoughts.

2. **How long:** You will never feel fully ready to begin creating something—you'll always feel like you need "just a little more time." Therefore, consuming nonstop won't ever result in a feeling of preparedness. While that may seem like bad news, it isn't. This truth gives you the freedom to jump in and start experimenting.

There are times when we must pull ourselves away from consuming, but there are also instances when we have to force ourselves to stop creating. There's a difference between pushing limits and exceeding capacity. If the average programmer can code for five hours and you can code for seven or eight, that's admirable. But if you try to go fifteen hours, it's likely that you're going to start doing poor work. The next day you may end up correcting a large portion of it with fresh eyes.

There is no one-size-fits-all ratio between consuming and creating. It's different for everyone. As a young designer, I spent as much time consuming design as I did creating it. Nowadays, though, I have a massive log of images and ideas in the back of my mind ready to go, so I spend more time designing.

Figure out what works for you and be open to experimenting.

Device Methodology

Learning has never been more accessible than it is today. Thanks to current technologies, the entire world and all of its history is at our fingertips. As Uncle Ben (from Spider-Man) said, "With great power comes great responsibility."

Technology, as powerful and useful as it is, is just as good at distracting us from everyday life. As mentioned in the previous section, it's easy to get caught up consuming too much non-useful content.[150] The best way to avoid that trap is to give each of your devices a job.

When your devices have jobs, you're more likely to spend your time in ways you can look back on with appreciation. Essentially, a little more learning and a little less lounging. Here's an example of how you can make your devices work in your favor, both for learning and creating:

PHONE
- **Learn:** Books / Web
- **Create:** Task Management / Quick Communication / Accounts Management

LAPTOP
- **Learn:** Web / YouTube
- **Create:** Design / Code / Business / Finance / Write / Detailed Communication

TABLET
- **Learn:** Books / TV and Movies / Web / YouTube
- **Create:** Write[151] / Brainstorm / 3D Model

These are the jobs I use. They change semi-regularly as I

---

150 I won't call it useless, because leisure and entertainment are necessary to happiness.

151 The entirety of this book's first draft was written on a tablet. Surprised? So was I.

introduce new skills, or one device becomes more suited to something than another. Everyone has their own workflow. Find what works best for you.

Summary

Bruce Lee said, "All types of knowledge ultimately mean self-knowledge." The act of learning is a journey that happens within yourself. While it's from the outside world that knowledge is gathered, it's inside that knowledge becomes something more. It melds with who you are. It dances with the ideas floating in your mind. And it contributes to the complex being that is you.

The more you learn, the more data points you have to mix and match. You can pair them like best friends working together, you can link them into an iron chain of sequential logic, or you can scatter them like sparks searching for a place to catch fire and spread.

On many mornings, you will wake up with facts but, after new light is shone, go to bed with them turned to falsities. Rather than fight, hand the reins to new information and ideas. Let them guide you on your journey. Keep in mind that you are what you eat, so be conscious of what you allow your mind to consume.

Over time, if done correctly, you will find yourself with more ideas than you have time to bring to life.

34
Treat Your Body Well

The Law of Symbiosis

Your body is more than just a container for your brain—it directly affects the quality of your thinking. Stay physically active and reap the rewards of improved cognitive performance.

Grandest of Slams

Professional athletes spend their entire lives improving their game. Whether it's basketball, tennis, cricket, football,[152] or any of the countless sports that populate history, one thing is certain: physical fitness matters. Top athletes, however, know there's far more to what they do than having physical prowess.

It was the last tennis match of the Australian Open in 2010: Serena Williams against Justine Henin. Each had won a set. They were on the third and final set to determine a winner. Both athletes had fought through multiple opponents to reach each other, and now they were just one step away from being the champion.

---

152 The one with hands or feet, pick your favorite.

Though Williams was the number one player in the world and the projected winner, Henin—an unranked German wildcard—took an early lead. Henin was, without a doubt, the underdog. And people love underdogs. Every time Henin scored, the audience erupted in cheer. When Williams scored, they booed.

At the top of her game, Williams had everything to lose while Henin had nothing. In addition to the stress of defending her title, Williams was dealing with several injuries. Her thigh and knee were taped, and she was fighting through a host of aches and pains that comes with enduring a multi-match event. Spectators could see the anger and frustration on her face as her hits landed out of bounds and her opponent's balls sailed just out of reach. Henin, meanwhile, was composed, even smiling.

It wasn't looking good for Williams. Henin grew more confident with every point. Williams started to lag behind.

Then something unexpected happened.

Someone in the crowd, anticipating a Henin victory, yelled, "You can beat her, Justine! She's not that good!" Williams stopped dead in her tracks and looked towards the source of the anonymous shouter. She wagged her finger in their direction and said to herself, *You don't know me.*

In that moment, the tide turned. Williams began scoring point after point. Her shots hit their mark. She returned even the best of Henin's attacks. The crowd quieted. Henin began to drag. Before long, Serena smashed one last, long shot into the back corner to win the final set.

Throwing her racket in victory, Williams ran forward and slid onto her back. Her hands covered her crying face. Against the expectations of some thirty thousand spectators that day, Williams retained her title as Australian Open champion.

Today, Serena Williams is considered one of the greatest tennis players of all time. She's won twenty-three Grand Slams,[153] more than any player in history, woman or man.

Zero in and Win

Over the years, Serena Williams has claimed on more than one occasion: "My greatest strength is my mental game." She is keenly aware of the connection between the body and the mind. What may come as an even bigger surprise is that Williams believes that "tennis is 70 percent mental."

Not only is Williams saying that the mind is a critical component of her success, she's claiming that it's even more important than her body's participation.

Think about it. How many people can successfully hit a tennis ball over a net? As per the Physical Activity Council,[154] over twenty-one million Americans picked up a racquet in 2020. Of course, not all of them are great (or even good), but even if we just take just the top 1 percent, that's still a whopping 210,000 players. Serena excels beyond them because, according to her, playing the sport well is more than just picking up a racquet or being able to send the ball back to an opponent.

In the match between Williams and Henin, Williams was undoubtedly mentally compromised by Henin's presence. No one expected Henin to get so far (remember, she wasn't even ranked at that point). By the time she got to the finals, her confidence was through the roof, and everyone was rooting for her.

---

153 Meaning she won all four major tennis tournaments in a single year.
154 I had no idea this was a thing either.

Henin's very presence made Williams uneasy, and it showed in her playing. If it weren't for that one crowd member's shouts, which altered Williams' thinking and shook her loose, it's likely she would've lost.

When that anonymous crowd member yelled, the scaffolding of unhelpful thoughts that led Williams to that point came crashing down. It reset her thinking and reminded her who she was—the number one player in the world! Afterward, she said the outburst helped her remember to "take it one point at a time," which she successfully did to beat back Henin and win the tournament.

The first part—Henin intimidating Williams—is an example of how our minds can detract from our performance. The second part—Williams overcoming it—is an example of the opposite. If we look closely, we can find the difference between the two.

When Williams' mind was detracting from her performance, she was thinking in the past. Aware of this danger, she's said, "One thing that makes me play poorly is if I'm thinking too much about my last match." When her mind was doing her favors, she was thinking only about the task at hand: "Even if you're going through something in life, you can't rush through it instantly. Take it one moment at a time. It's the same on a tennis court."

New Row Rafting, Neurorafting

We've established that the mind affects the body's performance. There's a clear connection between the two. Now it's time to close the loop and explore how the body affects the mind's performance. Wendy Suzuki, a neuroscientist and professor at New York University, proved the connection by unintentionally experimenting on herself.

Suzuki had been holed up in her lab for years studying the brain and its memory function. As a self-labeled Type A person, she went all in on her studies. She was so dedicated that everything else fell to the wayside, including her social life and her health. Eventually, she realized that she wasn't happy at all. "I was in New York, in my lab, eating takeout, and gaining weight." She goes on to explain that, without realizing it, she gained twenty-five pounds and found herself with few human connections.

So what did she do? She put the Law of Adventure to work and went on a whitewater rafting trip in Peru.

Suzuki left New York alone, but once in Peru she joined up with a group of adventurers and athletes. They all worked together to prepare for and navigate the waters. On the first night, the crew lined up and passed packs from the rafts to the campsite. Suzuki struggled with the heavier ones, and when she looked around at the rest of those in line, she realized she was the weakest link. "From that moment I vowed that I was never going to be the one who could not pull her own weight again," she recalled.

When she got back home, Suzuki redirected her Type A spirit towards exercise. Over the next several months, she got into fantastic shape. In addition to living up to her promise, she was about to get even more from the experience.

One evening, while writing grant requests, Suzuki had an epiphany. "I was sitting in my office, and I noticed something I hadn't noticed before. My writing was going well. Typically, writing never went well." She observed that her memory, attention, and mood were all far better than they had been in the past. She became determined to figure out why.

Right away, Suzuki entirely changed her research program from memory studies to exploring the effects of physical activity on the brain. What she learned proved that the body does in fact influence the mind's performance.

Physical activity affects two sections of the brain: the prefrontal cortex and the hippocampus. The former, located behind the forehead, is responsible for focus, attention, and decision making. The latter, located on the left and right sides of the brain, is the key component in forming and retaining memory. When you exercise, both sections improve their neurogenesis (creating new neurons) and neuroplasticity (strengthening existing neurons).

In effect, the brain's neurochemistry is bolstered through exercise. Which, in turn, positively impacts your ability to think, focus, and remember. Exercise, therefore, boosts your ability to be creative.

Another, simpler way to look at it: When someone eats poorly and lives a sedentary life, we expect their unhealthy habits to be reflected in their organs. Their heart is at risk, their liver processes blood less effectively, and so on. It makes sense, then, that the brain—also an organ—deteriorates in a similar way, and that poorer cognitive function is the result.

Furthermore, exercise indirectly enhances your ability to be creative by releasing serotonin and dopamine, improving your mood, sleep, and overall ability to self-motivate. When you're happy, it's easier to create. When you're well rested, it's easier to think. And when you're motivated, it's easier to get to work.

So—if the brain benefits from physical activity, how much exercise should you do?

Everyone's physical makeup and activity level is different, so there's no one-size-fits-all. But there are some guidelines. Suzuki suggests a minimum of three to four thirty-minute aerobic (high heart rate) sessions per week.

Some suggestions to get you started:

- **Walking:** As one of the most accessible forms of aerobic exercise, walking is surprisingly effective. It has been practiced by famous thinkers and creators such as Mary Oliver, the Pulitzer Prize-winning poet, and John Muir, environmental philosopher and father of national parks. For those who don't exercise at all, this is a great place to start.

- **Running:** Human beings are born runners. Our ancestors literally chased their prey until it collapsed using our energy-efficient bipedal mode of locomotion combined with our heat-dissipating superpower: sweating.

- **Active sports:** Cycling, basketball, tennis, soccer, swimming, the list goes on. These are harder to assimilate into the average lifestyle, but are more interesting and, consequently, easier to perform for extended periods.

- **Virtual reality exercise:** VR exercise is one of my favorite activities. It combines the full-body benefits of sports with the entertaining interactivity of gaming.

Whatever you decide, get yourself an activity tracker and log your exercise sessions. This will help you stay the course and track your progress as you improve. Ultimately, do what you and your doctors feel comfortable with. Every little bit contributes towards better thinking.

In all her talks, Suzuki makes a point of repeating her most fundamentally significant discovery: "Exercise is the most transformative thing you can do for your brain today."

Summary

Like a runner who must tend to the condition of their legs or a climber who must manage the stress on their hands, a thinker must actively tend to the health of their brain.

When you engage in physical activity, your brain develops new neurons and improves existing ones. This results in improved focus, memory, and overall ability to process thought. It also boosts your mood and helps you sleep better, both of which create a beneficial environment for creativity.

If you want to be great, follow Serena Williams' advice: "Don't let anyone work harder than you do." The healthier you are physically, the more effective you are mentally.

35

Locate the Present Moment

The Law of the Now

Connect to the present. Let time fall to the wayside, ignoring what was yesterday and what may be tomorrow. Let the now be all that exists—because it is—and you will go deeper than you ever thought possible.

Endless Invisible Pause

Part of what makes music so beautiful is that it is inherently fleeting. Music can't exist without notes, which can't exist without time. Which means that at any given moment, you can only experience a piece—a single blip—of a song. And when the musicians stop, so does the music.

Many of us listen to songs, but few take the time to truly hear them. Musicians, however, must simultaneously play and hear to successfully make music. Miles Davis, American jazz trumpet player, illustrated this idea on innumerable occasions throughout his career. Davis was a man of few words—he preferred that his trumpet do the talking—but thankfully, through others, we have tales of his genius.

Herbie Hancock was only twenty-three years old when he joined the Miles Davis Quintet in 1963. He would later go on to be one of the premier American jazz pianists of the era, but at the time he was still a young man with a lot to learn. Davis saw potential in Hancock. There was a flame inside him that burned bright, if a bit unrefined. With time and practice, Davis knew Hancock had what it took to be one of the best.

One particular night, the band was playing at a jazz club in New Orleans. Hancock sat at an upright piano. Miles was up front with both hands wrapped around a gold trumpet. The band had just eased into a new section of the piece, and it was Davis' turn to solo.

In jazz, the music isn't written note for note but rather in sections that follow a key with a few core notes and chords. The musicians take turns exploring ideas on their respective instruments, soloing one after another while the rest of the band supports the person who's currently playing. Such is the nature of jazz that no two performances of the same song are ever alike.

Davis stepped up to the mic, head tilted down, eyes closed, but ears wide open, submerged in the music. His cheeks tensed as he pressed air through the trumpet. A short sound cut softly through the background bass. Then another. He took a breath and dove into a solo that mingled long, sweet tones with quick, sharp ones.

Hancock, distracted by Davis' playing, for a split second let himself get caught up in the music and lost sight of the moment, playing the wrong chord right in the middle of Davis' solo. He was so distraught that he literally took his hands off the keys and put them over his ears. In the thick of it, emotions overtook him, and he was sure he'd be kicked out of the band after the show.[155]

Davis' eyes locked with Hancock's. Time stopped. The space between the last note and the next stretched for eons. Davis paused but for a moment, so quickly that only a musician on stage would notice.

The very next notes that came from Davis' trumpet blew young Hancock's mind.

Without missing a beat, Miles Davis changed the following notes so that they turned Herbie Hancock's "wrong" chord into the "right" one. The band kept playing. The audience continued to enjoy the performance. And Herbie Hancock put his fingers on the piano keys and got back to work.

A Gentle Realignment

Miles Davis was a master of his craft. He turned pro at age seventeen, and his career spanned over five decades. *Rolling Stone Magazine* named him one of the most important musicians of the twentieth century. His music, and his contributions *to* music, are studied to this day. When Herbie Hancock played the wrong chord, Davis knew just how to handle it.

In music, there are two concepts that describe the relationship between notes: consonance and dissonance. Consonance refers to notes that melodically align. It makes up the vast majority of music. Dissonance is when notes don't align. Instead, they sound harsh to the ear.

---

[155] Miles Davis was a notoriously no-nonsense band leader.

Hancock's chord was dissonant to what Davis was expected to play next, which is why he was so shocked. Although Hancock made the mistake, it wouldn't register to those listening until the next note. Which would make it seem like Davis, rather than Hancock, had made the mistake.

Davis, however, was keenly listening to the music as they played. He was connected to it rather than just going through the motions. Because of that, he was able to adjust on the fly. Instead of playing the expected notes, he made a slight alteration that sounded consonant to Herbie's accidental chord. His adjustment prevented the would-be dissonance, and then he gently guided the following notes back on track.

No one was the wiser.

"It astounded me. I couldn't believe what I heard. Miles was able to make something wrong into something that was right," Hancock recalled. "What I realized is that Miles didn't hear it as a mistake. He heard it as something that happened, just an event. That was part of the reality of what was happening at that moment—and he dealt with it." That's the benefit of connecting to the moment. By letting go of what came before and what should come after, Davis was able to take things for what they were as they came.

Hancock reflected on that night, saying that he learned, "The only way we can grow is to have a mind that's open enough to experience situations as they are—and turn them into medicine."

Now You See It

Connecting to the present moment is beneficial regardless of the medium. Hancock learned to be aware of the music actually being played, rather than the music that *should* be played. Personally, I found a deep connection to the present when I began to study drawing.

Like listening versus hearing, there's a difference between looking and seeing. In my very first drawing class at art school, I was presented with one of the most profound—and profoundly simple—creative challenges that had ever been requested of me.

It was our first day. We were in a huge, open room with dozens of windows on one side that looked out on the busy New York City street down below. The floor was flecked with dried paint, and wooden easels were standing at attention in a far corner. My teacher gave each of us a sketchbook and ushered us to a couple dozen chairs set up in a wide circle. A young man walked in as I put down my bag and got situated. He and the teacher swapped brief hellos, then the man began undressing off to the side. Before I knew what was happening, he was standing in the middle of the room, naked and frozen.

"Thirty seconds!" yelled the teacher.

I barely finished the head before the man swapped poses.

"Thirty seconds!" Again.

After several, we moved to sixty seconds, then two minutes. I learned later that what we were doing was called gesture drawing. They were warmups for the longer poses that followed.

And that's when I heard it. As the young man eased into a slightly less precarious stance so that he could hold it for ten minutes, the teacher said to us: "Draw what you see, not what you *think* you see."[156]

---

156 Mind. Blown.

Want to experience this idea in action? Grab a piece of paper and draw a person's face in ten seconds. Don't worry about it looking good or being accurate. If it makes it less intimidating, imagine you're drawing a diagram of a face rather than an actual face: make an oval for a head, add a couple of circles for eyes, a bowl-shaped line for a nose, and a nice round smile.

Did you do it?[157] Okay—now draw a line down the center of the head from top to bottom (right over everything); then do the same across the middle of the head, left to right.

When you're done, put the pen or pencil down and pick up your drawing. If you drew reality as it actually is, the horizontal line will go directly across the eyes as if they were slicing them in half. If it does, nice work. If not, don't worry—drawing what you think you see is a common mistake. Most people draw eyes above the midpoint because, as humans, we focus on other people's faces. Mentally, they take up our entire vision; their face becomes their head, in a sense.

Don't beat yourself up if you didn't draw the eyes in the middle of the head. For centuries, even the most celebrated painters missed what was right in front of them: They made paintings with sharp details in the background, no matter the distance.

Then Leonardo da Vinci came along. He not only painted, but studied optics, and formally introduced and popularized the practice of *sfumato*. In reality, objects become blurry the farther away they are, due to how light, air, and our eyes work together. Basically, da Vinci's practice of *sfumato* blurred objects

---

[157] If you didn't already do it, I *highly* recommend you do. It takes ten seconds. Once I explain this exercise in the next paragraph, you'll no longer be able to give it a go.

in the distance.[158] It instantly made paintings feel more realistic, changing the way painters created from then on.

Time Is a River

As you can see, plugging into the present moment leads to powerful results. It allows you to hear more, see more, and take advantage of what's often right in front of you. In psychology, aligning your awareness with the present is called Flow or being in a Flow State.[159] Most people call it being "in the zone."

Studies have shown that experiencing Flow can increase your effectiveness by 500 percent. Unfortunately, the average person spends less than 5 percent of their day in a Flow State. Which means that for an average eight-hour workday, they're in Flow for just twenty-four minutes.

So—how do you do it? How can you connect with the now? What do you have to do to be more productive, creative, and calm?

There are three techniques to activating Flow, each progressively more challenging. If you can integrate the following into your life, not only will you be more creative, you'll also be happier and experience less stress.

1. **Eliminate distractions.** To allow yourself to exist in the moment, you must remove the things that pull you away from it. Turn off your notifications, work in a quiet place or wear headphones, let those around you know that

---

158 Take a look at the Mona Lisa. Her hands, face, and clothes are sharp; the road behind her is less so; and the lake and trees in the distance are mostly indistinct swashes of color.

159 More on Float, Flow's sister state, in the Law of Stepping Away.

you've allocated time to active work, etc. Don't hide the things that distract you—remove them entirely.[160]

2. **Focus on the task at hand.** This one takes some mental gymnastics. You must literally redirect your thoughts from the end goal—the thing you're looking to ultimately accomplish—and focus on what's directly in front of you. Be aware of your thoughts because poor thinking can slip in silently and, before you know it, pull your mind away.[161]

3. **Meditate regularly.** Like running, the more you do it, the better you are at it both during and outside of the activity.[162] The more you actively connect with the moment, the more it will passively happen as well. After all, Flow State is simply a type of meditative experience.

These are not easy, and there's no doubt you will have difficulty trying each for the first time. Let go of concerns that you may not be doing them right. You aren't aiming for perfection, but improvement. Small changes add up.

Meditation in Particular

A few words on meditation are necessary here. In the previous chapter, we talked about the importance of physical health in relation to your mental effectiveness. Literally, a healthy brain

---

160 Learn more about your environment in the Law of Habitat.

161 We talk more about this in the Law of Wandering.

162 Watch a runner chase a runaway cart in the parking lot versus a non-runner. The activity comes back to serve them outside of the activity itself.

performs better. To achieve that necessitates sound nutrition and physical fitness of some sort. On the flip side, it's also important to practice mental fitness, and one of the best ways to do that is through meditation.

It's been shown that those who meditate for thirty minutes a day have over 400 percent more creative ideas. Even meditating for just ten minutes has been linked with over 20 percent wider range of ideas. And walking while brainstorming is said to increase creative thoughts by 60 percent.[163]

Don't get caught up in the numbers themselves. Measuring creativity is like trying to measure productivity. You may be able to see which person on the assembly line greases the most hinges, but that doesn't take into account how they're feeling that day, their physicality, how they contribute aside from the task (morale, etc.), and what the person before them in line is doing. What is important about these findings is that, across the board, meditation and mindfulness lead to improved creative output regardless of the exact measurement.

There are endless ways to meditate, but they all, more or less, aim for a similar experience. In a nutshell: pull your attention inward; fill your mind with an awareness of your breath, body, sights, and sounds around you; and hold that awareness, gently pulling your thoughts back if (when) they wander.

Personally, I find that taking a walk allows me to slip into the present with relative ease. The moment I step out the door, whatever problem I'm working on tends to expand and fill the world around me with invisible, floating thoughts. No longer

---

163 It even works if you're just walking on a treadmill facing a wall or pacing a room back and forth.

are they in my mind, bugging me, but bouncing along with each step as they orbit my head. What works for one person doesn't necessarily work for others, however. You may prefer formal meditation—sitting perfectly still—or an entirely different activity to get your mind in a calm place.

Again, the important thing is not that you have a perfect meditation, but that you have slices of serenity within your meditation. Over time, those slices may widen and, perhaps, even take up the entire session. As they say, the journey of a thousand miles starts with a single step—so just get going.

Summary

To connect with the moment is of utmost importance in truly creating something exceptional. You must switch from operating on routine and expectations to a present-minded awareness. If done correctly, your connection with the now allows you to interact with an activity as a conversation rather than a one-sided exchange.

Flow is the state of mind in which time falls to the wayside as you experience the present for what it is. Take the time to learn the techniques that foster a more frequent occurrence of Flow State: Eliminate distractions, focus on the task at hand, and meditate regularly.

Like music, any given moment in time is but a blip in the vast song of the universe—but it's the only part that truly exists. Connect with it.

36
Live the Golden Rule

The Law of Reciprocity

To reach the highest peaks, we must climb together. Focus on your fellow travelers rather than yourself and you will find yourself reaching new heights with less effort.

A Golden Emblem

War and strife were a part of everyday life in China in 551 BCE. Lords battled relentlessly, rising and falling like endless tides on a rocky shore. It was an era of great unrest, of moral darkness. It was also the year a boy by the name of Kong Qui entered the world.

Kong was born to the Shi class, a commoner who was allowed an education. His father died when he was three. Soon after, Kong and his mother were reduced to poverty. Without support, it fell on his mother's shoulders to raise him with strength during a period in which it was vital to do so.

She sent Kong to school to learn the Six Arts: rites, music, archery, chariot racing, calligraphy, and mathematics. In addition to the Six Arts—mastery of which was said to result in the pinnacle of humankind—Kong was fascinated with Chinese history. Particularly, the beginning of the Zhou dynasty. It was a period of serenity, of peace in China, bookended by constant violence. Kong became fixated.

He was determined to help the nation find its way back to peace—but how?

The answer was discovered in the royal archives. Thanks to a friend, Kong was able to access and read the ancient texts. It was in those hallowed halls, on pages deeply yellowed by time, that he uncovered a better way of leadership: through moral inspiration instead of fear and brute force. In bygone eras, moral inspiration led to widespread peace. If it worked before, Kong believed it would work again. In order to do that, he concluded, China needed a leader who was able to wield positive moral direction to bring its citizens into a new golden era.

Unable to affect change by working on a farm herding sheep and keeping their books, Kong quit and dedicated himself to teaching. As a teacher, he shared his thoughts on leadership, character, and life with anyone who was interested in listening. People came from all over to learn from him. Kong's passion was magnetic, and as the years went on, he gained many followers and much respect.

In his late forties, Kong was so well respected that he was asked to be the advisor for the ruler of his home state of Lu. Seeing an opportunity to finally put into action the ideas he had dedicated his life to, he readily took up the position. For a brief time, Lu grew in power and esteem under Kong's guidance. The neighboring state of Qi, however, became uncomfortable with Lu's emerging presence, and moved to foil Kong.

Live the Golden Rule

Disguising sabotage as a gift, Qi's leader sent a group of young dancers to Lu. Unable to resist, and against Kong's advice, Lu's ruler ignored his duties and instead spent days enjoying himself with the dancers. Kong, disappointed, resigned soon after. He immediately left Lu and his comfortable life in search of a leader who could inspire China.

Spending the next twenty years in self-exile, Kong traveled between states in search of the individual who could take his ideas and put them into action. Rulers invited him into their courts and listened to his thoughts, but ultimately rejected him each time. While he didn't have success convincing leaders, thousands of ordinary citizens were converted to his philosophies.

Kong returned home to Lu at close to seventy years old. Even though his passion had never waned, the arduous journey left him wanting. Despite all those miles and cities and leaders, he did not find the person he was looking for. China was still warring. Peace was only a pipe dream. And he felt no closer to making change than when he first started.

Resigned to failure, he went back to teaching and continued to do so until he died a few years later.

The story doesn't end there, however. Kong had close to eighty disciples. When he passed away, they collected his teachings and compiled them into a series of texts called *The Analects*. Over time, these texts spread far and wide. They eventually made their way into the hands of future rulers, ones who actually listened and employed Kong's ideas. Sure enough, a more peaceful China emerged.

Today, *The Analects* are one of China's most sacred texts. Countless Chinese citizens strive to live by the ideas held within, and they have been the foundation of Chinese education for close to two thousand years. His teachings continue to inspire new generations, not just in China but all over the world.

It is true that Kong never found the person he was looking for. But what he didn't know then was that one day, he would *become* that person. In the West, we know him better by the name Confucius.

To Give Is to Receive

One of Confucius' followers once asked him to sum up his teachings in a single word. Several moments passed as he pondered the question. "Reciprocity," he finally answered. "Never impose on others what you would not choose for yourself." We often call this the Golden Rule.

Across history's greatest teachers, a form of the Golden Rule always reveals itself. Over and over, it is repeated that to live a good life one must consider the lives of others. Confucius went a step further by directly drawing a relationship between oneself and the world as a whole. He said, "To put the world in order, we must first put the nation in order. To put the nation in order, we must first put the family in order. To put the family in order, we must first cultivate our personal life—we must first set our hearts right."

In essence, to improve the world we must first improve ourselves.

Confucius traveled China in search of a leader whose personal qualities embodied the raw materials needed to lead the country into a peaceful era. As we know, Confucius didn't find who he was looking for. Yet today, we all know him as one of China's greatest philosophers.

Perhaps ironically, Confucius' journey reflects the very thing he spent his life teaching. He could've tried to be that leader himself, but instead he wanted to help someone else achieve greatness. He focused outward rather than on himself, and in doing so changed the lives of thousands along the way. In the end, he embodied the very thing he was looking to find. Intentionally or not, he created a leader for future generations.

When you operate with love, honesty, and respect, you attract people who do the same. Together you enrich each other's lives. You teach and help one another. Through reciprocity, you lift yourselves higher and higher. It is in that place of maximum compassion and collaboration that your creations are able to bloom to their full extent.

Confucius said, "A person of humanity is one who, in seeking to establish themselves, finds a foothold for others, and who, in desiring attainment for themselves, helps others to attain."

Flora and Fauna

Has anyone ever told you that "You are not an island"? It's a phrase that's invariably thrown around when discussing the importance of asking others for help. The message is that you can't do everything yourself, that you aren't alone in the journey of life.

You've probably also heard the saying, "You can lead a horse to water, but you can't make them drink." No matter how much we try to help someone, ultimately it's on the individual to take the steps towards change. Curiously, the idea behind this phrase is seemingly in direct opposition with the previous one.

So which is true? If you can't succeed on your own in life, but others can't help you, are you alone or are you in collaboration?

The answer is both. On one hand, you *are* alone. No one can do the work—the stuff that's going to lead to personal growth or make change for yourself—for you. On the other hand, you do need assistance to make those things happen. Without people to aid you, you are a pale imitation of what you could be. But it will be on you—always—to make the decision to ask for help, as well as to toil away to change your reality.

Back when I was in design school, I noticed something peculiar. My fellow students all used two tools: a laptop and a notebook. But something was off. Every laptop was the same style and brand, but every notebook was different. They were different sizes, brands, paper types, and so on. I asked myself why there was ubiquity in one and not the other.

I didn't have an answer. So what did I do? I asked others.

I contacted as many thinkers as I could find (designers, writers, architects, accountants, etc.—anyone who used their brain to work) and asked them one simple question: "What do you like in a sketchbook or notebook?" Over a period of about three weeks, I sent more than five hundred emails, figuring I'd get a 10 percent response rate and have fifty solid conversations. Much to my surprise, 80 percent of those emailed (cold!) responded back. I ended up having in excess of *four hundred* conversations with people around the world. The threads took several months to reach completion. They resulted in our first product—the Confidant notebook—which sold so well that we launched Baronfig to continue making them.[164]

At the time, I was twenty-six and knew next to nothing

---

[164] Originally, making the Confidant notebook was just an itch I needed to scratch for myself. I didn't expect so many people to respond so positively (Law of Specificity).

about starting a business. Again, I sought guidance. I told close friends and acquaintances that I was looking for advice. Many of them introduced me to others who were willing to share their wisdom and experience. From those meetings, I was sent to even more people who could provide guidance. Nearly a decade later, links in that chain are still added regularly.

You would be surprised how often and how readily people will help. Over the years, I've sent countless emails—without introduction—to people who had knowledge I was hoping to learn from. Time and again, they'd respond even when I was almost certain my email had entered a black hole, never to be seen again. Similarly, I've received just as many emails asking if I would hop on a call or accept a free coffee while someone picks my brain, and I help whenever I can.

Effectively, we are each an island, but still connected. There's a word for that: an archipelago, a collection of islands. Our islands have ecosystems that are entirely their own, and it's up to each of us to decide when to hop on our boat and paddle over to the next one. This takes quite a bit of bravery the first time you do it. Once you become comfortable asking for help, however, you will also begin to offer it more readily. Helping others will become as natural and satisfying as receiving it. The more you do it, the more luscious your island becomes, as do your neighbors'.

Over time you will find that like-minded people will gravitate towards you. Help will be given to you as much as you give it to others. Help cannot, however, be given only to expect it back. It must be given without expectation at all.[165] It's in that place of generosity—of reciprocity—that you will flourish.

---

[165] Don't help others just so they'll help you. It's transparent and will most likely produce the opposite results: you'll push people away.

RULE OF SEVENTH MAGNITUDE

In my experience, there's a Rule of Seventh Magnitude that seems to be a decent predictor of the likelihood a response will come. Generally, if someone exists within a degree of seven from your position, there's a good chance they'll engage with you.

For example, if you're running a $5 million business, it'll be relatively straightforward to get in touch with other business leaders up to those who are running $35 million businesses. If you're an illustrator with two thousand followers, you're likely to get a response from others who have up to fourteen thousand followers. As an author with one book under my belt, it's possible for me to get in touch with someone who has a half-dozen releases to their name—but I doubt Stephen King will pick up the phone.[166]

Finding the correct metric to apply the Rule of Seventh Magnitude can be challenging—some endeavors are more transparent than others—but once you land on one, the results are generally predictable. There are always exceptions, of course (some people are more willing than others), but it's a surprisingly accurate rubric for determining where to place your effort. Ultimately, you won't know unless you try.

As Confucius once said, "The person who says they can and the person who says they cannot ... are both correct."[167]

---

[166] Dear Stephen, I'd love to be proven wrong. Thanks, Joey.

[167] Adjusted from masculine nouns/pronouns to gender neutral. Times change. Wisdom should be inclusive.

Summary

When we look at life like it's a race to the end, we tend to look at others as opponents in that race. If we aren't careful, we find ourselves in competition with everyone. We isolate ourselves for fear of being passed. Train yourself to appreciate the journey more than the destination and you will naturally begin to help those around you in their own journeys.

If you need help, ask for it. If you see someone who needs help, or they ask for it, take the time to give it. Do not expect anything in return. Let the act of giving be its own reward. The more you do this, the more often you will find yourself surrounded by people who are equally generous.

As you grow your archipelago of helpers, you will find you achieve far more together than alone.

37
Don't Give Up

The Law of Tenacity

Accept that the world and the people in it operate of their own accord. Despite your best efforts, you will face hardships of all magnitudes. It is in these moments of difficulty and despair that what you are made of is truly tested. To reach great heights, you must persevere.

A Force to Be Reckoned

Orpah Winfrey grew up in Mississippi in the 1950s and 60s. At the time, no one could have predicted the great heights she would reach despite the multitude of traumatic events that would block her path.

Winfrey's difficulties started almost immediately. She was raised by her grandmother, a loving but tough woman who didn't take kindly to trouble of any sort. Her grandmother taught her how to read by the time she was three years old … but she also frequently beat her.

"I went to a well to get some water and carry it in a bucket. And I was playing in the water with my fingers, and my grandmother had seen me out the window and she didn't like it. She whipped me so badly that I had welts on my back and the welts would bleed," Winfrey recalled. "And then when I put on my Sunday dress, I was bleeding from the welts. And then she was very upset with me because I got blood on the dress. So then I got another whipping for getting blood on the dress."

When Winfrey moved in with her mother at age six, the beatings were swapped for sexual abuse that was perpetrated by the men orbiting her mother's life. With no foreseeable end in sight, she did the only thing one could do in that situation: she ran away. It didn't solve all her problems, however, because although she escaped the abuse, she soon found herself pregnant at fourteen years old.

She moved in with her father and gave birth to a premature child. Sadly, the baby passed away shortly afterwards. Winfrey keenly remembers her father sitting her down, amidst the grief and confusion and darkness, and saying to her, "This is your second chance." It was at that point that the idea of renewal clicked, that within every loss was a lesson to be learned. And learn she did.

As Winfrey grew older, she began calling herself Oprah (as opposed to Orpah) because people kept mispronouncing her name.[168] She did so well as a student that she was transferred to an affluent high school. Academically, she continued to be a star. She was on the honor roll semester after semester. Socially,

---

168 Did you read it as "Orpah" or "Oprah" in the first paragraph? If the latter, that's why she changed it.

it was challenging. Her arduous upbringing made it difficult for her to connect with fellow students who had been raised in homes in direct contrast to hers.

While still a senior in high school, Winfrey was hired as a part-time news anchor at seventeen years old. She did well, and three years later she was hired at another station full time as both the youngest and the first Black anchor. She eventually worked her way up to the prime spot: co-anchor of the six o'clock news. It was a culmination of everything she had worked for, of everything she had overcome.

Then, suddenly, she was demoted.

For many, that would've signaled the end. To be demoted not just in front of her coworkers, but also to have to publicly face that truth every day on television—there are few who would endure. But endure she did. Winfrey held her head high and continued to persevere, taking in stride her new position as the co-host of *The People Are Talking*.

At this point, Winfrey began to shine. Her hard-earned life experience translated to powerful human empathy and wisdom. She transformed the average talk show into an endearing, hopeful program. The depth that made her high school years a challenge had made her a daytime phenom. Viewers couldn't stop watching as Winfrey got to the heart of all types of human truths, day after day.

Eight years later, in 1984, Winfrey took a new job as the host of *AM Chicago*. Ratings were low when she started, but in a matter of months it was the highest rated morning show in Chicago. Two short years later, it was rebranded as *The Oprah Winfrey Show*, got extended to one hour, and was syndicated across the entire United States in a record-breaking daytime television deal.

Not long after, *The Oprah Winfrey Show* became the top talk show in the country. It won forty-seven Emmys, and *TV Guide* listed it among the fifty greatest TV shows of all time. To this day, it remains one of the highest-rated talk shows in the history of American television.

Passion + Perseverance x Time

With the willpower to climb even more mountains, Oprah Winfrey went on to start her own production company, television network, magazine, and more—propelling her into billionaire territory and earning the nickname Queen of All Media. Her incredible path started with that little girl who saw the world as it was, rather than what she wanted it to be, and changed her name to adapt.

As the Tibetan Buddhist meditation master, Chögyam Trungpa, said, "It is easier to put on a pair of shoes than to wrap the earth in leather."

It was her adaptable nature that saw her through challenges time after time. Winfrey was repeatedly knocked down, often under immense pressure, yet at no point did she surrender. There were dark years, but in retrospect she still credits her successes to the harder parts of her life. When asked if she would go back and change things, she responded, "I would take nothing from my journey."

Winfrey's story is not the norm, however. Every day people fail because they quit in the face of adversity.

Angela Duckworth, American psychologist, spent years researching high and low achievers. To her surprise, it wasn't talent or intelligence that separated the top performers from the rest. There were skilled and smart people in both groups. Rather, the one thing the high achievers had that the others didn't is what she calls "grit."

Grit is defined, according to Duckworth, as "passion and perseverance for long-term goals." It is developed in a number of ways, most notably through struggle. Winfrey had a tremendously difficult childhood in which she was faced with challenges most of us will never have to endure. She learned, early on, that there were but two choices: quit or continue. She chose to continue, ingraining a grittiness that gifted her the ability to push through obstacles of all kinds.

A fair warning is necessary, however. Having tenacity is vital to reaching great heights. But it's important not to get caught up in the idea that you must persist at all costs. In fact, the truth is very much the opposite.

There is a grave distinction between needing to persist at all costs and needing to persist *at all things* at all costs. To operate under the latter belief will net you unnecessary, dragged-out struggles. To operate under the former belief, you must establish and nurture the ability to recognize avenues with potential from those without.

It is absolutely acceptable to cut your losses when you know the results you're looking for will not occur, or the odds are so strongly against you that to proceed would be foolish.

Moving on is different from giving up. Learn to recognize the difference.

You Can Do It

It's one thing to read about someone being resilient and another thing entirely to enact it yourself. After all, "Be tough!" is easier said than done. Like the rest of the laws, I wouldn't have included this one if I didn't personally validate its effectiveness. Unfortunately for me, but fortunately for this book, I've faced a multitude of challenges that have proven its accuracy.

In December of 1986, a boy was born in Newark, New Jersey—me. My birth parents were deemed unfit by the state to raise me, and I was immediately put into foster care.

A year later, just after my first birthday, I was adopted by a single woman. Thanks to her persistence, we discovered I was born with a genetic disease that rendered every tissue in my body weaker than normal. This was a foreshadowing of what has proven to be a lifetime of unending doctor visits. When I had my first major surgery, she was there to take care of me. Considering all that had come before, things were looking up.

Then my world was turned upside down.

When I was ten, my mother was diagnosed with cancer. In the early days, life seemed normal, at least from my young perspective. But as time went on, her condition visibly worsened. There came a point when she couldn't speak, let alone open her eyes.

Two weeks after my thirteenth birthday, she passed away.

I was unable to cry, left in a state of complete shock. My ability to feel seemingly disappeared overnight. The one person in the world who always put me first, was gone. Other family members were there for me, but I wasn't as important as their own kids and their own problems. It's a subtle distinction, but once I was no longer a priority to anyone, I felt completely alone.

Yet again, I was adopted. This time to my mother's ex-husband—whom I called my grandfather[169] and had a great relationship with—and his wife.

In an attempt to find normalcy, I built a relationship with my uncle, who I saw often while growing up. He and I grew closer as time went on. We'd watch movies together, and he'd discuss them with me—not as if I were a child, but a thinking person. It was because of him that I gained an appreciation for critical thinking and philosophy.

In the years that followed, things didn't get any easier: I had two chest reconstructions (the first one failed). When I was sixteen, my uncle passed away. Then I had open heart surgery, along with a difficult recovery. Soon after, my grandfather passed away. When that happened, my step grandmother kicked me out of the house, leaving me to live out of my car while I tried to figure out what to do next.

My heart was broken in more ways than one.

Luckily, a cousin had extra space in their basement and took me in. Afterwards, I moved to New York City, discovered my passion for design, met my incredible wife, and built a company that has touched the lives of millions of people around the world.

THREE STRATEGIES OF GRIT

As odd as it is to say, I was still happy throughout the difficult times. Sure, there were bad days, but for the most part I learned how to endure hardship and continue living my life. It wasn't easy, but I eventually came to understand that happiness and

---

169 Yeah, it's complicated. Just roll with it.

sadness are not mutually exclusive. In the end, I did the only thing I could: kept going.

I employed—and still employ—three strategies that helped me overcome anything and everything:

1. **Gratitude—for the past:** Nothing is immune to the effects of appreciation. When you look at the past through a lens of thankfulness, you realize that even the worst of times produce something to be grateful for, whether it's a lesson learned or a toughness earned. This allows you to recognize that no matter what happens, you will come out on the other side with *something* positive.

2. **Perspective—for the present:** In your mind, the world revolves around you. That's nothing to deny or be ashamed of. It's a fact—your eyes are the only ones you see from. But if you extend your awareness beyond yourself by considering other viewpoints, you can evaluate your current condition more objectively. This expands your world, often shrinking the challenges you face.

3. **Optimism—for the future:** You can't predict the future with certainty. No one can. That doesn't mean you're helpless, however. You *can* choose how you envision your future. If you imagine positive potentialities—and engage them—rather than negative ones, they tend to come to fruition far more often than not.

Combining these strategies, you appreciate what you have endured and achieved, minimize your challenges as they come, and live in the comfort of believing that things *will get better.*

With these beliefs, it's much easier to hold your chin up and keep going when times are tough.

Enduring the litany of hardships I was faced with gave me a special kind of superpower. As I entered my twenties and life finally started to normalize, I felt like I was wearing a bulletproof vest—nothing could hurt me.

When a challenge arose, I remembered to be grateful I was no longer sleeping in the backseat of my car. It put into perspective the difficulty at hand and how insignificant it is compared to other difficulties I and others have survived. And, because I've been through tough times and come out the other side, I stayed optimistic that I would do it again.

The more often you allow yourself to persevere, the more grit you will develop. Next time you have the option to face a challenge head on or steer clear, go forward. It may hurt, but, as we know, what doesn't kill you will only make you stronger.

They say half the battle in life is showing up. In terms of achieving greatness, the other half is sticking around.

Summary

Tenacity is not a trait that's inherited or randomly granted. It's a quality of character that's earned through perseverance. When you come up against hardship—which you inevitably will—acknowledge that, as distressing as it is, there's also good to it. Every trial you face is an opportunity to develop grit, which is one of the single greatest determiners of long-term success.

Remember, there's a difference between giving up and moving on. When you quit, you wave a white flag and resign yourself to stagnation. When you move on, you accept that the challenge, whatever it may be, no longer makes sense to face. Do not force yourself to endure the pain of persistence if it doesn't serve you in the end.

When the circumstance calls for it, however, you must bear the weight of the challenge at hand. Employ gratitude, perspective, and optimism like a hiker uses walking poles to take each step. Before you know it, you'll be at the top of the mountain looking down on where you have come from and all that you have learned.

EPILOGUE
Dream the Future

The Law of Vision

To achieve a thing, one must first envision a goal. Point yourself in a direction and let the process carry you forward. Ultimately, you must give yourself a purpose before you can fulfill it.

Mighty Morning

The sun peeks over the far ridge of the earth's curve. Its rays make their way through uncovered windows. Instead of gently tickling your cheeks and plucking at your eyelids, the sun's fingers find you already sitting in your favorite chair, book in hand.

What little that's left of your coffee is cold. Not because you ignored it, but because you enjoyed the first sip long ago and the bit at the bottom is the inevitable residue of progress.

The early morning was yours: You got out of bed and stretched, shaking from your body the stiffness of a good night's sleep. Then you sat with your journal and let a few thoughts drip onto the page, unjudged and unimpeded. After, you brought your mind to the center with a brief, but effective, meditation.

And finally, you picked up a book to fill your now-clear head with new ideas.

As the room erupts with light, so does your mind with thoughts. At this moment, with the entire day ahead of you, yet to be written, anything is possible. You embrace the potential outcomes, not anxious about another day to check off your list or fearful of what unknowns may come, but serene with the knowledge that today is a blank page and you are its author.

Create Your Future

Today is the future your past self could only imagine. The farther back in time you go, the less likely it is that you'd predict you'd be in the exact spot you are in now. Yet here you are. It makes little sense, then, to try and commit to details in the distant future. Instead, focus on the broad goal—the vision—and point rather than plan.

When you tightly plan your future, you anchor yourself to a set of expectations.[170] As we've uncovered, that's an unrealistic method for making progress. When you point yourself in a direction, however, you focus more on the present than the end goal. You accept that the future is a mystery, and though you aim yourself towards a vision, you also allow your path to be what it is rather than force a plan that may never be.

Grace Hopper did not know how she would get humans to communicate with machines via human-centric language, but she knew it needed to be done. Lonnie Johnson wanted to make

---

170 Be wary of setting highly detailed timelines beyond the next several months.

a toy, but he had no idea how it would make its way into the hands of children around the world. Jan Ernst Matzeliger didn't know how to democratize foot protection, but he was compelled to find a solution. Emily Dickinson didn't write poetry to be famous, she wrote because she had a burning desire to express herself. Dolly Parton, Sal Khan, Albert Einstein, Bruce Lee, and everyone you've read about in this book had a vision of the future long before they achieved it. It didn't always materialize the way they expected, but they made do with the hands they were dealt.

Of course, it's easy to point to successes that have already come to pass. It's also easy to point to big names doing big things today. Do not compare yourself. Rather, appreciate their successes and be inspired by them.

There are people everywhere with visions that have yet to come to life. Still, they work to transform the world—and our lives—because they have a clear idea of what they're hoping to change.

Vision is a benefit to all goals, big or small, and all people, famous or not. Inside of every single one of us lies the potential for greatness. That greatness manifests through a clear vision, if only you allow yourself the discipline to focus as well as the freedom to adapt.

Beginning of the Beginning

In the Introduction you first learned that creativity isn't magic, it's more like gravity: reliable and reproducible.

You read the Laws of Mindset, which gave you a foundation for seeing the world as a palette of possibility. You read the

Laws of Action, a step-by-step breakdown of the creative process. And you read the Laws of Greatness, where you got to peek behind the curtains into how some people rise above the rest.

If the ideas in this book take a while to understand or to assimilate into your life, don't fret. When that iconic apple fell and hit Isaac Newton on the head, he didn't discover gravity in an instant. It took him *two decades* to figure it out and publish his theory.

Similarly, it took me twenty-plus years (and a little help from a paper worm) to understand creativity and compile these laws.

At the heart of human nature is our ability to think abstractly—to be creative. The laws held within, then, are not just laws for creating, but for living. Writing this book not only helped me clarify my thinking, it helped me become more effective as a creator, writer, partner, leader, friend, and person.

Like Picasso said, "Good artists borrow, great artists steal." Now it's time to take these laws and make them your own.

Conclusion

The present day was built in all the days leading up to it. The future is built in the present because that's all that truly exists—this moment, right here.

What will you create today?

APPENDIX

The Laws of Creativity at a Glance

The thirty-nine laws distributed throughout this book are collected here for easy reference. They are organized in the same order as they appear in the text.

0: Law of Origin 15
Everyone, including you, started out creative. Creativity is not something you need to learn, but remember.

LAWS OF MINDSET 21

1: Law of Expression 23
Embrace the parts of you that others call weird. Don't hide what makes you different. Allow those parts to float to the top and be seen by all. Your uniqueness is what makes your creations original, effective, and memorable.

2: Law of Disruption 33
You have every right to challenge, question, and improve upon the ideas that are handed to you. At some point, these ideas evolved from and innovated on what came before them. It follows, then, that they themselves will eventually be replaced.

3: Law of Connection 41
Base concepts can neither be created nor destroyed, they simply merge to form new combinations. Creativity is not about creating—it is about combining.

4: Law of the Unknown 49
Fear is necessary to all creative acts. Your goal is not to eradicate fear, but to acknowledge it and continue in defiance of your mind's backward tugs. When you are afraid, you are on the right path.

5: Law of Continuity 57
Failure and success are directly proportional. The more you fail, the more likely you are to succeed. A failure is not a true end, but a lesson to apply going forward.

6: Law of Competition 65
Do not compare yourself to others, but rather compare today's you to yesterday's. Strive to be incrementally better and you will reach new heights, untethered by the unreasonable expectations derived from comparisons to an infinite supply of others.

7: Law of Play 77
When you are having fun, you are doing something of your own free will. In this state, you go further, longer, and harder with less overall effort. Identify the things you enjoy and put them at the heart of your creations—then you will find true freedom.

LAWS OF ACTION 89

8: Law of Curiosity 91
The only way to know what is not known is by asking. Do not fear answers, for they hold no power over you. Questions are journeys: the ones worth going on hold unknown destinations.

9: Law of Precision 101
Sharpen your understanding of a problem through investigation. Peel back the layers until you are left with a single question that, when answered, resolves the heart of the matter.

10: Law of the Muse 111
Do not start from zero. Do the necessary research to collect relevant ideas. Use these as inspiration, plucking the best parts of each to combine into something of your own. Don't wait for the muse to strike—reach out and strike it yourself.

11: Law of Simplicity 123
While counterintuitive, the more options you have, the less likely you are to make progress. Keep your parameters tight, your path narrow—and you will find that innovative thinking appears faster and more reliably.

12: Law of Beginning 137
By its very nature, your creative destination cannot be perfectly predicted or precisely planned for. Do not waste time wondering about what could happen. Instead, take sensible precautions and simply begin.

13: Law of Ideation 147
Take your idea and make it real, no matter how rough. The final step is only attainable by taking the first step. Once you have something to look at and adjust, you can begin the journey towards completion.

14: Law of Grounding 159
Find a problem or concept to anchor your idea. If a problem is your anchor, experiment with concepts to solve it. If a concept is your anchor, use different questions to express it.

15: Law of Wandering 169
To create something new, you must allow the process to lead—inviting serendipity to work in your favor—rather than force expectations of the final result. If you do not wander, then you will only encounter what has already been created.

16: Law of Iteration 177
Do not concern yourself with quality. Rather, prioritize quantity through iteration—even at the expense of quality. Over time, quality will emerge. The more versions you make, the better the results.

17: Law of Specificity 187
Make for yourself and you will appeal to many. Make for many and you will appeal to none.

18: Law of Plain Sight 195
Many answers lie in the open. They do not need to be uncovered, but, rather, recognized. Fight the urge to discount ideas that are not derived from toil. Judge each idea on its merit alone.

19: Law of Obscurity 203
Do what others do, and you will get results that others get. Instead, do what is not being done to get results that are fresh and novel.

20: Law of Collaboration 213
Join forces with others to maximize knowledge, speed up ideation, and minimize wheel-spinning. Share what you know and you will, in turn, have others share with you. Multiple heads truly are better than one.

21: Law of Stepping Away 227
Over-familiarity is poisonous to creativity—it produces boredom and blindness. The cure is space and time. When progress stagnates, take a break.

22: Law of Vulnerability 235
To be vulnerable is to be true. Exploring truths, especially those that are below the surface, reveal a piece of what it means to be human. You become relatable—and your message speaks to the heart of what matters most.

23: Law of Rebellion 243
Progress, innovation, and the unknown are nearly always met with opposition. Stand up for your ideas or they will never take flight. What's resisted is often what matters most.

24: Law of Good Enough 255
Aim for perfection and you will find yourself smothered by perpetual searching and disappointment. Instead, publish the simplest, clearest version of your creation, and go from there.

25: Law of the Finish Line 263
The end is a fallacy. You don't reach it, you choose it. And when you do, when your creation leaves your hands and enters the world—it is no longer yours.

LAWS OF GREATNESS 277

26: Law of Showing Up 279
Do the work and you will reap the rewards. Attempt to skip to the end or cheat the process and you yourself will be skipped over or cheated out. Instead, convert passion into energy, believe in yourself, and begin.

27: Law of Order 289
Greatness requires great effort. No one can actualize your potential but you. Develop the discipline to go longer and further than you originally thought possible.

28: Law of Chaos 299
Learn to be adaptable rather than presupposing an outcome. You will not only mine the most from the immediate circumstance—you will also enjoy yourself more.

29: Law of Habitat 309
Tend to your mind and your surroundings before you tend to your work. To do so is to leverage probabilities in your favor. Otherwise you force yourself to put in more effort than necessary.

30: Law of Intention 319
Practice at the edge of your capabilities and steadily broaden their borders. Focus, and spend little energy to great effect; slack, and you will go to great lengths just to find yourself exactly where you started.

31: Law of the Will 329
Often the deciding factor between success and failure is not skill, timing, or luck—but the willingness to endure. Success has its own timeline, one you cannot control. Patience, then, is the most powerful tool against failure.

32: Law of Adventure 339
Routinely venture into the unknown so that your pool of inspiration never grows stagnant. New ideas come from new experiences. Allow yourself to engage in opportunities you might initially reject.

33: Law of Growth 351
Learning has no limits. Don't be content to master one skill and neglect others. Without diversification, your strengths can turn into weaknesses. Commit to being a student for life.

34: Law of Symbiosis 361
Your body is more than just a container for your brain—it directly affects the quality of your thinking. Stay physically active and reap the rewards of improved cognitive performance.

35: Law of the Now 369
Connect to the present. Let time fall to the wayside, ignoring what was yesterday and what may be tomorrow. Let the now be all that exists—because it is—and you will go deeper than you ever thought possible.

36: Law of Reciprocity 379
To reach the highest peaks, we must climb together. Focus on your fellow travelers rather than yourself and you will find yourself reaching new heights with less effort.

37: Law of Tenacity 389
Accept that the world and the people in it operate of their own accord. Despite your best efforts, you will face hardships of all magnitudes. It is in these moments of difficulty and despair that what you are made of is truly tested. To reach great heights, you must persevere.

38: Law of Vision 401
To achieve a thing, one must first envision a goal. Point yourself in a direction and let the process carry you forward. Ultimately, you must give yourself a purpose before you can fulfill it.

Download a free printable cheat sheet at
lawsofcreativity.com/cheat-sheet

Common Creative Doubts and How to Overcome Them

Doubt is a natural part of the creative process. You never know what's around the corner when exploring the unknown. Sometimes you find everything you're hoping for, but often you're met with yet another mysterious tunnel and yet another corner. This can cause self-doubt.

Below is a collection of the most common doubts associated with creativity and the creative process. For each, you'll find a short list of chapters that speak to it. If any of these doubts resonate with you, it is recommended that you read the chapters in the order they are listed.

I don't know if I am creative (or I am not sure what creativity is).
- Introduction, 1
- Law of Origin, 15
- Law of Expression, 23
- Law of Connection, 41

I don't feel ready to create (or I don't have the time to be creative).
- Introduction, 1
- Law of the Unknown, 49
- Law of Competition, 65
- Law of Play, 77
- Law of Beginning, 137

I am starting too late (or I am too old).
- Law of the Unknown, 49
- Law of Competition, 65

I am afraid to fail.
- Law of the Unknown, 49
- Law of Continuity, 57
- Law of Competition, 65
- Law of Wandering, 169
- Law of Vulnerability, 235

I don't have any good ideas.
- Law of Disruption, 33
- Law of Connection, 41
- Law of Curiosity, 91
- Law of the Muse, 111
- Law of Ideation, 147

I am not sure how to start creating.
- Law of Curiosity, 91
- Law of Precision, 101

Common Creative Doubts and How to Overcome Them

- Law of Simplicity, 123
- Law of Beginning, 137
- Law of Iteration, 177

I am trying to create but not getting anywhere.

- Law of Ideation, 147
- Law of Grounding, 159
- Law of Wandering, 169
- Law of Iteration, 177
- Law of Specificity, 187
- Law of Plain Sight, 195
- Law of Obscurity, 203
- Law of Collaboration, 213
- Law of Stepping Away, 227
- Law of Tenacity, 389
- Law of Vision, 401

I don't think my creation is ready to be seen.

- Law of Vulnerability, 235
- Law of Rebellion, 243
- Law of Good Enough, 255
- Law of the Finish Line, 263

I am not enjoying what I create.

- Law of Play, 77
- Law of Specificity, 187
- Law of Chaos, 299
- Law of Adventure, 339
- Law of Growth, 351

- Law of the Now, 369
- Law of Reciprocity, 389

I can't create anything good.
- Law of Competition, 65
- Law of Iteration, 177
- Law of Showing Up, 279
- Law of Order, 289
- Law of the Will, 329
- Law of Adventure, 339
- Law of Growth, 351
- Law of the Now, 369
- Law of Tenacity, 389

I will never be a great creator.
- Law of Competition, 65
- Law of Order, 289
- Law of Intention, 319
- Law of Symbiosis, 361
- Law of the Now, 369
- Law of Tenacity, 389
- Law of Vision, 401

How to Be More Creative at Work

While writing this book, interviewees and early readers regularly asked me for suggestions on how to apply these laws in the workplace. It became clear, depending on the job, there is a spectrum of ease in which creativity can be integrated. To answer this question requires a broader perspective than the book allows. Though this How-To does not fit with the core mission of *The Laws of Creativity*—to explain creativity, creative thinking, and the creative process—I decided to write a chapter to help with this problem.

Download the bonus chapter at
lawsofcreativity.com/creative-at-work

How to Be More Creative at Home

As children, it was easy to be creative because we played all day without a care in the world (or very few cares). As adults, however, our lives fill up with responsibilities that demand our time. In building a company and managing a team, my free time became increasingly scarce. There was much I wanted to do, but little time to do it. I was compelled to overcome this challenge. Over the years, I've collected a set of creative activities that anyone with five to ten minutes can do. They'll help you keep your creative muscle in shape. And, best of all, they're enjoyable.

Download the bonus chapter at
lawsofcreativity.com/creative-at-home

Index of Original Terms

While writing *The Laws of Creativity*, I was faced with putting names to various concepts that had not previously been labeled.[171] Below is a list of terms I coined to better convey the ideas behind creative thinking and the creative process.[172]

Active Inspiration, 116
Adjacent Exploration, 344
Attention Pie, 130
Concept Anchor, 164
Device Methodology, 358
Do Board, 291
External Habitat, 315
External Questions, 96
Failure by Action, 62
Failure by Inaction, 62
Five Rules of Play, 304
Float State, 231
Grok Threshold, 131

---

171 To the best of my knowledge after extensive research and discussion.

172 For a select bibliography, visit lawsofcreativity.com/bibliography.

Internal Habitat, 313
Internal Questions, 96
Macro Will, 334
Micro Will, 334
Order of Five, 232
Passive Inspiration, 116
Prime Construct, 261
Problem Anchor, 164
Problem Method, 108
Remote Exploration, 344
Rule of Seventh Magnitude, 386
Think Units, 218
Zeitgeist Inflection, 282

Acknowledgments

An immense, lifelong thank you to my wife, Ariana. From the day we met, you have inspired me to be the best version of myself. Thank you for giving me the kick I needed to start writing, for suggesting stories when I hit dead ends, for reading every chapter out loud and giving me feedback, and for cheering me on as I slowly progressed. This book would never have been written without you.

To Chantel Hamilton and Jeff Goins, thank you for guiding me along the journey of creating my first book. None of this would have been possible without your encouragement, feedback, and insights. I am grateful to have you in my corner.

Jay Desai, this book wouldn't have entered the world if you didn't make it so. Thank you for all the effort you put into bringing it to life both physically and digitally. And thank you for being such a good friend all these years. I'm glad we still get to make things together every day.

Thank you to Andi Talarico for being so supportive. You helped with research, lifted me up when I was frustrated, gave me real talk when I needed it, and whenever I was unsure if a sentence made sense, you were always there to help. This book—and my writing—is better for it.

Thanks to Laura Toffolo for helping me find the space to write. Your design work constantly inspires and surprises—which is the highest compliment I can give a fellow designer. Without your help this project would've taken twice as long.

To Adam Kornfield, thank you for believing in my idea. Together we've built something that has positively impacted countless people in all corners of the planet.

Thank you to Ariel Curry and Lauren Terrell. From the biggest ideas down to the smallest punctuation, you helped me refine these words into engaging stories, sharp points, and clear language. I couldn't have done it alone.

Thanks to Chris Golinski for answering the phone at all hours so I could talk out ideas. From five in the morning to five times in one day, your conversations kept the steam engine running.

A necessary thanks to Peter Guzzardi. You shot down my first book idea and said, "Now if you wrote a book on creativity, that's something I'd read." It was the tipping point that made me believe I just might have something to say.

Thanks to James Clear and Josh Kaufman for providing advice from the other side of Author Mountain. Your suggestions were the ropes I used to pull myself up when there seemed to be no passing.

Unending thanks to Aunt Carol and Rita Longo for seeing me through life's darkest times. You were a mother to me when I lost my own and the sister I didn't know I needed.

Tremendous thanks to Inez and Florian Dziedzic for all the love and support. Having you in my life has been a gift I never expected and am so grateful to have.

As always, thank you to Lara McCormick for introducing me to design. You gave me the answer before I even knew the

Acknowledgments

question. That gesture continues to reverberate through my life.

To all my early readers—Najeebah Al-Ghadban, Ken DeTizio, Inez Dziedzic, Marcus Ellison, Chandler Reed, Carol Scrivo, and Dan and Richard Stern—thank you. Your feedback shaped this book.

Thank you to those who were kind enough to lend a hand or share your thoughts along the way: Gail Anderson, Eric Baker, Stuart Blitz, Justine Bloome, Naomi and Ziggy Bornas, John Castrillon, Marc Champagne, Theresa Cocuzza, Brian Collins, Tom Critchlow, Puja Desai, Hamdy El-Shamy, Dylan Fogarty, Roxane Gay, Danielle "Eagle Eye" Golinski, Howard Gray, Grace Han, Marc Jansen, Chris Kaiser, Chip Kidd, Andy Kukula, Kevin Lehmann, Rosemarie Loescher, Iker Maidagan, James Mazza, Debbie Millman, Matthew O'Boyle, Scott Robertson, David Sax, Paula Scher, Sumeet Shah, Khoi Vinh, Courtney and Ellie and Tom Voorhees, Adam Wahler, Paddy Walsh, J.Q. Whitcomb, Brad Whitley, Elizabeth Wimer, Joe Woelful, Adam Wood, Robbie and Katie Young, Tanner Zachem, Zipeng Zhu, and anyone else I may have missed. Without you, this book would not have reached its potential. I am lucky to have so many people in my life who are willing to help.

Finally, thank you to Luigi for being the best writing buddy a guy could ask for.

Notes

Notes

Notes

About the Author

Joey Cofone is Founder & CEO of Baronfig and an award-winning graphic designer and entrepreneur. His work has been featured in *Fast Company, Bloomberg, New York Magazine, Bon Appétit, Quartz, Mashable, Gizmodo,* and *Print,* among others. Joey was named a New Visual Artist and, separately, Wunderkind designer, by *Print* magazine.

He strives to make work that appeals to curious minds—work that's beautiful, smart, and communicative. He believes that design is the least of a designer's worries, that story is at the heart of all tasks, and jumping off cliffs is the only way to grow.[173]

Joey lives in New York City with his wife, Ariana, and his dog, Luigi.

See more at *joeycofone.com*

---

[173] He is also a massive fan of macaroni and cheese.

About Baronfig

Baronfig's mission is: *To champion thinkers around the world through inspiration and imagination.*

What's a thinker? If you have thoughts, you're a thinker.

Literature expands knowledge, inspires ideation, and encourages conversation. From creating tools to imparting wisdom—Baronfig provides an ecosystem for thinkers to thrive.

See more at *baronfig.com*

Final Note

Remember, creativity isn't perfect. In a book with many words and ideas, there are almost certainly mistakes. If you spot anything (or have suggestions), reach out and let me know via *joeycofone.com/contact*.

If you're feeling chatty, say hello on Twitter *@joeycofone*. I'd love to hear which parts you enjoyed the most.

Thank you for reading.